Profitability in Law Firms

Insight and Analysis

EDITED BY ALEX DAVIES

Commissioning editor
Alex Davies

Managing director
Sian O'Neill

Profitability in Law Firms: Insight and analysis
is published by

Globe Law and Business Ltd
3 Mylor Close
Horsell
Woking
Surrey GU21 4DD
United Kingdom
Tel: +44 20 3745 4770
www.globelawandbusiness.com

Profitability in Law Firms: Insight and analysis

ISBN 978-1-78742-997-0
EPUB ISBN 978-1-78742-998-7
Adobe PDF ISBN 978-1-78742-999-4

Contents

Executive summary

Profitability – on the face of it – should be simple enough to determine. But once you start to lift the lid, there is much more than meets the eye.

This book provides practical and proven strategies for law firm leaders and managers who want to take their firms to the next level of performance and profitability. How can they increase their profitability and efficiency without compromising their quality and reputation? How can they leverage the power of technology, data, and innovation to create value for their clients and themselves? Law firms are facing unprecedented challenges in the current financial climate and therefore need profitability strategies to survive and thrive in a competitive and changing market.

Our opening chapter, by Toby Brown, CEO at DV8 Legal Strategies, suggests that profit calculations for most businesses are not as simple as they may first appear. Of course, most businesses go to great lengths to understand their margins as well as they can. But in the end, most profit is an estimate. That being said, it is an extremely important metric for a business to make strategic and other key business decisions. In this space, law firms are at the back-of-the-business pack when it comes to calculating profit and using that metric in their decision-making processes. Chapter one is an effort to help law firms and their owners better understand the profitability of their businesses and ultimately to make better, more informed business decisions for their firms.

Leading and lagging indicators are two types of metrics that can help you measure and improve your business performance. Leading indicators are forward-looking and predictive, while lagging indicators, like profitability, are backward-looking and descriptive. You need both types of indicators to provide a balanced view of your performance, align your actions and goals, and enable continuous improvement. To use leading and lagging indicators effectively, you need to define your goals and objectives, select relevant and meaningful indicators, set realistic and achievable targets, monitor and report your indicators regularly, and review and revise your indicators periodically. Chapter two by Steven Campbell, consultant at Acumen KPI, explains how by doing so you can optimize your business performance and achieve your desired outcomes.

At the onset of the pandemic, law firm leaders were forced to assess their business differently – in crisis mode – which is an unfamiliar perspective from what they know. Even cost-cutting discussions that take place in short-term recessions aren't really an existential crisis to the firm so much as a self-induced "crisis" to preserve partner incomes at all costs. But COVID-19 forced leaders to think differently because no one truly knew at the beginning whether there'd be any revenue at all during the remainder of the year. The triage that took place was much more focused and helped separate critical priorities from nice-to-have efforts and expenditures. Chapter three by Tim Corcoran focuses on applying those "battlefield" lessons during peace time, looking at how law firm leaders can use the discipline they needed for survival in a once-in-a-lifetime crisis to help their firms thrive in better times.

There are many ways to compensate partner performance in law firms. They include:

- The partner with the biggest book of business.
- The partner who is most forceful in arguing why they deserve more.
- The partner who threatens to leave the firm if they do not get more.
- The partner whose father founded the firm…

Some of these strategies work, or at least they appear to do so for a period of time. But, to build a strong, prosperous firm, a firm that will withstand the economic challenges over the decades, law firms need to directly link partner pay to the achievement of the firm's business strategy. To accomplish this, a law firm needs a clear, widely understood, and universally supported business strategy rooted in fact and driven by metrics that are clear, a process that is transparent, and which can be validated by all the partners. Chapter four by J. Mark Santiago of SB2 Consultants explores how a law firm can develop and implement such a program.

The "death of the billable" hour has been mooted for some time. Fixed pricing is clearly now fairly well-engrained. However, the concept of so-called "value pricing" – explicitly setting fees based on an understanding of the value to the individual client – seems to be becoming more recognized as an option. In chapter five, Shaun Jardine of Big Yellow Penguin draws on research carried out in 2022 on law firm profitability, which demonstrated how different pricing approaches affect (professional service) firm profitability. The chapter looks at the opportunities to generate more value for professional service firms and their clients, and to create a better work-life balance for employees.

In chapter six, John McCarthy, profit coach at Summit Business, looks at the fundamentals behind improving cash flow, increasing profits, the need to implement good systems, and to engage the whole team. John shares the key to achieving sustainable and profitable growth by following the world-class "P.R.O.F.I.T." business building system. He discusses the "business blueprint", which will help you to know exactly where to prioritize when growing and managing your business, as well as five cash flow levers that will show you how to immediately boost your cash flow. John explores real-life success stories of law firms that have embraced these principles and achieved remarkable results and provides practical exercises designed to improve cash flow and substantially increase your profits in the coming year and beyond. As an experienced lawyer, you understand the value of structured, evidence-based approaches for optimal client outcomes. With John's help, you can apply the same philosophy to your law firm's success.

In chapter seven, Jack Kingston of BigHand, a 20-year veteran of the legal software industry, shares his insight into how a sound matter pricing strategy can drive profitability. He explores the importance of client transparency throughout the life cycle of the matter, the importance of staffing models, and project planning. Furthermore, the chapter discusses the importance of the use of AI to help firms code their data for use in future matters, resulting in a more predictable framework.

For decades now, it has become common practice for many law firms in North America to offer up "discounted" hourly rates to their corporate clients in exchange for potential legal work. These are typically benchmarked against what many in the legal industry refer to as a law firm's "rack rates", which are almost always some of the highest rates a firm will charge clients. This law firm practice is referred to as *rack rate benchmarking* or "RRB", which has become entrenched as a mechanism by which law firms can maintain rate predictability and increase profitability for themselves while also providing the optics of trading off "discounts" in exchange for potential legal work from some of their clients. In chapter eight, Richard Brzakala, senior director at Global External Legal Services, explores the concept and determines whether this approach is actually valuable to the firm's bottom line.

After a decade of buildup, the most recent generation of AI technologies are starting to realize some of the potential for augmenting legal work that has been predicted would be possible. Integrating these technologies into traditional legal service delivery models not only changes the amount of work to be done, but also the mix of skill sets and professionals required to do it, and what this means to a law firm commercially. Along with these changes, firms and clients have to reassess what drives value, and how law firm pricing strategies must change in order to reflect the new service dynamics. The traditional hourly rate model is no longer fit for purpose, especially when adopting these more contemporary approaches. Chapter nine by Stuart Dodds, principal at Positive Pricing, highlights what successful pricing executives (or those supporting the pricing of legal technology) need to consider in these situations from a functional, firm-wide, and client perspective.

We are standing on the precipice of an unfathomable change in legal service delivery. GenAI has captured the imagination of the general public across the world with the latest release of Large Language Models (LLMs) like ChatGPT, and there is specific interest in the partnership between Allen & Overy and legal AI tool Harvey. But how will this new dawn in technology affect law firms, and their underlying profitability? Chapter ten by Phil Nixon looks at the law firm of tomorrow, and just how far AI and technology can go in changing the fundamentals of law firm service delivery and operations. How can a law firm embrace this change when the technological foundations of their firm are often undervalued? The chapter focuses on the potential impacts of GenAI on law firm operations, cashflow, and profitability – both as an internal and external use case. It encourages law firms to embrace technological change across the board, providing a roadmap of areas to consider to ensure the correct foundations are in place to best face and embrace the coming wave.

Chapter 11, by Wayne Hassay of Maguire Schneider Hassay, looks at what AI means for law firm profitability. There exists a palpable objection among lawyers in firms of all sizes about integrating AI into their practice. In fact, in the current environment, the objection seems to have taken on mythical proportions, like a boogeyman. Granted, all industries and professions are struggling with how AI will change the world. The common struggle is rooted in ethical concerns. This is a comfortable posture for the legal profession because ethical grounds are generally the objection when the legal profession has been faced with change. The open-source information revolution of AI has the unprecedented potential to quickly marginalize lawyers and therefore do the public more harm than good – the latter being a very worthy basis for an ethical objection. In the past, ethical objections have maintained the status quo of how the profession works with the public. This time, Wayne believes, the status quo cannot be maintained. The AI revolution is just that, a revolution. Historically, the profession has always been able to maintain its grip on the one core thing that lawyers use to be in control – information. This time, lawyers will lose their leverage.

Just like many facing the AI conundrum, lawyers unquestionably fear something that could significantly marginalize them, as some of their work product becomes more accessible, and more easily produced. Regardless of the trepidation, the marketplace will drive the needle. Lawyers must find a place in this new paradigm. How the overall risks of AI are managed will likely make the difference between success and catastrophe for society in general. The legal profession, while infamously risk averse, must face the existential threat head-on. Lawyers must be candid with themselves and the public and stand firm on the true value of their services. Properly managed, AI is not here to disbar or replace lawyers, but rather will empower them to be more successful and help the public that they serve.

Profitability is a journey, and chapter 12 attempts to navigate the way with the aid of four key markers. The first of these is positioning – designing the initiative and integration into the firm culture and leadership. The second is communication – successfully educating people and immersion of the program into the firm's DNA. The third is using legal project management to embed the profitability initiative, before, finally, looking at practical ways to incorporate profitability throughout the matter lifecycle. Madhav Srinivasan, CFO at Proskauer, and Mitch Spradlin, pricing director at Hunton Andrews Kurth, look at how each can help improve a law firm's profit and performance.

Legal practitioners often assume that the benefit of higher profits is inextricably linked to the burden of working more hours. Chapter 13, by Michelle Peters, founder of The Business Instructor and creator of the "profitable practice" program for small law firms, debunks this myth and explores how small changes in each of the seven "profit zones" in a legal practice can dramatically increase profits without needing to work more hours. The key to this lies in moving focus away from constantly looking for new clients and instead focusing more on the "assets within" – especially the firm's current and past clients – and creating internal systems and processes that maximize profitability without requiring repeat manual labor by fee-earners.

In the classic law firm business model, there are various ways to increase profitability, many of which may be unhealthy for the people involved. Most lawyers come into the profession with a purpose and values not (solely) about money. The tension between their personal purpose and the relentless pursuit of profit creates incongruence and mental distress. One alternative approach that can mitigate some of the stress is the Mindful Business Charter, a movement designed to remove the unnecessary stress in the ways we work so as to work more effectively and more healthily. In our final chapter, Richard Martin, principal consultant at Byrne Dean and CEO of the Mindful Business Charter, looks at the human cost of boosting profitability and how we can work smarter.

About the authors

Toby Brown is the CEO of DV8 Legal Strategies, which provides high-level strategic consulting to law firms, legal providers, and corporate legal departments. He is also CEO of NextGenLPM, which provides executive LPM coaching for LPM professionals and lawyers. Prior to this, Toby served as chief practice management officer for Perkins Coie. In this role, Toby worked with firm partners and clients in developing pricing arrangements and service delivery models that drive successful relationships. The role included practice management, pricing, legal project management, lateral partner acquisition, practice innovation, and client relationship management. Before Perkins, Toby served as the chief practice officer for Akin Gump and served in pricing roles for both Vinson & Elkins and Fulbright & Jaworski. Before joining Fulbright, Toby served as a director for the Utah State Bar. Toby presents nationally on legal pricing, practice innovation, lateral partner acquisition, marketing, technology, and law firm management for associations, law firms, legal departments, and law schools. He is the founder of the P3 Conference and is a founder of the Legal Value Network, which is building a community of pricing, LPM, and innovation people. Toby is also the founding president of the board for SALI, the standards body for the legal industry. Toby has served on a number of legal services boards, bar association task forces, and legal market organizations. He was named to *The National Law Journal*'s 2013 list of Legal Business Trailblazers and Pioneers and received the Peer Excellence Award, the President's Award, and the Anne Charles Award from the National Association of Bar Executives. Toby received his BS and MS in Economics from the University of Utah.

Richard Brzakala is a published author, speaker, panelist, podcaster, and a recognized legal marketplace expert in legal operations, sourcing, and cost efficiency strategies. He has been a trusted advisor to many executives and general counsels, having consulted for numerous FIs, law firms, and companies. Richard is a contributing author for Thomson Reuters Legal Executive Institute, chairs a variety of legal ops groups, and acts in an executive advisory capacity for various global legal services companies. A leading US global publication once recognized Richard as a global trailblazer for developing a standardized cyber security evaluation process to monitor law firm compliance with cyber security standards. Richard currently works as the senior global director of external legal services at a large FI in Canada.

Steven Campbell is a consultant with Acumen Consulting, LLC. He helps law firms develop strategies to improve performance, leveraging innovative analytics and his extensive law firm experience to provide insight and encourage action. With over 25 years of experience in AmLaw COO and law firm consulting roles (including Thomson Reuters Elite's Business Intelligence team), Steven has pioneered data-driven profitability analysis and performance management in law firms. Steven's deep understanding of law firm operations and challenges has enabled him to partner with firms to successfully design and implement data-informed strategies, achieving significant transformational results in profitability and client value.

Tim Corcoran is a former CEO who now guides law firm and law department leaders through the profitable disruption of outdated business models. Tim is a fellow and former trustee of the College of Law Practice Management; he served as president of the Legal Marketing Association and is a member of its Hall of Fame; he's an American Lawyer research fellow, a teaching fellow in the Masters in Legal Business program at the Australian College of Law, and a frequent presenter at lawyer retreats and legal conferences. Tim is a writer whose articles and book chapters are published regularly in leading legal publications. Legal journalists and podcasters regularly seek his perspectives because of his ability to get right to the heart of complex issues and for his wit and candor. Tim's practice focus has been dominated lately by partner compensation redesign, governance reviews, and succession planning.

Stuart Dodds is co-founder and principal of Positive Pricing. Previously, he was one of the first and longest serving pricing and LPM directors in the legal industry, working firstly with Linklaters and then Baker McKenzie. Since co-founding Positive Pricing, he has subsequently worked with over 80 leading professional services firms. Stuart is a fellow of the College of Law Practice Management, a founder and board member of the Legal Value Network (a professional organization with 1,600+ members), and holds a number of professional accreditations (including as a Certified Pricing Professional (CPP)). He is a frequent speaker at conferences, and is extensively quoted in pricing and project management publications and journals.

Wayne Hassay began private practice in 1991 as a civil litigator and is now the managing partner of Maguire Schneider Hassay, LLP, in Columbus, Ohio. He is past president and serves on the board of directors of the American Bar Association affiliated Group Legal Services Association. His law firm serves as a provider firm for the legal service plan, LegalShield. As managing partner of MSH, his mission is to bring innovation and technology to the practice of law for the benefit of clients and lawyers. The philosophy is to broaden access to justice by using technology in a way that helps clients afford the legal services they need. Wayne believes this will achieve the best possible result for clients and lawyers.

Shaun Jardine is unashamedly and unapologetically a disruptor. As a solicitor (now non-practicing) and former CEO of a top 250 law firm, he has an insight into what makes law firms tick. Shaun founded Big Yellow Penguin in 2021 with the aim of encouraging and helping lawyers and law firms to move on from the 20th century and adopt practices, including value pricing, which will make their futures more secure, both financially and operationally, and enjoy practicing their craft again.

Jack Kingston has been working in the legal software industry for the better part of the past 25 years. He has a passion for working with firms within the AMLaw 250 and beyond to drive productivity and profitability and enable firms to serve their clients more effectively.

Richard Martin is the CEO of the Mindful Business Charter, an increasingly global member organization with strong roots in the legal sector whose purpose is to address the unnecessary stress in the ways we work so as to work more healthily and more effectively. He is also a principal consultant at leading workplace consultancy Byrne Dean. Richard chairs the steering committee of the Lord Mayor of London's "This is Me" campaign, which uses the power of storytelling to challenge the stigma that still exists around mental illness. He is a mental health first aid instructor and qualified coach. Previously, Richard was a senior law firm partner in London before experiencing serious mental illness. Richard is a regular speaker on mental health and wellbeing at conferences around the world.

John McCarthy guides owners of law firms to grow their practices, increase profits, and create world class teams so they can reduce their working hours and live healthier and happier lives. With ten years' experience as a multi-award-winning business coach, and 30 years as a sports, military, and corporate trainer, he has developed a disciplined mindset and unique style of coaching, mentoring, and training. He has guided over 100 clients to transform their businesses and their lives.

Phil Nixon has worked in the legal technology industry for over a decade, working for multiple providers of legal technology to all different sizes of law firm, both in the UK and across Europe. Currently working for Elite Technology as a senior sales executive, Phil is experienced in helping law firms transition their foundational software to new platforms and understand and realize the benefits of these tools for their firm. Phil often writes articles concerning the areas of both legal technology and law firm profitability. Prior to this, Phil was a lecturer in law at the University of Central Lancashire in the UK. Phil completed his thesis on intellectual property, with a specific focus on technology and the impact of virtual piracy on copyright law.

Michelle Peters, founder of The Business Instructor, is a former practicing solicitor who trained at a "Magic Circle" firm in London and specialized in intellectual property and advertising law for seven years. She then spent the following five years as the co-owner of a small franchisor business where she discovered her business skills and developed them through training and coaching her franchisees to grow their own businesses. Since setting up The Business Instructor in 2010, Michelle has focused on helping the owners of small law firms to develop and create a more profitable practice by attracting more of their ideal clients and increasing their fee income and profits without working more hours. Michelle provides a blend of strategic advice, coaching, and skills training through her "profitable practice" program for small law firms.

J. Mark Santiago is the managing partner of SB2 Consultants, headquartered in New York City. Mark holds an MBA from Fordham University, is a certified management consultant (CMC), and a member of the Accounting and Financial Planning Newsletter Board of Editors. He has consulted to the legal profession for more than 30 years in the areas of financial performance improvement, partner compensation systems, merger/acquisition due diligence, and integration and administrative support outsourcing. While a partner at Deloitte & Touche he led the two largest law firm administrative outsourcing projects in the United States and one of the three originators of the Legal Tech Conference series, and was a member of its board of advisors. Mark is a frequent public speaker and author and was the chairman of the Am Law CFO conferences for 11 years.

Mitch Spradlin is the pricing director at Hunton Andrews Kurth LLP, leading the global pricing function, and holds industry certifications in both pricing and legal project management. He is a regular speaker and panelist on a variety of topics related to pricing and profitability. He has served in leadership roles in legal pricing industry groups. Since joining Hunton in 1994, Mitch has held a variety of leadership roles within the finance function.

Madhav Srinivasan is the chief financial officer at Proskauer. He has extensive experience in legal financial management, and a deep background in corporate finance, financial consulting, capital markets, and international business. Madhav has taught at Columbia Law School in New York and the University of Texas Law School. He is a guest professor at the Wharton School of Business. He is an ALM intelligence fellow and on the advisory board at the Future of The Profession Initiative at UPenn Law School. He has published in leading journals and is a frequent speaker at major conferences.

Chapter 1:
The law firm profit primer

By Toby Brown, CEO, DV8 Legal Strategies

Profit. What a simple term. To determine it, all one needs to do is take revenue and subtract costs and there you go: profit. From there, it's easy to determine a percentage and margin. So what's so hard about law firm profitability?

First, we should realize that profit calculations for most businesses are not that simple. Of course most businesses go to great lengths to understand their margins as well as they can. But in the end, most profit is an estimate. That being said, it is an extremely important metric for a business to make strategic and other key business decisions.

In this space, law firms are at the back of the business pack when it comes to calculating profit and using that metric in their decision-making processes. This chapter is an effort to help law firms and their owners better understand the profitability of their businesses, and ultimately to make better, more informed business decisions for their firms.

The first step on this path is understanding the current state on this topic. A legacy aspect of law firms that has kept them in the dark on this topic is that they are run on a cash basis. What this means is that revenue and expenses are booked at the time the cash enters or exits a firm. Most businesses of any size ($1m and up) are run on an accrual basis. This means the revenue and expenses are booked when transactions are signed. For this discussion, we won't go into the accounting principles behind these two options. It's enough to say that law firms are out-of-step on this issue.

What this cash basis approach has brought to law firms is a cash basis mind set. In this mind set, all revenue is good. A large firm COO I spoke with recently commented that his firm was mainly covering expenses up through October, then it was all profit after that. At a firm-level, through a certain lens, that is actually true. At every other level it is not useful, and in fact will negatively impact a firm's margins. It drives law firm business owners to focus more on costs than profitable revenue. This leads to sub-optimal business decisions.

Let's get started

So how should we calculate profit on legal work? We'll go back to our Revenue - Costs = Profit, but we will apply that at a matter level.

Revenue equals hours times effective rates, where effective rates are the dollars collected per hour on a matter after discounts, write downs, and write offs. Cost equals hours times the cost of those hours. For law firms and any professional services firm, cost of hours is boiled down to cost rates. There are two cost rates for each timekeeper. These are Direct costs (aka Compensation) and Indirect costs (aka Overhead). In simple math, this looks like like Figure 1.

Rate	Effective rate	Revenue	Direct cost rate	Indirect cost rate	Full cost rate	Profit
$500	$425	$425	$125	$130	$255	$170

Figure 1.

This covers one hour from one timekeeper. Simple, huh?

And now it gets complicated.

For a partner there is a challenge deciding on the Direct cost rate. Partners, especially equity partners, have higher compensation that includes a component that rewards originations in addition to work (aka hours billed). The originations piece is the tricky part. Since that is profit, it should not be included in a direct cost rate. The hard part is determining how to draw that line between originations and work for a partner's compensation. Partner compensation systems can be complicated, making it difficult to draw that line in an equitable way across the partnership. So firms have to build models that treat this as thoughtfully as possible.

There are three primary ways law firms approach this:

1. Treat all partner compensation as cost.
2. Treat all partner compensation as profit.
3. Find some formula for dividing it out as noted above.

Each of these methodologies has pros and cons. Starting with the first, this is the least used and most problematic method in my opinion. I refer to it as the Contribution Model, since any profit shown at the matter level means the work is "contributing" to profits, versus pulling them down. This approach breaks down with higher compensation partners. This means the best originators in your firm will overly damage margins every time one of their hours is billed against a matter. So I don't recommend this approach.

Next up is the second approach, which I refer to as the Net Margin model. It's not overly difficult to come up with a formula for dividing out profit from compensation; the challenge comes in selling it to partners. Since it can never be truly equitable across all partners, there will be debates. These debates typically focus on how much overhead a given partner feels they consume. Yes, I know. Overhead is not part of the direct cost rate. It's just a convenient way for partners to attack the model. Ultimately through some negotiating a firm can establish a net margin model.

Side note

Some firms do not include indirect costs in their methodologies under the logic that partners don't have control over overhead. This approach does reduce arguments over components of overhead, but I do not recommend it for two reasons. First, indirect costs matter and should not be left out of the metrics. Second, partners do have control over overhead. They are great consumers of overhead. They just think all of the overhead they are creating has value and that other partners' does not.

Once a method is established, the firm average net margin becomes a default and convenient way to assess any matter or client's impact on profit, which leads to impact on total partner compensation.

The last method I like for several reasons. First, it focuses partners on profit instead of revenue. It brings a focus to enhancing margins in order to increase profit dollars and partner comp. I have developed an extension of this model that transforms the profit into a Profits Per Equity Partner (PPEP) number. This makes it very easy for partners to understand how their work and clients fits within their firm. If their work supports a PPEP number above the firm's current number, they know they are being accretive.

Figure 2 shows what that looks like.

Time-keeper	Hours Worked	Stan-dard Rate	Rlztn	Effec-tive Rate	Revenue	TIC	TDC	Total Expense	Profit	PPH	PPPH	PPEP
EP	80	$1,000	88%	$880	$70,400	$15,200	$–	$15,200	$55,200	$690		
SP17	100	$895	88%	$788	$78,760	$19,000	$29,500	$48,500	$30,260	$303		
10yr	125	$735	88%	$647	$80,850	$18,125	$30,625	$48,750	$32,100	$257		
7yr	90	$660	88%	$581	$52,272	$13,050	$19,350	$32,400	$19,872	$221		
3yr	55	$595	88%	$524	$28,798	$7,975	$10,175	$18,150	$10,648	$194		
Totals	**450**				**$311,080**			**$163,000**	**$148,080**	**$329.07**	**$1,851**	**$2,591,400**

Figure 2.

Here's a breakdown of this type of view of a single matter.

We start with a list of timekeepers from most senior on down (EP = Equity Partner). Next is Hours worked followed by Standard rate. This matter has a Realization of 88 percent (one industry average) resulting in the Effective rate and the Revenue generated by each timekeeper. Next up is Total indirect cost (TIC) and Total direct cost (TDC) followed by Total expense for each timekeeper. Then we see the Profit in dollars generated by each one. The next column, PPH, is Profit per hour. That is used to generate the PPPH, which is Profit per (equity) partner hour. I then use that along with the Total profit to determine a PPEP outcome. In this example, this matter supports a PPEP of $2.6m.

Stay with me. I know this appears a bit complicated, but it is really Revenue - Cost = Profit. It's just broken down to the timekeeper level then transformed into a PPEP number.

Whichever method a firm may choose, they will need buy-in from the partnership and for the partnership to understand it.

Moving right along

So now that we have a basic understanding of how we calculate profit, we will delve into the profit drivers. Spoiler – it's not costs. Law firm profit has four basic drivers – Rates, Realization, Utilization, and Leverage. We will tackle these one by one to see how they work.

Rates

For a long time, billing rates have been the top driver of both revenue and profit for firms. Firms that aren't raising their rates with the market are forgoing significant revenue. To demonstrate how and why, we will start with a simple baseline matter. We will then move on to each lever to see its impact. For this exploration we will be using the Net margin methodology to simplify the numbers, which means the equity partner will have a direct cost. The rates and cost rates used are AmLaw averages. Figure 3 shows the baseline matter.

Time-Keeper	Hours Worked	Standard Rate	Rlztn	Effective Rate	Revenue	TIC	DCR	TDC	Total Expense	Profit	Net Margin
EP	40	$1,000	90%	$900	$36,000	$7,600	$500	$20,000	$27,600	$8,400	
JP	50	$895	90%	$806	$40,275	$9,500	$295	$14,750	$24,250	$16,025	
10yr	75	$735	90%	$662	$49,613	$10,875	$245	$18,375	$29,250	$20,363	
7yr	65	$660	90%	$594	$38,610	$9,425	$215	$13,975	$23,400	$15,210	
3yr	45	$595	90%	$536	$24,098	$6,525	$185	$8,325	$14,850	$9,248	
Totals	**275**				**$188,595**				**$119,350**	**$69,245**	36.72%

Figure 3.

Notice that leverage is about 2:1 – meaning for every hour a partner bills, two hours are billed by non-partners. Realization is at 90 percent, resulting in Profit of $69,245 and a Net margin of 36.72 percent.

To test the impact of rates on profit, we will hold everything else but move rates up by one percent. This would come about when a firm implements a one-point higher rate increase than they would have done. The results are shown in Figure 4.

Time-Keeper	Hours Worked	Standard Rate	Rlztn	Effective Rate	Revenue	TIC	DCR	TDC	Total Expense	Profit	Net Margin
EP	40	$1,010	90%	$909	$36,360	$7,600	$500	$20,000	$27,600	$8,760	24.09%
JP	50	$905	90%	$815	$40,725	$9,500	$295	$14,750	$24,250	$16,475	40.45%
10yr	75	$740	90%	$666	$49,950	$10,875	$245	$18,375	$29,250	$20,700	41.44%
7yr	65	$670	90%	$603	$39,195	$9,425	$215	$13,975	$23,400	$15,795	40.30%
3yr	45	$600	90%	$540	$24,300	$6,525	$185	$8,325	$14,850	$9,450	38.89%
Totals	**275**				**$190,530**				**$119,350**	**$71,180**	**37.36%**

Figure 4.

The Net margin is up to 37.36 percent and profit up three percent to $71,180. How did a one percent increase in rates yield a three percent increase in profit? Because every extra dollar was pure profit. For Rates and Realization, a general rule of thumb is three-to-one, so that a one percent increase or decrease in either of those will generally result in a three percent impact to profit.

To put this in partner lingo, think about it this way. If your firm has $100m in revenue, for every point of rate increase you add, you add $1m to the partner profit pool.

Realization

Now let's see what a hit in Realization does. We'll lower it from 90 percent to 89 percent in Figure 5.

Time-Keeper	Hours Worked	Standard Rate	Rlztn	Effective Rate	Revenue	TIC	DCR	TDC	Total Expense	Profit	Net Margin
EP	40	$1,000	89%	$890	$35,600	$7,600	$500	$20,000	$27,600	$8,000	22.56%
JP	50	$895	89%	$797	$39,828	$9,500	$295	$14,750	$24,250	$15,578	39.17%
10yr	75	$735	89%	$654	$49,061	$10,875	$245	$18,375	$29,250	$19,811	40.44%
7yr	65	$660	89%	$587	$38,181	$9,425	$215	$13,975	$23,400	$14,781	38.80%
3yr	45	$595	89%	$530	$23,830	$6,525	$185	$8,325	$14,850	$8,980	37.72%
Totals	**275**				**$186,500**				**$119,350**	**$67,150**	**36.01%**

Figure 5.

Compared to the baseline of $69,245, Profit has dropped to $67,150. This is a four percent drop. This is above our predicted three percent, but still demonstrates the magnified impact.

A big point to make here is about protecting your rates. Too often, partners are willing to give clients discounts as a perceived way to win work. As an aside, I can tell you from years of experience, price is number four or five in a client's firm selection consideration. But when clients ask, partners give additional discounts without much questioning. Many times, this can mean a jump from a ten percent discount to 15 percent. The extra five percent discount will result in a 15 percent or so reduction in profit. That's a lot of profit to give away without question.

Utilization

Our next test is on Utilization. The math for this needs some explaining. Indirect cost rates are determined by taking the total overhead cost for a firm and dividing it by the number of timekeepers. With this cost per timekeeper, you divide that by average billable hours to get to the cost rate. For Direct you take the total comp and divide by the same hours. For our model, the average billable number used is 1,800 hours. If these hours drop by one percent to 1,782, the impact as shown in Figure 6 is seen.

Time-Keeper	Hours Worked	Standard Rate	Rlztn	Effective Rate	Revenue	TIC	TDC	Total Expense	Profit	Net Margin
EP	40	$1,000	90%	$900	$36,000	$7,680	$20,200	$27,880	$8,120	22.56%
JP	50	$895	90%	$806	$40,275	$9,600	$14,900	$24,500	$15,775	39.17%
10yr	75	$735	90%	$662	$49,613	$10,988	$18,563	$29,550	$20,063	40.44%
7yr	65	$660	90%	$594	$38,610	$9,523	$14,105	$23,628	$14,983	38.80%
3yr	45	$595	90%	$536	$24,098	$6,593	$8,415	$15,008	$9,090	37.72%
Totals	**275**				**$188,595**			**$120,567**	**$68,030**	**36.07%**

Figure 6.

Profit has dropped by two percent to $68,030. Not exactly the three-one ratio we noted above, but still a magnified impact.

Leverage

This brings us to Leverage. From our baseline of 2:1 Leverage, we will increase that a full point to 3:1 and see what happens. (see Figure 7 overleaf).

These results require a bit more explanation than the others. First, there is no easy three-to-one rule, since the impact of leverage is dependent on what you start with – 2:1 in our example – and where you end, 3:1. We

Time-Keeper	Hours Worked	Stan-dard Rate	Rlztn	Effec-tive Rate	Revenue	ICR	TIC	DCR	TDC	Total Expense	Profit	Net Margin
EP	25	$1,000	90%	$900	$22,500	$190	$4,750	$500	$12,500	$17,250	$5,250	23.33%
JP	40	$895	90%	$806	$32,220	$190	$7,600	$295	$11,800	$19,400	$12,820	39.79%
10yr	85	$735	90%	$662	$56,228	$145	$12,325	$245	$20,825	$33,150	$23,078	41.04%
7yr	75	$660	90%	$594	$44,550	$145	$10,875	$215	$16,125	$27,000	$17,550	39.39%
3yr	50	$595	90%	$536	$26,775	$145	$7,250	$185	$9,250	$16,500	$10,275	38.38%
Totals	**275**				**$182,273**					**$113,300**	**$68,973**	**37.84%**

Figure 7.

could have started at 4:1 and gone to 5:1. Even though it's still a full point of change, the magnitude is lower. In any event, let's discuss the outcome. First, we can't use the simple profit in dollars number, since our overall revenue decreased. It dropped from $188,595 to $182,273. This is a four percent decrease. The number we'll use here is the Net margin number. It went from 36.72% to 37.84%. This is a three percent increase. The bottom line here is that this leverage improvement does result in less revenue, but better margins.

For partners, this can sound counterintuitive. A logical reaction is, "Why improve leverage? I have the highest rate, therefore my hours generate more profit." We will add in another metric in Figure 8 to explore – Net margin per timekeeper.

Time-Keeper	Hours Worked	Standard Rate	Rlztn	Effective Rate	Revenue	TIC	TDC	Total Expense	Profit	Net Margin
EP	25	$1,000	90%	$900	$22,500	$4,750	$12,500	$17,250	$5,250	23.33%
JP	40	$895	90%	$806	$32,220	$7,600	$11,800	$19,400	$12,820	39.79%
10yr	85	$735	90%	$662	$56,228	$12,325	$20,825	$33,150	$23,078	41.04%
7yr	75	$660	90%	$594	$44,550	$10,875	$16,125	$27,000	$17,550	39.39%
3yr	50	$595	90%	$536	$26,775	$7,250	$9,250	$16,500	$10,275	38.38%
Totals	**275**				**$182,273**			**$113,300**	**$68,973**	**37.84%**

Figure 8.

This shows the Net margin for the EP at 23 percent versus 41 percent for the tenth year. This answers our question above. Although the EP does have the highest billing rate, she is also the most expensive resource. Her time is better spent originating more matters like this versus billing time. That is how she will drive profit and partner compensation to higher levels.

Putting it all together

Partners have material control over all these profit levers.

- They can be supportive of getting their rates up to a market level.
- They can be confident in their value, to hold the line on discounts.
- They can proactively manage their work to reduce write downs.
- They can communicate effectively with their clients to reduce write offs.
- They can make sure work is done at the lowest cost, appropriate level.

Profit is not everything, but it is a very important thing

Now that we have established a reasonable method for determining profit and that partners can take action to impact it, we need to move a level up in our discussion. For most businesses, profit is a key element in decision-making for everything from what to produce and sell, to how tech and other investment decisions are made. Currently, most law firms lack this decision-making tool.

Take this scenario, for example. A firm is considering an investment in an emerging technology like AI. How and where it deploys this is a very important business decision for the firm to make since these are shaping up to be high-dollar investments. What appears to be happening is that the decisions are made around the willing and able partners. These are partners with some interest in technology or perhaps some perception that their practice should have more tech within it.

Two ideas to consider:

1. Is this a practice that has strategic value for the firm? Is it a practice that generates high margins and generates other related work (aka cross-selling)?
2. What will the ROI on this investment be for the firm? Will a $250k investment lead to additional, higher margin work?

What we are seeing in the AI space is a likely negative ROI outcome for these types of investments. Yet firms are making these decisions with little to no view into the impacts on profit and the likelihood of a positive ROI.

Take this scenario and spread it across every decision a firm makes on – lateral partner acquisitions, new office openings, billing rate setting, the billing and collections program, paralegals, e-discovery, office space renovations, etc. The real challenge would be finding decisions that won't benefit from having a profit aspect included.

It is clear law firms will benefit from understanding their profitability and having a clear view into all aspects of it when making business decisions.

Core challenge

#1 – Actionable information

For law firm partners to effectively manage profitability, they need real-time, actionable information. What do we mean by that? An easy example is that of time entries and billing information. Typically, partners don't see that information until it's too late. At the beginning of the month they get their pre-bills from the prior month's work. They then don't review those bills until the end of that month. This means they don't even know where they are against any budget until weeks after problems occur. Of course this means it's too late to do anything about it. The result is write-downs (reductions before an invoice is sent).

Now take that problem and spread it across the spectrum of the points made above in our exploration of profit. Partners can't see if work is being done at the right level of expertise. And they're unable to provide meaningful updates when a client calls.

What partners need is a real-time view into this information. They need to see what types of work are being done and by what level of timekeepers. They need to see budget information including all A/R and WIP. And they need a sense of where they are in the progression of a matter.

This challenge is not simple to resolve. But it is important for a firm to start on a path to do that. First they should clean up their data, since it is likely not well structured or categorized.[1] They should set policies for good time entry hygiene so the information they see is timely. They should set standardized processes and develop tools for real-time information reporting. Finally, the reporting should be easily understandable and not just a data download into spreadsheets.

Investments into these processes and tools will have a positive ROI, by the way.

#2 – Partner compensation systems

Sadly, the vast majority of partner compensation systems are not well-aligned with profitability. They heavily weigh hours-billed by partners and do not consider the profitability of revenue generated. Therefore, a partner with high billable hours, big discounts, and bad leverage could easily be paid more than someone with the same originations, but with better margins and lower personal billable hours.

What's worse is that altering partner compensation systems may be the most challenging project a law firm can undertake. Changes to this will mean some partners earn more and others less. Every partner will be focused on staying in the former category and avoiding the latter. Expect a ton of friction when dealing with this issue. But a firm should make an attempt in any event. I would suggest setting out an end-goal and then planning a multi-year transition to give partners time to adapt and change their behaviors.

Conclusions

Law firms should put profitability at the center of their decision-making processes. They should establish an understood and communicated methodology to the partnership. It will likely take a few years before this is fully integrated into partnership thinking. This critical first step should be followed with numerous other programs that build on this foundation to establish the tools and processes to integrate profitability into all law firm business decision-making. The result will be a more profitable and resilient firm built for the future.

References

1 Firms would be wise to leverage the SALI code sets for this, since they are becoming industry standards. Check out www.sali.org.

Chapter 2:
KPIs for aligning strategy to enhanced client value and partner profitability

By Steven Campbell, consultant, Acumen Consulting LLP

Tracking Key Performance Indicators (KPIs) is essential for aligning daily activities and priorities with the firm's strategic objectives. KPIs provide valuable insights that enable firms to identify areas for improvement or opportunity, track progress against specific goals, and make timely data-driven decisions.

In this chapter, I discuss how KPIs can be essential for supporting and guiding firm strategy. In addition to common financial and operational metrics, I show how some less familiar KPIs can help drive successful firm performance through the hiring and retaining of top talent, and the provision of exceptional service that exceeds client expectations. I demonstrate the link between these activities and improved Profits per Equity Partner (PPEP).

Despite their potential, however, the majority of KPIs being tracked by law firms today are not conducive to guiding transformational change. In many firms, the focus is on too many broad operational KPIs that do little to help achieve the necessary changes required to build effective teams, alter service models to enhance client value, and improve long-term performance. Partners are often inundated with so much data that it becomes impossible to determine where effective action should be taken.

KPIs should be designed to measure progress against firm or practice objectives that are aligned to the firm's strategy. They should be timely, intuitive, and relevant to their consumers (firm leaders, practice leaders, partners, timekeepers, administrators, etc.). Dashboards should be visual but not at the expense of focusing on the most crucial KPIs to drive actionable insights and decision-making. For KPIs to be impactful, it is imperative that people are trained to understand the purpose for the KPIs and how to use them to make effective decisions or course corrections to optimize performance.

Avoiding unintended consequences

It is important to recognize how common KPIs can result in unintended consequences. For example, Profit per Equity Partner (PPEP) might be considered a single metric, but the formula to calculate PPEP is a little more complex and must be fully understood to maximize PPEP.

$$\text{Revenue-Expenses} = \text{Net Income} / \#\text{ of Partners} = \text{PPEP}$$
$$\text{Revenue} = \text{Billable Hours} \times \text{Standard Rate} \times \text{Realization}$$
$$\text{Expenses} = \text{Direct} + \text{Indirect Costs}$$

No single part of the formula can accurately predict PPEP, as the following example will demonstrate. Each measure should be optimized to the client's situation. To illustrate, we will compare two staffing models for the same theoretical matter and assume that the client received the same quality of service and legal outcome.

When profitability is calculated below the firm level, direct costs are assigned to the timekeepers who incur them. Partner compensation is not considered an allocated expense in most profit models as it is paid from profits.

Overhead costs are usually allocated based on the full-time equivalent (FTE) and title of the timekeeper. Senior timekeepers are assigned a larger percentage of overhead expenses.

In Scenario A, the partner and associate each worked 350 hours. Expenses are calculated by multiplying each timekeeper per hour cost (calculated in the first table) by their billable hours to determine expenses associated with their time spent. Since they both worked the same number of hours, matter leverage is 1 to 1.

In Scenario B, the partner worked 200 fewer hours on the matter. The associate is not as experienced, so they work 300 more hours than Scenario A. In this case, leverage is 4.33 associate hours to each partner hour.

Comparing scenarios A & B, many would conclude that Scenario A outperformed B because the measures accurately reported the highest standard rate, realization, net income, margin, and fee revenue.

However, Scenario B better achieved the firm's vision of providing exceptional client value through lower fees, and while net income in Scenario A was higher, it resulted in lower PPEP compared to Scenario B (as explained below).

Timekeeper expenses / Cost rate		
	Associate	Partner
Direct (Comp and benefits)	$150,000	$0
Overhead	$150,000	$225,000
Total expenses	*$300,000*	*$225,000*
Hours worked	1,900	1,600
Compensation / hour	$78.95	$0.00
Overhead / hour	$78.95	$140.63
Total per hour cost rate	*$157.89*	*$140.63*

Scenario A	Associate	Partner	Matter summary
Hours	350	350	700
Standard rate	$300	$550	$425
Realization	94%	94%	94%
Effective rate	*$282.00*	*$517.00*	*$399.50*
Revenue (hrs × effective rate)	$98,700	$180,950	$279,650
Expenses (hrs × cost rate)	-$55,263	-$49,219	-$104,482
Net income	*$43,437*	*$131,731*	*$175,168*
Leverage			1.00
Margin (net income)			62.6%
Return per partner hour			$500.48

Scenario B	Associate	Partner	Matter Summary
Hours	650	150	800
Standard rate	$300	$550	$347
Realization	94%	94%	94%
Effective rate	*$282.00*	*$517.00*	*$326.06*
Revenue (hrs × effective rate)	$183,300	$77,550	$260,850
Expenses (hrs × cost rate)	-$102,632	-$21,094	-$123,725
Net income	*$80,668*	*$56,456*	*$137,125*
Leverage			4.33
Margin (net income)			52.6%
Return per partner hour			$914.16

Matter summaries	Scenario A	Scenario B
Hours	700	800
Standard rate	$425	$347
Realization	94%	94%
Effective rate	*$399.50*	*$326.06*
Revenue (hrs × effective rate)	$279,650	260,850
Expenses (hrs × cost rate)	-$104,482	-123,725
Net income	*$175,168*	*$137,125*
Leverage	1.00	4.33
Margin (net income)	62.6%	52.6%

Return per partner hour	Scenario A	Scenario B
Net income	$175,168	$137,125
Partner hours	350	150
Return per partner hour	$500.48	$914.16
Average annual ptn hours	1,600	1,600
Profit per equity partner (PPEP)	$800,768	$1,462,663

Figure 1: Two staffing models for the same matter.

Don't confuse margin (net income) and profits per equity partner (PPEP)

Although Scenario A resulted in a greater net income, it would be incorrect to assume that it also created a higher PPEP. We can explain why by referencing the investment community's earnings-per-share (EPS) concept.

EPS is calculated as net income divided by the number of shares outstanding. An entity with a higher net income but proportionally more shares (lower EPS) will be considered a less attractive investment opportunity than a company with a lower net income but proportionately fewer shares.

A KPI that measures "return-per-partner hour" is similar to EPS. Assuming a partner has the capacity for 1,600 billable hours (# of sweat equity shares), then scenario A service model could support PPEP of $800K while a service model like Scenario B could support a PPEP of $1.46M.

As an alternative, a partner with a practice that reflects the Scenario B service model could work fewer billable hours and invest more time to client development and mentoring associates to create stronger long-term success and still make a greater PPEP than a partner with a Scenario A type practice.

Dashboards should focus on areas of greatest impact

This section uses fictitious data to demonstrate that, even within a practice group, dashboards should prioritize metrics that will have the greatest impact on desired performance, in this case, PPEP. To illustrate, assume the profit dashboard in Figure 2 reports profit metrics for an Intellectual Property (IP) practice group.

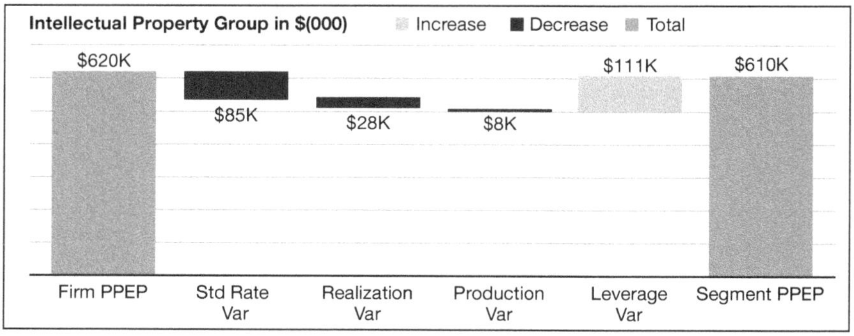

Figure 2: Profit metrics for an Intellectual Property practice group.

This PPEP dashboard adopts a unique approach to evaluating profitability metrics. Instead of assessing rates on a dollar basis, realization as a percentage, utilization as hours, and leverage as a ratio, the PPEP variances are measured in dollars from firm average to the filtered context.

For example, a lower average standard rate reduced PPEP by $85K, while higher-than-average leverage made a positive PPEP contribution of $111K. Drilling down to the timekeeper title level revealed that most of the standard rate variance was due to a greater use of lower-rate timekeepers. The interrelationship is made clearer in the Waterfall visualization than if each measure was reported independently as standard rate per hour and leverage as a ratio.

Despite negative variances for standard rates, realization, and productivity, the practice's overall profit was respectable due to strong leverage.

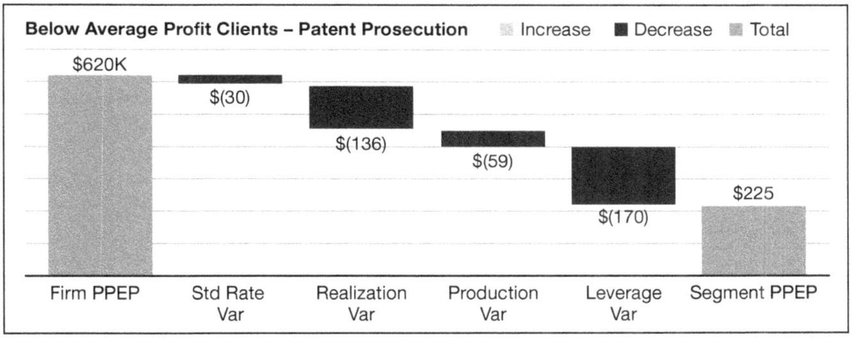

Figure 3: Below average profit clients – patent prosecution.

Filtering the dashboard between litigation and prosecution practice areas revealed that litigation matters achieved an average PPEP of $659K (higher than the firm average). Prosecution PPEP, on the other hand, varied widely when further segmented by high-profit and low-profit clients, yielding PPEP of $864K and $225K, respectively (Figure 3).

Additional research was needed to identify the causes for the weak PPEP performance of the below-average profit client group. Let's assume that we learn from the practice group leader that these clients were primarily serviced by a smaller office that was not fully staffed with experienced patent agents, resulting in partners doing most of the work and splitting their time between litigation and prosecution work, doing the latter when not pressed for time by litigation matters.

Using a what-if feature of the dashboard revealed that increasing leverage by a factor of 1.5 would increase PPEP to $654K. The current leverage for the low profit clients was only .38, so a target leverage of 1.85 would be clearly achievable as it is still less than most firms in this market.

Surveying the clients confirmed that they valued the firm's expertise in the relevant technical fields, which enabled the partners to communicate effectively with inventors on patentability, validity, infringement, and freedom-to-operate analyses. Yet these clients would not recommend the firm if asked, due to the following concerns:

- Matters took longer than expected to close, exposing them to "first to file" risk from their competitors.
- The timekeepers handling their cases seemed less interested in their matters (citing low attentiveness, responsiveness, and a lack of general business advice).
- The firm could make better use of recent advances in patent prosecution technology.
- The fees per matter were too high, leading to frequent negotiations for rate reductions (resulting in a lower realization percentage).

Clearly a change in service model was required. The following transformational changes were made to improve client service and value as well as profitability:

- Prosecution matters were centralized, and additional patent agents and associates were hired to handle the work. Delegating the work to lower-rate timekeepers increased leverage and reduced client fees.
- A new metric was created to track matter turnaround time, which improved significantly with the new service model.
- A team of patent agents and associates was assigned the task of evaluating the latest patent filing technology and making recommendations for change where appropriate.
- Clients were contacted periodically to measure their satisfaction.
- A PPEP target of $500K was set for the Prosecution practice to be achieved within 12 months.

This example highlights that a single dashboard cannot cater to the needs of everyone. Dashboards should be tailored to a level where the strategic objectives are the same for the filtered group. By drilling deeper into the IP group's practice segments and client clusters, we uncovered the root causes for the lower performance of a segment of the Prosecution clients and provided insights to guide impactful changes that could be taken to improve both client value and profitability.

Vision drives strategy – strategy drives effective KPIs

Let's review the relationship between mission, values, vision, and strategy.

- *Mission*. The mission sets the foundation for planning. It outlines what the firm will do to achieve its vision. It answers the question of "why" the firm exists.
- *Values*. Values represent the firm's principles. They define the character and identity and guide the firm culture.
- *Vision*. The vision establishes the desired future state for the firm and why it matters. It answers the question of "where" the firm is headed.
- *Strategy*. A well-defined strategy is like a roadmap that guides a firm from its mission to its vision. It sets out the goals, professional standards, and go-to-market approach to help achieve the vision and mission.

Example law firm mission, values, and vision

Our *mission* is to provide legal and business advice that goes beyond expectations. We accomplish this by adopting a practical, innovative, and cost-effective approach to law practice. Furthermore, we prioritize creating a welcoming environment that attracts and nurtures top talent. We are deeply committed to our community, clients, and their businesses.

Our firm is guided by four *core values* – integrity, excellence, respect, and commitment. We uphold the highest ethical standards, aim for excellence in our work, and always treat our clients and colleagues with dignity and respect. Our unwavering commitment drives us to always act by these values.

Our *vision* is to become the top law firm in our practice areas by delivering exceptional value and results while attracting and retaining talented and collaborative professionals.

Many law firms have developed well-crafted mission, values, and vision (MVV) statements. Too often, however, these statements are not explained or adopted widely throughout the firm and are not taken into consideration when creating KPIs. To track progress against specific objectives and provide actionable insights, KPIs should be based on the strategic goals and initiatives of the firm (or practice). As strategies change, in response to performance or external factors, so should KPIs be adjusted.

Non-financial KPIs

Research indicates that managing predictive leading indicators can positively impact attracting and retaining top talent, creating loyal clients, and achieving financial success. Although metrics like client satisfaction and partner/employee engagement can be difficult to quantify, making the effort to develop and track KPIs relevant to strategic objectives in these areas will help focus action to ensure progress in achieving critical goals that will enhance firm performance.

Balancing quantifiable metrics like staff attrition with data from partner/employee engagement surveys will not only identify a potential problem but also provide insights into possible actions for course correction to alleviate the problem.

Sample questions for a partner/employee engagement survey could include the following.

On a five-point scale, ask how well the firm is doing in the following areas:

- Do you understand our firm's mission, values, and vision statement and how you can contribute to achieving strategic goals?
- Are you happy with your work/life balance? Do you feel supported by the firm in managing your stress and wellbeing?
- Are you satisfied with your career development and progression opportunities at the firm? Do you have access to mentoring, coaching, and training programs?
- How do you rate the firm's diversity and inclusion efforts? Do you feel respected and valued for your unique contributions and perspectives?
- How do you rate the firm's pro bono and community service initiatives? Do you participate in any of them?
- How likely are you to recommend the firm to a friend or colleague? What are the main reasons for your recommendation?
- Does the firm adhere to its core values of Integrity, Excellence, Respect, and Commitment?
- Do you feel that people prioritize the needs of the firm over their own?
- What should we do to improve? (This is an open-ended question.)

Similarly, while there are a number of financial metrics that might indicate that a client is satisfied (or not), clearly the most effective and informative method is listening to the client – both objectively through a survey and talking to the client directly.

Sample client survey questions might include the following.

On a five-point scale, ask how well the firm is doing in the following areas:

- How satisfied are you with our firm's communication with you?
- How satisfied are you with the outcome of your matter(s)?
- How likely are you to refer our firm to colleagues?
- How well do we perform relative to the measures you use to track us and other outside law firms that you use?
- How well do you feel we know your business and industry?
- How do you rate our quality of service and value compared to other firms?
- How do you rate our fees compared to other firms?
- Do you feel the firm is maximizing the benefits of new technologies?
- What should we do to improve? (This is an open-ended question.)

In addition to survey data, there are some reliable internal predictive indicators that can be effective when trended over time and benchmarked between high and low-performing segments (i.e. practices).

A few examples:

- Client/staff growth/attrition as a satisfaction rating.
- Average hours per similar matter – indices to measure efficiency gains.
- Percentage of matters with retainer agreements, project plans and budgets – reduces the risk that the client did not understand the billing arrangements, scope of work, or estimated fees.
- Investment hours spent with clients – legal department surveys show this as a measure they use to evaluate legal providers.
- Hours spent on continuing development.
- Number of new software applications evaluated and percentage implemented.
- Number and quality of client referrals.

- The average number of practice areas used by clients – clients that use more practice areas are stickier and identify areas of law for additional cross-selling

"Measure what is measurable and make measurable what is not so."
Galileo

New tools to help measure and prioritize strategic action

With the help of machine learning and AI, it is now possible to determine the impact of financial and non-financial KPIs on related metrics such as PPEP, member attrition, and client satisfaction.

In Figure 4, the metrics that cause PPEP to increase are ranked by dollar impact. By selecting the circle beside the influencer metric, the data referenced in the calculation are represented in a scatter diagram – in this case, client scores for matter turnaround. The data suggests that improving turnaround scores by one standard deviation (an average of 0.13 on the five-point scale) can increase PPEP by $13.51K.

The majority of clients in this small sample have given a good rating of

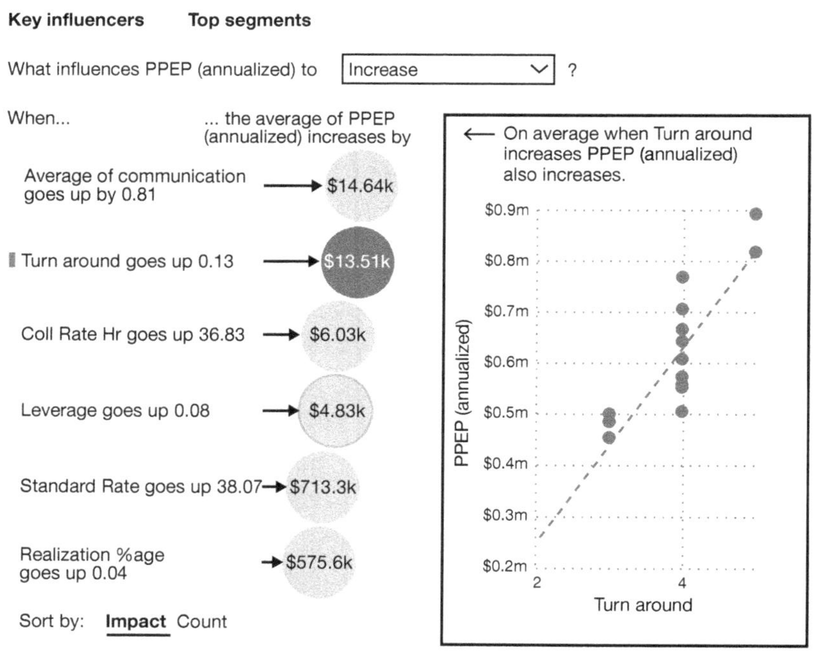

Figure 4: Key influencers.

four for matter turnaround time. However, there are a few clients who have rated this metric at two or three. By clicking on those dots, the client's name and other relevant data is presented in a summary box. One of the plans for this practice group should be to look for other data that might suggest why the client gave a low rating; perhaps a litigious counter-party that refused to settle. In such cases, little can be done, but if the ranking cannot be explained internally and the client is important to the firm, someone should reach out to them to understand the reason(s) and determine what the firm can do to improve going forward. This effort could make the difference between retaining or losing an important client. The fact that the firm expressed interest in finding out why the client was unhappy may even improve their loyalty to the firm.

Based on the results of this analysis, the practice group leader should focus on managing the top four influencers to improve PPEP. The last two influencers have a minimal impact on PPEP and should not distract attention from the first four.

There is virtually no limit to the number of KPIs the analysis can rank. The program logic will automatically exclude KPIs that have no statistical correlation to PPEP. This ranking tool can also be filtered for strategic business units such as practices, offices, client industry, etc. The influencers are recalculated and reranked as new filters are applied.

Finally, the analysis can benchmark results over time, so progress can be measured and strategy adjusted as required.

Effective KPIs should inspire action

In many law firms, partners still have to wade through reams of reports to find a single nugget of actionable information. Too often, new dashboards are created with pretty charts depicting numerous traditional metrics without highlighting areas for strategic action that actually deserve a partner's attention.

KPI dashboards should be targeted to their particular consumers. As discussed earlier, practice areas will have different strategic objectives and, therefore, different KPIs for tracking progress against them. Administrators may see more comprehensive operational metrics, while partners should see only those operational KPIs that require their attention, ideally on an exception basis.

In many cases, issues that require partner intervention can be handled more effectively with exception-based KPIs, such as email alerts when certain client-level metrics move out of acceptable range. Instead of having to spend time searching a dashboard or report for issues needing attention, only the critical data is delivered on a timely, as needed, basis.

It is critical that dashboards focus on the KPIs that have a high impact on the objectives that the firm (or practice) is trying to achieve. The sample dashboard shown in Figure 5 has nice-looking visualizations but requires too much effort for the user to find any actionable information.

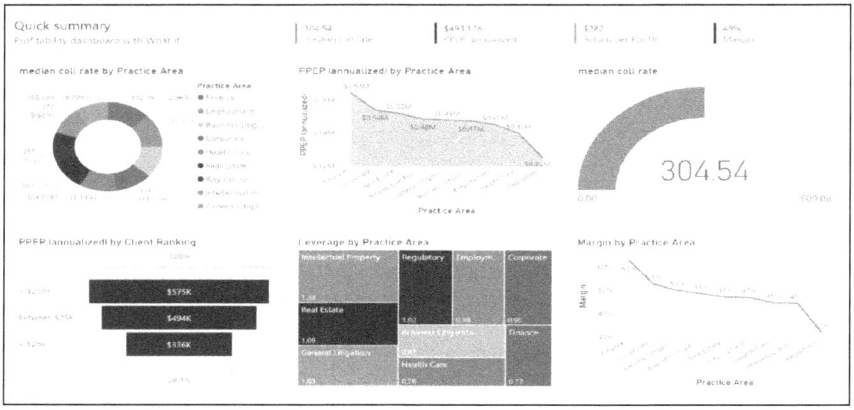

Figure 5: Sample dashboard

> *"The ability to simplify means to eliminate the unnecessary so that the necessary may speak."*
> Hans Hofmann, artist

Conclusion

KPIs should be metrics that matter – designed to track progress against strategic objectives and provide timely insights to facilitate course correction and meaningful action to build effective service teams, enhance client value, and optimize partner profits. Just because you can measure something and make it visually appealing does not mean it deserves the attention of firm leaders. Too much valuable time is spent on activities that do not result in exceptional client service or attract and retain top talent.

It is important that KPIs support firm strategy, keep focus on important continuous improvement initiatives, and provide timely, actionable insights. People should be well trained to understand why KPIs are being tracked and how to interpret them for effective action.

Caution should be taken to ensure that metrics are not misleading or lead to unintended consequences. Too great a focus on billable hours, for example, can lead to a high-pressure culture that could drive associate attrition or, in lean times, induce partners to do work that should be delegated to lower rate professionals.

Analysis of KPIs should include trending over time, benchmarking against firm averages, segmentation by practice, client, industry, and various other parameters, depending on the particular insights required. KPIs should be updated in response to changes in performance, goals, and objectives or external factors.

With firm strategy (and its mission, values, and vision) as a guide, actionable goals and strategies are developed at the strategic business unit level (i.e. industries, practice areas, key clients, etc.). KPIs and dashboards need to be tailored to their specific goals and opportunities. From there, financial results happen as a "result" of building the right foundation that attracts the best talent, supported with training, processes, and leading technology to anticipate changing demands and provide exceptional service that exceeds client expectations and eventually leads to enhanced profits per partner.

Chapter 3:

Applying battlefield lessons during peace time – learnings from the COVID-19 pandemic

By Tim Corcoran, BringinTim

The disruption caused by the COVID-19 global pandemic presented law firm leaders with unprecedented challenges. Many were forced to make decisions that, based on the limited information available at the time, could very well have had life-or-death implications for fellow lawyers and staff. The rapid-fire pace and sheer magnitude of operational decisions required of these leaders far exceeded what any had encountered previously. Further compounding the challenge, governments across the world imposed mandatory lockdowns nearly simultaneously.

Law firm leaders didn't have the luxury of time to explore the past actions of their predecessors or even to observe the current actions of their peers since so much was changing in real-time. They had to make critical decisions by first filtering and then assessing the reliability of the deluge of information coming their way. Then, by relying on their instincts and gathering advice from those they trust, these leaders chose what they deemed to be the optimal course of action for their circumstances.

Depicting leadership as a battlefield is a familiar trope in pop-management literature. Every airport bookstore has a display of books written by academics or bigshot executives that offer some gimmicky, non-scientific, but *absolutely guaranteed* approach to solving the complex puzzle of management. Leading any complex business in a competitive and fast-evolving marketplace is not easy. Most days, however, leading a business bears little resemblance to actual war. Combat veterans generally find it reductive and disingenuous when businesspeople compare the experience of "taking fire" in the trade press or in Yelp or Trustpilot reviews to dodging live gunfire. Still, leading through the pandemic was at times harrowing.

The managing partner of a 150-lawyer US law firm shared the agony of having to decide who would visit the shuttered office to pick up mail. Notwithstanding the unimaginable volume of email sent to law firms every day, most law firms continue to receive a high volume of posted mail and packages. This posed a serious logistical challenge for law firms in jurisdictions where government and health officials commanded all offices to be closed.

> *"We simply had no choice but to send someone to retrieve important documents, including numerous cheques from clients. My dilemma wasn't finding someone to visit the office. It was choosing from among several options. Our mailroom is staffed by a third-party provider. The team was essentially out of work because theirs is a job that can't be done remotely. The compassionate response was to keep several of them busy."*

Surprisingly, not everyone took the dire health warnings seriously.

> *"A few partners were angry at being locked out of the office. One was so insistent on securing the single daily exemption allowed by building security that he offered to pick up all the mail! But I did take the health warnings seriously. I agonized over whether I could authorize anyone to visit the building if this meant exposing them to a deadly virus that was spreading quickly and had no cure. Never in my life before or since have I been responsible for a decision that might result in someone's death."*

In the following discussion of lessons learned – and lost – from this period, let's show proper respect and acknowledge that leading a business through COVID-19 was, for most, not equivalent to leading soldiers on a battlefield. It was, however, a very complicated, uncertain time with, at times, as much economic peril as health peril. When those who held positions of authority during this dramatic time look back one day, many will recognize it as the single most impactful period of their career.

The standard playbook

A key observation from the pandemic era is that law firm leaders engaged in processes and made decisions that, in a law firm context, were extraordinarily unusual. Before we can properly understand the stark differences, we need to establish a baseline for how law firms operate.

The legal marketplace tends to follow some predictable patterns. During times of high demand, when billable hours increase, revenues increase too. Law firms gear up to quickly hire more lawyers to meet growing demand, and the competition for a limited pool of talent generates a spike in remuneration. The headlines start to report huge increases in salaries and bonuses for graduates of leading law schools as, one by one, leading law firms play "follow the leader". In a reaction as predictable as day following night, some clients will begin to grumble and threaten not to pay higher rates for these "baby lawyers". So long as there are plenty of other clients with a backlog of legal work, law firm leaders can safely ignore these threats. Some go even further and ask their finance teams to compile lists of unprofitable clients, defined as those with billing or collection realization far below the firm average. Partners are encouraged to contact these clients to advise that the volume of work or the billing rates, and preferably both, need to increase or, unfortunately, the firm won't be able to work them any longer.

Mid-level associates who have successfully survived the first few years of practice and are now generating healthy profits know their market value is high, so they demand higher pay and more flexible work arrangements, and many change firms in search of a more lucrative or balanced opportunity. Lawyers at all levels lucky enough to be part of a hot, fast-growing practice, including service partners who are in high demand for their team and matter management skills, gain negotiating leverage and start to demand more rewards and recognition. Not surprisingly, rainmakers with lucrative client relationships are more likely than ever to jump to a competitor willing to pay far more, often with multi-year guarantees. The fault lines between high-rate and low-rate practices, or between busy junior partners and less productive senior partners, begin to fracture. However, so long as partner profits rise each year, law firm leaders can usually forestall any major conflicts.

Meanwhile, law firm leaders are busy acting on back-burner investments like network and hardware upgrades, cyber security measures, and office renovations. The various business teams may commence a once-a-decade project like installing a new time and billing system or rebranding and relaunching the firm website. Leaders with an interest in workplace and social causes may authorize new diversity, equity, and inclusion campaigns, or recruit a chief wellbeing officer to operationalize work–life balance programs. The firm's operating costs grow quickly, so annual revenue targets and hourly rates are increased to keep pace. The firm is generating a lot of profit but, due to their chosen business form, or the insatiable appetite of the partners, or both, they can't or won't retain earnings and build a reserve for a rainy day. And then the rains come.

Multi-practice law firms are well-designed to withstand the ebbs and flows of business cycles. It may not have even been a conscious choice when a group of lawyers launched a new law firm all those many years ago. The founders may simply have been friends or classmates who wanted to go into business together. But conscious or not, the way to mitigate risk in a business is to sell services to different market segments, to offer both high-priced and low-priced services, and to expand across geographies. This increases the likelihood that some services are always in high demand even as other services falter. When some client segments experience a downturn, others may experience a counter-cyclical boon. The same goes for operating in multiple jurisdictions. On day one of business school, professors advise that the best path to immense profitability is to find a niche that addresses an unmet or under-served need, outperform everyone else in that niche, and ride the wave of increasing profits until the market inevitably moves on and your business dies overnight. Lawyers who, by and large, deplore risk don't find this model at all compelling. So, law firms grow big and wide and offer many services to many clients and this is how law firms pass through every economic downturn unscathed. Or at least they would fare better if law firm leaders paid closer attention to business cycles.

Law firms don't create economic downturns. The marketplace is quite capable of triggering these, sometimes in isolated regions or industry segments, but in a connected global economy, it's increasingly likely that a downturn in one segment will quickly spread to others. When interest rates rise, the higher cost of capital stifles corporate investments and acquisitions. Trade disputes or military actions between countries or regions disrupt supply chains and trigger consumer price increases. Political actions, whether populist or oligarchic, can quickly impact wages, labor supply, unemployment, money supply, or manufacturing productivity. The characteristics and scope may differ each time, but there's a certain inevitability to business cycles. What's up will eventually come down.

The defining characteristic of leaders is that they influence others, they're storytellers, they have followers, or they get things done through others. When it comes to economic downturns, the defining characteristic of many leaders too often seems to be surprise. Those heady with success, certain they have solved an elusive formula and joined an exclusive club of perpetual winners, tend to not plan ahead for the inevitable rainy day. Law firm leaders are not immune from this, as they follow a predictable pattern of reactions.

The first signs typically appear in the form of reduced billable hours, longer collection times for outstanding receivables, a marked increase in fee negotiations, and histrionic headlines in all the leading trade publications. To protect partner profits in the short-term, firm leaders implement measures that impact primarily everyone but partners – a staff hiring freeze, a ban on unnecessary travel, a pause on major expenditures, and an aggressive collections effort. As the slowdown advances, so do the remedies. There are staff layoffs, some characterized as "realigning to industry standard lawyer-to-staff ratios", while others, such as chiefs overseeing cost centers, are done more stealthily. The current approach is more humane than a few cycles ago, when leaders were more likely to announce any workforce reductions as "overdue actions to address underperformance", though this fooled no one. There's typically a major rollback of big-ticket marketing expenses, and firm events such as holiday parties and the annual partner retreat are downgraded if not canceled outright.

Sooner or later, the actions begin to impact the lawyers. The start date of incoming graduates is delayed. Departing associates are not replaced. Requisitions for open positions at all levels are canceled. Leaders begin to study productivity metrics more closely and make the rounds to hold tough conversations with lawyers whose hours or rates or collections are lagging. Top rainmakers and partners who own significant client origination credit will schedule meetings with firm leaders to discuss their concerns with subsidizing unproductive partners. If the slowdown endures, senior lawyers, including partners, will be exited.

Simultaneously, there's a big push for partners to generate more revenue. Every idle partner starts to bombard the marketing team with clever ideas, with at least one suggestion per day to call the editors at *The Financial Times* or *Wall Street Journal* to secure an above-the-fold bylined article placement for the partner's latest 40-page white paper. Practice groups start to forward every RFP or tender, many with hourly rate caps that a year or two previously would have relegated the opportunity to the bin. Partners will request intel on past clients, including many that were unceremoniously terminated for being undesirable, in advance of an awkward "Good news! We'll take you back!" outreach. Curiously, this push tends to take place just as marketing headcount and budgets are reduced and contracts with external business development coaches are terminated.

What's usually not at the top of the recession task list, often missing entirely, is counter-cyclical investing. Law firm partners have been conditioned to perceive every dollar or euro or pound sterling spent to be gone forever, so they feel the best way to safeguard the remuneration pool is to avoid spending. There's a world of difference between an expense and an investment, however. Purchasing new office chairs is an expense that generates a modest return, if you make the connection that comfortable chairs make employees happy and employee satisfaction reduces unwanted attrition. The point of an investment is to put in a pound and receive three pounds, or 15 pounds, or 60 pounds, or more, in return.

Experienced business leaders will often increase investments in the exact areas where competitors are decreasing. Whether this is marketing, manufacturing capacity, fill-in acquisitions, or recruiting talent, they know that the right investments during a downturn can generate significant returns, in much the same way that purchasing shares of blue-chip stocks at a low point allows for a much greater upside when the share price recovers. The extreme focus in law firms on preserving partner profits leads to miserly penny-pinching, and this is exactly why the recovery from a downturn is often so challenging.

Sooner or later, a new coalition or party takes office. Military skirmishes cease. Regulators resolve trade conflicts. Central Banks signal a financial recovery. And many businesses dust off delayed initiatives and get right to work. Law firms often have a more uphill battle. The two most common challenges for a law firm trying to jump back into the fray are a depleted bench (talent pool) and a partnership reluctant to spend. Lawyers have a somewhat unique perspective as business owners. As owners, they expect to be insulated from any economic downside and benefit from any economic upside. There is no circumstance in which it's acceptable for a partner to receive a distribution that's lower than the year prior. When this horrific reality happens, or comes close to happening, during an economic downturn, partners take a more active role policing the firm's operating expenses, or at least make it a point to remind firm leaders of the importance of not spending the partners' money.

As a consequence, when client calls begin to increase, when practices start to get busier, they quickly realize they cut too deep. To be ready for a client call that puts a team to work right away, the firm often needs to add more people. This can be lawyers, paralegals, or staff. To be in a position to receive that client call, the firm often needs to boost its visibility by expanding its outreach. This is not the best time for law firm leaders to accede to partner demands to hold operating budgets flat until the economic forecast is more certain. Eventually, every firm is compelled to act and will spend money, but it often costs a lot when trying to catch up to more nimble competitors. The frenzied pursuit of legal talent creates – surprise! – a sudden spike in salaries. After a brief interval of being treated as chattel, trainees and associates are again in high demand and may receive a starting salary higher than their unlucky predecessors received during the downturn. Lateral partners are on the prowl again. Price-conscious clients who had once been lost but were joyfully welcomed back into the fold by idle partners may have their distracting low-rate matters delegated to juniors. And so it goes.

We've taken a little license here to paint a bleak picture, primarily to illustrate the immense inefficiency that can come from appointing firm leaders whose full-time day job may be practicing law. Even those who suspend their law practices during their terms as elected firm leaders face an inefficient learning curve. Few partners have had in-depth training as leaders or managers. Leaders who have learned the ropes and are stepping down are often faced with restarting a moribund practice, so some can't afford to spend a lot of time transitioning and sharing information with successors. We certainly don't intend to convey that law firm leaders are incapable of learning. Indeed some, without any formal training at all, quickly become fantastic leaders and managers. Even for smart lawyers, it takes time to learn the craft of leading a complex business. Ironically, operating with these blind spots may have increased the effectiveness of law firm leaders during the COVID-19 pandemic. Unlike their peers in other business segments, they had less management dogma to un-learn.

The onset

Most of us can recall exactly where we were when the world seemed to come apart. In mid-March of 2020, this author delivered a talk to law firm leaders in Sydney, Australia. Our host firm had just started to implement safety measures in its conference space. None of us had masks at this point, but we were instructed to use toe or elbow taps instead of shaking hands, and this became a source of endless amusement. Four days later I was in North Carolina in the US, presenting to another group of law firm leaders. There were no safety measures in place at all. Arriving home two days later, I sought treatment for an unknown respiratory ailment and was attended to by a single doctor in a vivid yellow spaceman suit, or so it seemed. In the next few days, while confined to my bed, I watched news reports of surrounding states enacting travel bans, then my state, and then most of the country and the rest of the world were directed to shelter at home until further notice. It was another 734 days before Australia re-opened its borders, and I was able to return to Sydney to visit my daughter, who resides there. This anecdote perhaps serves the purpose of illustrating the intensely personal nature of the pandemic. Everyone has a story to tell. My family had the good fortune to experience mostly inconvenience and no tragedy. Still, it may take years to determine the mental health toll of the pandemic on our then pre-teen who spent almost two years in complete isolation from his peers.

In some jurisdictions, law firms were deemed in their entirety to be essential services providers not subject to shelter-at-home restrictions. In other jurisdictions, the nature of the legal practice dictated whether barristers or solicitors were allowed to visit their law office or another essential facility, such as a courthouse. In the end, a very high proportion of lawyers and law firm personnel were required to stay home and work remotely. Four years hence, quite a few have still never returned to the office. They're happily toiling away without the burden of a rush-hour commute, they're wearing casual clothes, periodically hidden under a "Zoom shirt" for client video calls, and they're enjoying more time with their families. If leaders from 1,000 different law firms of all sizes and locations were polled in early 2020 about the feasibility or desirability that such a working arrangement could exist, let alone thrive, at least 950 leaders would have confidently stated it to be impossible. On this note, let's turn to the challenges faced and actions taken by law firm leaders as the impossible became possible.

Lessons learned

Each vignette below describes a challenge that law firm leaders faced, how they handled it, and how their actions may have been atypical, at least in a law firm. To the extent there's any discernible pattern, we'll also point out lessons potentially at risk of being forgotten.

Communication style

Law firm leaders initially went through the normal process of vetting internal communications prior to circulation. Fast-moving circumstances at the onset of the pandemic caused many leaders to dispense with the formality pretty quickly. The most expedient way for leaders to convey important messages was simply to send frequent, concise, and specific emails without a lot of extraneous puffery. Some messages focused on logistics, such as how to obtain a laptop for home use. Others shared practical details of health and safety measures undertaken by building management, such as capacity limits in lifts, or public transport restrictions. The law firm caste system was suddenly irrelevant. Everyone needed information quickly, and everyone received it quickly. Few leaders had time to circulate a detailed partner-only memo and then wait a suitable time for partner reactions before sending a firmwide memo containing far less detail. It may have seemed a modest shift to partners, but to junior lawyers and staff in the most hierarchical firms, it was quite refreshing to be treated as equals.

Many leaders took to writing more personal notes that shared details of how they and their families were coping with the sudden changes and offered encouragement to those struggling to adapt. Everyone could relate to the challenge of working amidst household chaos, with toddlers seeking attention, schoolchildren consuming the WiFi signal, and the family dog entering the frame during every Zoom call. During a recent conference session on the topic of post-pandemic changes, attendees from numerous firms shared how delighted they were to receive genuine, heartfelt messages from colleagues, particularly at a time when the absence of in-person connections was so acute. The frequency, informative content, and tone of communication from leadership prompted one attendee to state, "*We have never communicated so well as a firm. Despite not seeing any colleagues in person for several months, we all felt even more connected than when we were together in the office every day.*"

Sadly, as everyone settled into a new normal, law firm leaders reverted to the usual impersonal and paternalistic mode of intra-firm communication. Firm chairmen who once shared amusing anecdotes of their families' struggles to adapt rarely communicate now outside the usual memos with updates on the firm's performance. In firms where new leaders have taken the reins, now nobody knows their dog's name, or even if they own a dog. Law firms are people-intensive organisations. People are tribal and like to feel a connection and a sense of common purpose. Leaders who take the time to communicate regularly, who let their personality shine through, and even show some vulnerability, can engender great loyalty and respect.

Setting priorities

The onset of the pandemic was a critical time. For several months, no one really knew if the volume of client work would hold steady and if clients would pay invoices, or if clients would hoard cash while putting a halt to all but the most essential business processes. A common question among firm leaders at this time was, "How long do we have until we run out of cash?" Even in law firms unconcerned about an imminent cash flow threat, the immediate rise in unexpected expenditures, such as laptops, chairs for home offices, firmwide Zoom licenses, and so on caused a modicum of panic. One of the most compelling lessons learned by leaders at this stage was the importance of *triage*.

Many leaders facilitated a conversation about financial priorities:

> *"I need all department heads to look closely at their operating budgets. Please identify expenditures in terms of one or more of the following criteria:*
> *1. How does it directly generate new revenue?*
> *2. How does it protect current revenue?*
> *3. How does it reduce our operating costs?*
> *4. How does it help us avoid incurring new operating costs?*
> *5. How does it provide a demonstrable competitive or operational advantage?*
>
> *Be specific and explain your rationale. We meet in two days to review and decide what expenditures continue and what we will immediately halt."*

This may sound like a simplistic approach, but at the heart of it is the foundation for every strategic and operational planning process. Every line manager and division head of every business of any scale has had to prepare and defend a budget in this manner. Corporate boardrooms are the original Dragon's Den or Shark Tank. Executives are competing for access to a limited amount of capital and their fiercest enemy is not the competition but their colleague from another department or division who has a more compelling investment opportunity. Law firms do not operate this way.

Law firms are not designed to maximise profits, notwithstanding the relentless pressure to generate profits. Nor are they designed to delight clients or deliver the highest possible quality. Law firms are primarily designed for partner comfort. Within certain boundaries, the partnership hierarchy means that a senior partner's wish is equivalent to a sound business decision. As an example, there is not enough time in the day for marketing professionals to manage the deluge of terrible ideas presented to them by earnest and well-intentioned lawyers who confuse their preferred tactic with reasoned analysis. Should a marketer feel sufficiently bold to present data indicating the futility of a proposed tactic, the partner will as often be confused as angry. *"I don't need to counter with my own data. My desire to proceed is all the justification I need to access firm resources that I pay for."*

There's generally no neutral court where informed analysis drives the decisions. This occurs in law firms every day in many different ways, from hiring a lateral whose book of business is sizable but has little in common with the firm's current practices or clients, to launching a new sub-practice specialty that seems hot because numerous competitors have done the same, or favorable discounts offered by partners to clients who haven't asked, and more.

Again, we exaggerate a bit here for effect to make the point that partners are not accustomed to hearing no, and certainly not from staff. But that's exactly what happened. It was prompted by a panicked sense of the unknown, but law firm leaders, in their quest to hoard cash in case the pandemic ground business to a halt, stumbled on the simplest method for sorting the necessary from the nice-to-have. As they examined major expenditures using some variation of these five criteria, they discovered a lot of nonsensical line items. In one notable example shared by a chief financial officer, an executive committee finally got a look at the RoI report for an annual golf outing that the marketing team had prepared, only for the partner in charge of the event to bury it. It turns out the firm had spent over a quarter million dollars annually for over ten years for an event that primarily involved 20 clients and friends of two partners. Two-thirds of the attendees showed recent billings, though their combined annual fees exceeded the annual cost of the event only about half the time. One-third of the attendees had never hired the firm. The partner who planned and hosted the outing defended it by stating that it had been in the budget for years and no one had ever questioned it.

We advised multiple law firms in the early days of the pandemic on how to undertake this streamlined budget review exercise. Every firm was able to identify significant expenditures to be canceled. Some line items were put on a list to restore once there was more budget certainty, often to keep the peace with influential partners. Practice group and business department leaders were directed to apply this five-point framework to any new expenditure requests of a certain size and they were deputized to reject those that didn't qualify. Somewhat surprisingly, the increased scrutiny and the rejections of partner ideas were accepted fairly well, though by most accounts the partners didn't complain solely because they too were spooked by the uncertainty. We'd like to report that this framework has successfully remained in place, but no, it has not. The year the pandemic started and the year that followed turned out to be two of the most financially successful years in the history of many law firms. The fiscal discipline that helped many law firms prepare for a time of uncertainty was discarded once it was clear that revenues would continue unabated. Further eroding the need for discipline was the enormous reduction in travel, entertainment, and sponsorship expenses, and the infusion of income from government-subsidized loans. We followed up with several chief financial officers and learned that the annual budgeting exercise is back to being complex, opaque, and rife with pork barrel spending.

Technology

There have been breathless headlines for decades announcing the growth of technology usage in law firms. Indeed, many law firms have a sophisticated "tech stack", as those in the business refer to it. Many firms are still light on cyber security measures and continue the reputation of law firms being the weakest link in the chain of custody for business data. Others are heavily invested in bespoke software development to meet finicky or one-off demands for features or functions that enterprise software providers don't offer (because finicky or one-off features are, by definition, not of interest to most customers). But most sizable law firms have established sensible rigor in hardware and software policies, such as imposing limits on BYOD (bring your own device) options. A partner demanding to use a

2009-era Blackberry would be denied today, unlike a partner in 2009 demanding to use a 1999-era wireless Palm Pilot 7, whose wish would have be accommodated. From an operations perspective, law firms are generally all-in on the use of technology. Where many firms lag is the use of technology to improve the delivery of legal services.

Still, there was a pretty intense learning curve as lawyers and staff fled the well-appointed confines of their central business district offices and set up shop in their suburban houses and condos. No one will forget the adorable senior lawyer who went viral after using his assistant's laptop to join an online court hearing, only to discover that his assistant's children had previously activated a filter that presented his surprised visage with fluffy white fur and whiskers. Luckily, he was able to assure the judge that he was not a cat.

There were several lessons learned during this time. Despite the prevalence of office technology, many lawyers were uncomfortable using these tools because there had been no reason previously to step outside their comfort zone. A decade ago, Casey Flaherty, a tech-savvy in-house counsel, administered a basic office technology test to his outside counsel. He posited that those incapable of performing the most fundamental tasks using ubiquitous office technology are more likely to practice law in other inefficient ways.[1] With an economic model that rewards inefficiency, this was no great leap. It would be easy to characterize this as a generational issue, as lawyers approaching the end of their careers now didn't regularly see a computer in their law offices until well into their careers. However, the pandemic demonstrated that tech blindness affects a much wider swath, young and old, lawyers and staff. Fumbling with technology is not the best way to impress a client, particularly one whose business is heavily reliant on technical innovation.

Another important lesson was more subtle. A popular comic has a routine where he goes back in time and struggles to convince anyone that he's from the future. He can describe a mobile phone, but he has no idea how it works. Does any of us really know how they work? Lawyers tend to operate like this in their own firms. There's an entire infrastructure built around law firm partners to help with whatever they need. It's not surprising that many have no idea how things get done. Experienced staff members make it look easy, so naturally some believe it is easy. Until they try to do it from their quiet sitting room after everyone has retired for the evening. During the pandemic, law firms that offered nighttime clerical services still offered nighttime clerical services. But assigning tasks in the matter management system, online court filing, approving and routing prebills, even creating PDFs, can be a bit more challenging to those accustomed to handing off an assignment in person.

As one chief technology officer shared:

> *"When we were building our new system, every time we scheduled a review of the latest screens and functions to gather feedback, the lawyers were too busy to attend. In the first few months of the pandemic we logged hundreds of design or feature suggestions from lawyers on how to make things easier. I wish we had received this level of interest before we launched!"*

The use of technology appears to be a lesson that took hold. Anecdotal reports from firms of all sizes indicate that lawyers who were forced to fend for themselves while isolated at home have now taken a more active interest in how internal systems are built. Many law firms now offer more robust technology training as part of the onboarding process, and it's been quite a while since the last sighting of the cat barrister.

Adaptability

The expanded use of technology is but one example of the flexibility and adaptability demonstrated by law firms during the pandemic. Darwin is often misquoted, but his work clearly conveyed that the strongest survive in large part because their strength enables them to overcome challenges when adapting to a changing environment. A key lesson law firm leaders learned is how fundamentally adaptable lawyers and business professionals can be when the times require it. But there won't often be a global pandemic to put wind into the sails of a leader's next bold idea.

Law firms are not unlike other businesses in which starry-eyed leaders envision a bold new future and then implement plans to achieve that future – and the first time those who will participate in or be impacted by that future hear about it is when it's launched as a fait accompli. Law firm leaders, relying on the support of the hierarchical system, often adopt a directing management style. This means exactly what it sounds like. Rather than embracing a democratic process or coaching others into developing innovative ideas, law firm leaders often believe their role is to make decisions and take action. This goes only so far. When it comes to impacting their daily routines and processes, people will only accept so much directed change before they revolt. Imagine a celebrity chef visiting your home and immediately rearranging your kitchen. One could stipulate that the chef is well-equipped to identify a more efficient use of space, but directing a homeowner to fundamentally alter their way of operating without so much as an inquiry let alone a discussion will lead to good ideas being rejected, even when the idea could confer desirable benefits to all involved.

There are lot of principles of change management that law firm leaders can better embrace. Foremost is that people who will be impacted by change will instinctively resist change unless they can contribute to designing the change. The pandemic was unique in that the circumstances didn't really give anyone an opportunity to weigh in or vote. The health crisis was upon us, and no amount of wishing it weren't so (and there was plenty of that) would make it go away. For future changes, the lesson for law firm leaders is that their teams have demonstrated extraordinary adaptability. To unleash that power again and again, leaders will benefit from dialing down the directing style in lieu of a more inclusive approach that invites more voices to the discussion. Including more voices is not the same as ceding authority to the mob. Rather, it helps secure buy-in and leads to greater adoption of the contemplated change, even when the specific change is not exactly what the mob wants. The power to unleash change comes as much from including others in the process as it might lead to incremental improvements of an idea.

Management styles

Another key lesson learned by leaders in the pandemic is that job titles may convey positions of authority, but not everyone with a title is an effective leader. We have consistently used the term leaders rather than managers in this chapter. While there are a variety of ways to distinguish the two, for simplicity we'll say that leaders establish a vision and empower others to act while managers oversee the execution of the vision. In the early days of the pandemic, there were a lot of decisions to be made. There wasn't a lot of time to debate or seek clarity. Action was preferable. More than a few leaders and managers wilted under the pressure. More than a few with no organizational authority stepped into the breach to take charge.

One executive committee chairperson from a six-office law firm shared how a simple one-off gesture to satisfy one request turned into a firm-wide effort, none of it planned. When the state governor announced an imminent lockdown, everyone scrambled to gather necessary belongings from the office so they'd be equipped to operate from home. A young administrative assistant in one of the smaller offices asked a colleague, a senior paralegal who served as a point of contact for building management but otherwise had no operational authority, if she was permitted to take home her desk chair. Evidently, the small flat she shared with her companion had no suitable chairs she could use, especially on camera. Overhearing this, another paralegal asked if she could take home her large screen computer monitor that she used because smaller screens taxed her eyes. The senior paralegal said neither request would be a problem, since the accommodations were reasonable and this situation had not been addressed in any senior leader communications. Knowing that building security required a pass to remove equipment from the premises, the senior paralegal sent a memo to all other colleagues in the office asking for a list of equipment, supplies, and/or furniture they'd be taking so she could make arrangements with building security. Within an hour, she received a frantic call from the office managers of two larger offices. The paralegal's email was making the rounds and contradicted what most office managers had done in response to similar requests. They were concerned that the removal of these items hadn't been specifically authorized and partners may not like the optics of employees and lawyers wheeling desk chairs topped with boxes of office supplies to the parking lots.

The chairperson was looped in within two hours and shared her initial reaction:

> *"I almost literally smacked my head, like an emoji character, wondering why we hadn't anticipated this. I immediately shared the paralegal's note in a firm-wide memo and confirmed that lawyers and staff were authorized to take whatever they needed to work from home for a few weeks and to please document what they needed. I wasn't worried that our desk chairs would come back ruined by coffee spills or that a devious employee would start a black-market pencil store from our supply cabinet. The senior paralegal in that small office took the right action because it was the right thing to do. A month later when it was clear the lockdown would be extended, she stepped up again to arrange for the mail clerk to fulfill resupply requests and drive the orders to each colleague's homes. We eventually expanded that to allow employees to order directly from a national office supply store. I appreciate that this woman simply acted on what she felt was right without seeking explicit permission. I don't fault others for their hesitation, but it did help me understand how our love of detailed and often proscriptive policies can overlook that when we hire smart people, they shouldn't need constant guidance to do the right thing."*

Despite the relative insignificance of this gesture when compared to life-or-death decisions being made elsewhere, it helps showcase how organizations can thrive when leaders set a vision but leave it in the hands of capable managers to execute the vision, authorizing them to make suitable decisions within certain boundaries without constantly seeking approval.

A senior partner who serves as both practice group leader and office managing partner for a regional office of a national Australian law firm recounted how his colleagues essentially ran for cover when big decisions were made.

> *"Our wider management committee consisting of all office managing partners, all practice heads and second chairs, the executive committee, managing partner, and three of our business chiefs, typically meets only quarterly. Most of the firm's day-to-day operational decisions are made by the managing partner and business chiefs, with any thorny issues raised to the EC. When lockdown happened, the entire group began to meet more frequently. Our operating agreement allows us to give our proxy to a colleague to speak or vote on our behalf if we miss a meeting for a client meeting, family holiday, or some other unavoidable conflict, but with standing quarterly meetings we didn't have too many conflicts. A few weeks in, people began to miss the calls so colleagues would start each call by reporting who was holding a proxy. The issues we discussed started to escalate. A returning citizen broke quarantine and spread the virus to one of our employees, and she was in the office for a couple of days before we learned of it and triggered our own lockdown. Quite a few people died from that outbreak, though none of ours. Then state governments closed the borders to travelers from neighboring states, which had never happened. Over half of the attendees from two of our larger offices had stopped attending entirely at that point. The rest of us were quite capable of making decisions without them, but it was telling that colleagues who had been elected or appointed to take on important leadership roles couldn't find the time to engage. It's taken us a while, but we've now implemented some minimum expectations for partners holding key roles and we've made some distinctions between titles that are for marketing purposes and titles for those actually governing the firm."*

The final management anecdote has to do with the challenges line managers faced when their entire teams worked remotely. Numerous press reports within and outside the legal sector have cited research illustrating how employee productivity generally improved, sometimes dramatically so, when lawyers, paralegals, and administration staff didn't have to commute to an office. The purchase of employee-monitoring software or "bossware" spiked during the pandemic. Nothing demonstrates trust in an employee like installing a tool to monitor a user's mouse, keyboard, and eye movements to ensure they're not napping.

Some tasks require close supervision. Some people require regular supervision. But knowledge workers hired for their expertise, especially those who record and bill time to clients, may not need the same level of supervision as an entry-level data entry clerk, notwithstanding a manager's preference for micromanagement. At a roundtable of small firm executive directors discussing operational challenges during the pandemic, several noted how productivity had increased and paid time off and sick leave requests had decreased. After applauding themselves, they moved on to the next topic – how to require reluctant remote workers to return to working in the office. I pointed out the incongruity of demanding workers to revert to quantifiably lower productivity. The only other argument beyond the vague assertion that *"Workers belong in the office"* was *"Unless supervisors periodically walk the halls to ensure people are working, people's attention will inevitably wander"*. None had a persuasive argument. I gently pointed out that continuing to hire staff consistently at risk of failing such a simple test is a poor reflection of the capabilities of the hiring manager. In an old joke, a patient enters a doctor's office. *"Doctor, it hurts when I do this"*, the patient says, to which the doctor immediately replies, *"Then stop doing that"*. If a manager can never trust employees to work diligently during the workday, it may be time to question the effectiveness of the hiring manager or supervisor. Many law firms have enjoyed sustained increases in productivity post-pandemic. To accomplish this, many managers were forced to adopt new approaches. Often different members of the same team require different levels of oversight, depending on the complexity of the task and the experience of the employee. A fundamental tenet of "situational management" is that not everyone needs to be treated exactly the same for everyone to be treated equitably.

The pandemic helped law firm leaders see that not everyone with a title is able or willing to engage when leadership is needed and that many with no formal titles or organizational authority are quite capable of stepping up and contributing at a high level when others falter. As circumstances change, management styles have to change as well. Any firm lacking a clear set of expectations for its leaders should remedy that right away.

Remote work

We've already touched on remote working. The single most impactful lesson brought about by the COVID-19 pandemic is that common approaches to running a law firm are not etched anywhere in stone. Law firm leaders' reluctance to change the formula and provide more workforce flexibility has been proven to emanate from the leaders' risk-aversion and preference for familiarity, and not by any market constraint or client requirement. Several generations ago, someone's great-granddad and his peers designed a law firm operating model that suited them, and precedent-driven lawyers have been perpetuating this model ever since. Knowledge workers are capable of being highly productive without gathering in an elegant office in a central business district. Meetings can take place virtually. Lawyers and staff can recapture time and money lost to commuting and obtain more balance in their personal lives.

Cynically, if law firm leaders wanted to free up commuting time that lawyers could devote to billing more hours, encouraging remote working would be an easy solution. Instead, many simply encourage a high number of billed hours on top of long days that often include lengthy commutes. For lawyers of any generation who value family and health and recreation, this forces a choice between what fills the firm's revenue ledger and what recharges their mind and body. Renee Branson, a wellbeing advisor to law firms, explains that, "The billable hour helps to perpetuate a system that discourages efficiency and encourages the churn and burn that results in middle-of-the-night emails".[2]

In a recent study of RTO (return to office) policies at S&P 500 companies, researchers found that in-office workers aren't more productive.[3] With no financial incentive to return to the office, it's puzzling to learn of a Forbes report[4] that "90 percent of companies will return to the office in 2024, with 28 percent threatening to fire workers who don't comply". The researchers concluded that it's about reasserting workplace control and leaders satisfying their own best interests, even if it costs the firms money. RTO mandates are more common among male CEOs and more powerful CEOs, who may feel they're losing power in their firms as employees have become more aware of their rights and options. Secondarily, ascribing the firm's poor performance to lazy employees working at home deflects responsibility from management's own bad decisions. Could there be a more poignant demonstration of the notion that law firms are designed for partner comfort above all else?

The pandemic taught law firm leaders that law firms can be run differently. This should come as no surprise as most law firms have business clients that operate across borders with far-flung operations and a distributed management class. If it were optimal to run a business by having everyone sit in the same city postal code at all times, business leaders with a lifetime more experience managing complex organisations would have reached that conclusion long ago. Hopefully, law firm leaders will retain this lesson and strike a balance between workforce flexibility and partner comfort.

Intentionality

Some common objections to remote work policies are the inevitable collapse of law firm cultures, the challenge of training and mentoring young lawyers and onboarding new employees virtually, or the inability of colleagues to effectively communicate or collaborate. These have already been disproved. It may also be helpful to question the premise. Who believes that law firms have ever been paragons of collaboration and communication? Numerous law firms have invested millions in developing well-appointed and comfortable collaboration spaces with cozy seating and walls that serve as giant erasable whiteboards. Many sit empty for simple reasons – lawyers travel regularly, and deal teams and client teams in larger firms are regularly comprised of lawyers and business staff in multiple offices, so at least some participants are always remote. Prior to the pandemic, if a good portion of a working group were going to be on-screen only, it was a lot more convenient for others to remain in their offices and join virtually as well.

Few law firms have provided specific training on how teams can effectively collaborate. Having trained numerous groups of lawyers and staff in project management and process improvement, we can report that the most common experience with collaboration among many thousands of lawyers across hundreds of law firms globally is that the most senior partner in the room speaks the most and directs the action. A more effective approach for many collaborative exercises relies on mixed or cross-functional groups with absolutely no hierarchy, since a common factor in key breakthroughs is the naïve questioner challenging conventional wisdom and groupthink.

As we noted previously, the pandemic disrupted normal patterns of communication so much that lawyers and staff in many law firms enjoyed an unprecedented sense of shared purpose. Lawyers and staff members who previously sat near each other but never saw each other were communicating far more effectively when they had to be proactive and thoughtful. Managers accustomed to walking the floor to monitor activity realized that unstructured wandering generates a lot less insight than holding a series of brief one-on-one on-screen conversations. Partners who rarely stopped by the Friday night drinks and nibbles on the sunny veranda on the firm's main floor found themselves delighted to participate in virtual wine tastings with colleagues. Other team members were more eager to participate in online pet costume contests or a virtual candle-making class or to read the "Meet the Family" section of the managing partner's weekly email that shared a few interesting tidbits about a few firm families, including at least one awkward adolescent photo of the lawyer or staff members whose family was profiled.

Whether it's culture, communication, collaboration, or training, the fundamental catalyst for improvement isn't dedicated space, or proximity to others. It's *intentionality*. For some leaders, being thoughtful about developing such programs comes naturally. For others, there are plenty of experts in corporate communications or culture-building or team-building who can help. A key takeaway from the pandemic is the importance of intentionality over proximity.

Talent

Law firm clients have long lamented the endless rate increases pushed out by law firms every year, or nearly every year. Law firm leaders who have been conditioned to operate solely in a cost-plus framework will look at the growing costs of healthcare, office leases, or associate salaries and scratch their heads, puzzled as to why clients don't see the inevitability of price increases when the law firm's costs increase. Rest assured, business leaders are quite familiar with the rising costs of doing business. The difference is they aren't victimized by it. When law firm operating budgets dropped to a mere fraction of pre-pandemic levels because of the overnight elimination of travel and entertainment and the reduction of many marketing and operational expenses, clients exclaimed, *"Perhaps now you understand what we've been talking about!"* Law firm leaders have always had the ability to better manage their cost base. Some simply choose not to. Unless leaders are constantly seeking ways to deliver legal services more efficiently, the growing cost case will always push up hourly rates. Clients don't wish to pay higher prices just because law firms are locked into a rigid operating model that leaves little room for efficiency.

Leaders who, even inadvertently, combined the lessons mentioned above stumbled upon one of the single greatest opportunities to manage law firm costs while improving quality and profitability. In years past, when a highly valued lawyer or business professional relocated across the country to follow a spouse's career or to be closer to family, we threw a bittersweet party and sent them away, never to be seen again. During the pandemic, it dawned on numerous law firm leaders that highly valued lawyers or business professionals who had a proven ability to operate effectively remotely could remain, even if they moved. In fact, in many law firms, what drove this point home was partners moving permanently or semi-permanently to their summer home in warm climates or to their winter home in a posh ski town. When the global economy began its pandemic-fueled meteoric rise and associate salaries began to rise, these clever leaders realized they could recruit capable lawyers in lower-cost regions, pay wages below those demanded in large cities, yet set billing rates in the same range as their big city counterparts. It was like a magic formula – lower cost base, higher timekeeper revenue and profit margin, a reduced learning curve if they can better retain lawyers who might have otherwise left the firm, and no need for a lease expansion to accommodate new offices for lawyers who will only rarely work from the office.

Of course, even more leaders discarded this notion due to the inexorable pull to return to the familiar operating model of all lawyers and staff working from expensive offices in the highest rent district of each major cities, where on a given day only 60 percent of the office was occupied due to business travel, holidays, paid time off, or reduced capacity. It's in this context that clients shake their heads at law firm leaders who reject opportunities to manage their business more effectively and at a lower cost, and then pass on a surcharge for their resistance to change to clients. Law firm leaders have been led to believe that "competing on price" means lowering rates until the work becomes unprofitable. During the pandemic, some leaders realized that by lowering operating costs through clever geographic talent arbitrage, they could hold on to existing rates or request more modest increases than the competition, thereby boosting demand for the many price-sensitive services they offered, while pocketing more profits than a much higher rate increase would have ever netted them.

The long view

The same part-time leader challenge that causes law firms to fall into the same recurring patterns of short-sighted behaviors during an economic downturn has now surfaced in a post-pandemic world. Four years after the onset of the pandemic, many of those who held leadership roles during the pandemic have moved on. Some have retired, and some have stepped back into law practice. And who can blame them? They led their organizations during a global event of unprecedented scope, they presided over two years of financial performance that many firms declared to be their best ever, and some continued to lead as the legal sector entered a downturn. Those who remain for a bit longer will struggle to embrace pandemic lessons on a more permanent basis. Their own or their partners' comfort zone will exert strong pressure to migrate back to a more familiar and comfortable, albeit less profitable, operating model.

For those who need a slight push toward retaining all the lessons learned during the pandemic, here's some added incentive – most law firms will revert in large part to their pre-pandemic comfort zone. This means that leaders who stay the course and embrace the above lessons have the potential to exploit a compelling economic advantage – to access a much wider, more diverse, and less costly talent pool; to reduce operating costs by shrinking office footprints to properly reflect who's actually in the building rather than reserving a space for everyone who might be there; to foster a culture that values lawyer and staff wellbeing and is intentional about collaborating and communicating in a remote or hybrid environment; and to maintain fiscal discipline by constantly assessing which expenditures or programs drive revenue, reduce costs, or provide a market advantage.

The COVID-19 pandemic was an unprecedented, disruptive, horrific, and traumatic event that everyone on the planet, if we were blessed with the ability to wave a magic wand, would wish had never happened. But it did. And it presented numerous compelling lessons for law firm leaders on what the future of legal practice could look like if the rigid, current rules were miraculously suspended. It doesn't take a miracle. Law firm leaders have always had the ability to rewrite the rules and run a law firm in the manner that the pandemic showed was possible. How many will embrace these lessons long-term? Time will tell. But each day, the time in office of those who were in the unenviable position of leading a law firm during the pandemic is coming to a close. As new leaders take charge, the unfortunate and inefficient but inevitable re-learning of the law firm cycle of life will start anew. Let's make sure these leaders have the benefit of embracing during peacetime what their predecessors learned on the battlefield.

References

1 www.washingtonpost.com/news/capital-business/wp/2015/02/23/lawyers-could-you-pass-this-test/

2 "When Altruism is Not Enough: The Economics of Well-Being in the Legal Profession," by Renee Branson, LegalBusinessWorld, 2020

3 www.businessinsider.com/rto-policies-dont-improve-employee-performance-company-value-controlling-bosses-2024-1?r=US&IR=T

4 www.forbes.com/sites/shephyken/2023/09/24/nine-out-of-10-companies-will-require-employees-to-return-to-the-office/

Chapter 4: Linking partner and associate compensation to the achievement of a firm's strategy

By J. Mark Santiago, managing partner, SB2 Consultants

There are approximately 1.3 million attorneys in the United States, working in 421,643 law firms.[1] In Great Britain, approximately 185,000 barristers and solicitors work in more than 11,500 law firms.[2] In most of those firms the rules for compensation usually boil down to the decision(s) of the firm's founders, the partners with the largest book of business (originations), or in some cases the partner(s) with the best argument at year-end about their performance and why they deserve X amount of the firm's profits.

The focus of this chapter is not only to present a better way to apportion the profits that a law firm produces but to increase those profits as well. By linking a law firm's compensation program to the achievement of its strategic objectives, law firms and their partners can better realize the old proverb that "a rising tide does indeed lift all boats".

Strategy is an activity that has as many meanings as the number of people you ask. Foremost, it is some combination of analysis, proactiveness, defensiveness, and futurity blended into a lengthy document that only business school professors and consultants understand and love. I have seen many strategy documents on MPs' bookshelves gathering dust. Beyond the initial excitement of receiving the documents, it would appear (based on the amount of accumulated dust) that they have been seldom read.

Having been a consultant for almost 30 years with an MBA in strategy from a major business school, I have developed (over the years) my own definition of strategy – a far less complex view than what I learned in university but one that still addresses the four components of strategy noted above.

My short definition of law firm strategy is:

How a law firm chooses to invest its limited capital (both monetary and human) in advancing the ongoing success of the firm.

Vision and strategy development

Vision and strategy development are the logical starting points for a firm's partner compensation program. After all, if a firm does not know where it is going, how can it direct and reward the partner actions that will get it there? Indeed, how will it even know if it has gotten there?

Strategy development can be a long and arduous process and is best undertaken by an outside consultant/expert who reports to either a strategy development committee or the firm's management committee. Outside experts begin with a clean-slate mentality and no preconceived ideas about the firm. They can therefore produce a strategy document that stands a better chance of acceptance than a document produced by in-house resources that some partners might believe were biased.

The consultant should begin by conducting interviews with a significant number of the firm's partners (leadership, significant originators, up-and-coming younger partners, and those partners who, if they were not involved, would be disruptive because they were left out of the process). My experience is that at least 25 percent of the partners should be involved to ensure the broadest scope of opinion is gathered. However, in smaller firms the percentage should be increased (firms with ten partners or fewer should interview all the partners) and, depending on a firm's culture, the percentage of partners may increase. At one client firm, I interviewed all 67 of the partners.

During the interview process a consensus will begin to emerge about what are the firm's strengths, weaknesses, and potential new practice areas. Validation of the initial findings should be obtained through a detailed analysis of the firm's financial records; this is an important step in this process. Often, practice areas that are perceived as profitable are not, while other practice areas considered breakeven or even a drag on profits are profitable.

Questions that should be explored in the partner interviews include:

Competitive advantage:

1. What do we want to be famous for?
2. What competitive advantages does the firm currently have?
3. What are the weaknesses within our competitive advantages?
4. Would an additional practice area or strengthening an existing practice area improve our competitive advantages?

Firm culture:

5. What is the firm's culture?
6. What aspects of the firm's culture are non-negotiable?
7. What behavior does the firm want or need to change?
8. Who "owns" the firm's clients?
9. What actions by the partners does the firm want to reward/discourage?

Firm resources:

10. How large an investment in "firm building" does the partnership want to make?
11. For how long is the firm willing to invest before it receives a return on its investment?
12. Would the firm consider a merger to deepen its competitive advantages or broaden its service offerings?
13. Should the firm borrow money to achieve its strategic objectives?

This list is by no means exhaustive, but it demonstrates the breadth of issues that a strategy and its supporting compensation system must address. A firm's responses to these questions will also help to identify partner roles (a key part of any new compensation system) and what success in those roles will look like.

The importance of a clear, widely understood and supported-by-the-partnership firm strategy/vision cannot be overemphasized. Many law firms have floundered in the perilous sholes of ill-defined strategy, lack of partner understanding of the strategy, or outright opposition to the firm's strategy.

How did we get here?

Not so long ago, it was not uncommon for attorneys to spend their summers between classes working in a law firm as a summer associate. In those days, while training was a large part of the summer program, an equally important part was the determination (by both the summer associate and the hiring committee) as to whether the summer associate was "one of us". For the hiring committee the question was "Does this person match our idea of what an XYZ partner is?", and associates tried to determine if XYZ was the place where they wanted to spend a significant part of their lives. In those days, lateral partners were few and far between and in many instances were attorneys leaving high-level government positions.

I met my first former US ambassador at Donovan Leisure, my first former Dutch counsel at Hersh Dudeck, and my first former state governor at Winston & Strong.

The managing partner of one of my clients was retiring in his 70s, having worked at the firm more than 50 years. As he said on many occasions, "I bleed XYZ firm green". The days of bleeding XYZ green (or any other color) is not very common in any recruiter's office or hospital these days.

In many law firms the unwritten, but widely understood and accepted, compact among the lawyers required that younger, more productive junior partners and associates were to defer significant income to the older senior partners. In return, less experienced lawyers were trained in the practice of law and those associates who ultimately made partner received a stream of virtually guaranteed income until retirement – again, because younger attorneys were deferring part of the value they created. The fact that senior partners' income would often exceed the current value of their contributions to the firm compensated them for their prior lean years as associates. And the circle of professional life was complete.

Today the situation is very different. Although many attorneys will still spend their entire professional careers at the same firm, a growing number of partners can cite two, three, even four previous firms on their resumes. Just as corporate clients shop around for legal services, partners are shopping around for career opportunities that will offer more compensation and better meet their work and lifestyle expectations.

Law firms contribute to this instability by actively recruiting (cherry-picking) partners and attorneys from rival firms to bolster specific practice areas or start new ones.

With few exceptions, law firms no longer command all of a large corporation's legal work. Gone are the days when a specific firm rendered day-to-day legal advice and handled everything from the CEO's will or divorce to the purchase/sale of a subsidiary or the issuance of new stocks or bonds. By and large, corporations are now shopping for service among panels of law firms to meet their diverse needs. These companies base their selections on a number of criteria, including perceived expertise in the required field, the cost and timeliness of the needed service, and the level of attention the clients believe the firm's attorneys will be able to give to their matter.

Just as fewer attorneys are satisfied to stay with one firm their entire careers, firms are more aggressively evaluating performance at all levels. Partnership is no longer a guarantee of lifetime employment. Firms increasingly evaluate partners' performance and contributions based on absolute standards. Those who fail to meet the firm's criteria are frequently asked to leave – something that was unheard of several years ago. Firms are also more willing to lay off partners to "clean house" of ineffective colleagues, thereby improving the profit per partner reported in the annual AmLaw charts and improving their ranking.

These shifting loyalties have made law firm compensation an increasingly complex and dangerous endeavor. Complex because of the myriad compensable factors that firms now want to incorporate into their partner evaluation criteria, and dangerous because at no other time have firms been at such risk of losing key contributors to rival firms.

There are also other variables to consider – globalization, mergers, and acquisitions among them. After all, what worked for ten partners in a single office with similar backgrounds and long work histories together simply will not work for a firm with hundreds of partners with diverse backgrounds, spread throughout the world who have been brought together by plan, merger, or happenstance.

Compensating the rain dancers

The best way to drive a strategy is to link the achievement of the strategy to the firm's compensation system. In order to do that, a firm must identify and define the actions that partners need to do to help make the strategy succeed. We call these activities "compensable factors" and while the factors are the same for all attorneys, the amount of expected contribution varies between the firm's contribution roles.

Compensable factors include:

- Originations (individual and team);
- Individual (recorded and billed) hours;
- Client-managed hours (total client hours recorded, billed, and collected);
- Collection velocity/docket-to-pocket days (average collection cycle from recording to collection);
- Attorney development (number of attorneys mentored and success level, associate turnover on client matters managed and cost to the firm);
- Firm and practice development (number and quality of articles written, speeches given, and seminars presented; Bar service).

Additional non-financial factors need to be considered in the compensation process, including:

- Client tending, which includes maintaining superior ongoing client relationships and forging multiple contacts at different levels within the client and among other attorneys at the firm.
- Attorney development, including improving personal legal skills, as well as enhancing the technical legal, marketing, and presentation skills among junior partners and associates.
- Practice development, by increasing the public's awareness of the firm's expertise or specialty practice areas through public speaking, writing, or participation in Bar events.
- Administrative management at the departmental, practice, office, and firm level.

Contribution roles

As attorneys gain more experience and improve their skills, we find that various levels of contribution to the firm are identifiable. While age is not the sole determiner of a role, it plays an important part. We find that more mature partners develop skill sets that are compatible with different contribution roles.

There are many individual contribution roles and, within each role, a number of contribution levels. Therefore, most firms should make their role definition as broad as possible to recognize a broad scope of contribution within a role but also to make identification of roles very apparent to all the partners.

We recommend a three-category approach that provides a broad framework that captures all of the ways that partners can contribute to the firm's success without creating an overly complex system that results in dozens of distinctions with few real differences. The three categories and their broad outlines are as follows.

Client partners

This group of partners is usually more senior in tenure and has originated significant books of business. They have been at the firm for an extended period of time and served their clients for years, if not decades. While they are intimately familiar with their clients and are trusted advisors to them, often times they do not directly manage every active matter the client has at the firm. If the client partner is not directly involved in the day-to-day management of a matter, she would have consulted with the engagement partner as to strategy and staffing and ongoing progress in the matter.

Engagement partners

This group of partners manages individual matters. Either for client partners or, in many cases, for clients that they have developed independently, they are the client partner for that particular client. The difference between a "client" and "engagement" partner is the size and number of the partner's clients. A partner with five to ten or more clients with more than $1m in annual billings would be a client partner. A partner who manages a number of matters for other partners and has a single $200,000 (whom she developed) client would be an engagement partner. They are responsible for matter strategy, resource utilization, and day-to-day management decisions.

Specialty partners

This group includes three different types of partners. They are subject matter experts, administrative partners, and recently elected partners. Subject matter expert partners are the partners who "wrote the book" on a particular legal issue and work on numerous matters, providing critical insight into complex issues. Administrative partners are responsible for the management of a practice, office, or the firm in general. The final category of specialty partner includes all newly elected (usually for three to five years) and lateral partners until they become acclimatized to their new firm.

Once a firm has identified its evaluative criteria and the partner roles it will recognize and reward, it must determine by each role and each evaluative criteria what success looks like for each role.

Beginning with the premise that, while every partner is expected to contribute in every factor, the expectations will vary between roles. As an example, a client partner may be expected to develop $2m in new originations every year. A newly elected specialty partner's originations might be expected to be $250,000 (or even less).

Additionally, a client partner might be expected to record 1,200 billable hours in addition to the $2m in originations, while the specialty partner's hour target might be 1,800 or more. These contributions and their contribution level in the non-financial factors will form the basis of the partner's year-end performance evaluation.

To assist in the year-end process, we recommend that each partner develop a set of goals based upon their contribution role and the expectations for their role.

Individual partner goal setting

This phase has two distinct steps. First, each partner develops an individual plan outlining how he or she will contribute to the firm's overall success. I like to refer to these documents as "Partner Performance Contracts" or PPCs. The PPCs are developed late in the year in connection with the firm's business planning cycle for the coming year. These plans are based on the clearly defined and different roles – client partner, engagement partner, and specialty partner – conceived during the vision and strategy development phase. The strategic plans should also include specific milestones that, when reached, produce identifiable results to help achieve the firm's overall strategy. PPCs should be developed in cooperation with either the partners' practice leader, office MP, or the firm's MP. The documents should be clear in identifying goals for each compensable factor that supports the firm's strategy, based upon the partner's role.

Assessment and evaluation

At the end of the year, the assessment process begins. Individual partners meet with the partner with whom they worked to develop their PPC – department head, office manager, compensation committee member, or managing partner – to review their prior year's achievements. This conversation is based on the individual partner's PPC compared to the actual year's results. Individual partner performance data – the numbers – are still a major topic of discussion, but performance in the more subjective areas, such as attorney development, practice enhancement, and firm management are also included.

At the conclusion of individual meetings, the evaluators get together and, based upon the firm's overall strategy and needs, evaluate the partners relative to each other. This process groups partners into various hierarchical levels and allows for a firmwide "equity" evaluation.

Before beginning the evaluation process, some firms establish expected distribution percentages. For example, "Relative to our firm's standards, we expect five percent to substantially exceed expectations; ten percent to exceed expectations; 75 percent to meet expectations (with gradations in the "meets" category); and ten percent to fail to meet expectations". Such a distribution ranks partners and helps the firm and the individuals involved make long-term career planning decisions. The ultimate outcome of this phase is, of course, pay and bonus decisions.

It is important that a partner is able to independently confirm his or her performance evaluation on a periodic basis and, at the end of the year, validate the firm's pay decisions. Therefore, whatever criteria a firm uses to evaluate its partners – client development, management, billing, collections – the firm's management information system must provide a ready means for individual partners to assess their performance. If partners are measured on something, appropriate information should be available so they can "keep score".

Communicating pay decisions

The final phase of any compensation program – and the one most frequently overlooked – is communicating final results to the individual partners. Firms that downplay the importance of effective communication squander one of their best opportunities to direct partner behavior and affect firm performance.

An appropriate member of the firm (department head, office manager, executive committee member) and the affected partner should discuss individual partner pay and bonus decisions. These discussions should clearly and directly link the pay and bonus decisions to the partner's actual performance, compared with the goals set in their individual strategic plans and previously defined roles in the firm. This is an opportunity to explain "why you got what you got" and to discuss how the individual partner's strengths can be leveraged and what weaknesses need to be addressed. It may also be an appropriate time to discuss a partner's long-term career goals and opportunities at the firm, as well as that individual's role in the firm.

Although all partner compensation systems are different, the one common characteristic is their frequent lack of functionality. Many of the problems that a partnership encounters from its pay decisions are rooted in the system itself. For example, many systems have individual components that are poorly documented and misunderstood by those involved. In addition, the linkages between the various components are unclear – to firm management and to individual partners – or simply are not there.

The partnership compensation system

A complete partnership compensation system can be broken down into the following four key phases, as illustrated in Figure 1 on the next page.

This annual review is also the starting point for the following year's compensation cycle when partners prepare their new individual strategic plans for the coming year based on these discussions.

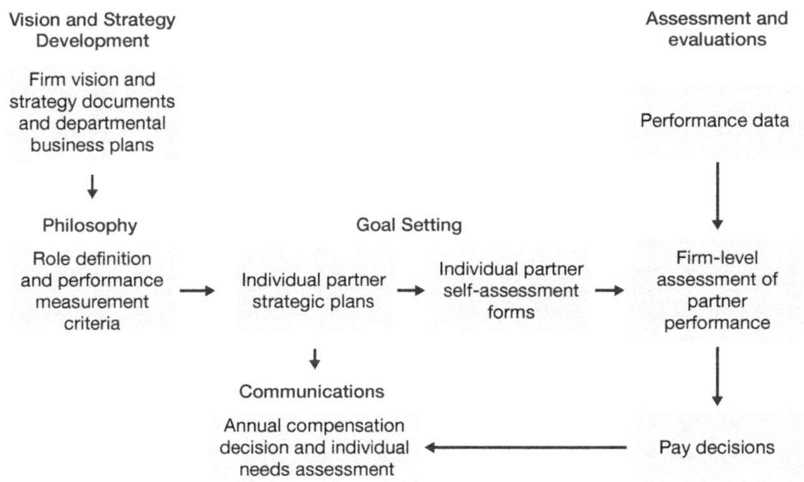

Figure 1. 360-degree performance feedback system.

Closing the loop

By closing the compensation "loop", the compensation system becomes an effective mechanism for directing partner behavior and achieving the firm's strategy. As firms recognize their changing environment and adapt to succeed within it, the compensation system can help individual partners appreciate the integral part they play in their firm's long-term success. As in all change, the most difficult step is the first. Before embarking on a major overhaul of its compensation system, a firm needs the following components:

- A clear, broadly shared, articulated vision of where the firm is going.
- A management group that is committed to undertake the substantial changes required to achieve the firm's vision.
- A managing partner with both the patience and the drive to take day-to-day responsibility for implementing and managing the necessary changes.
- A partnership that understands and supports the firm's vision and strategy, as well as the behavioral changes required to achieve the firm's goals.

Revising a compensation system in a partnership is a long and arduous process. It strikes at the foundations of the firm and any revision has as much potential for ill as good effects on a firm. Change should be undertaken neither lightly nor with the expectation that any fix to the compensation system is permanent. Compensation systems need annual reviews and periodic adjustments to ensure that they correctly reflect the firm's current thinking about its strategy and how best to achieve success.

References

1 https://www.americanbar.org/news/abanews/aba-news-archives/2022/06/aba-lawyers-survey/
2 https://www.statista.com/statistics/319220/number-of-solicitors-in-the-uk/

Chapter 5:
Pricing approaches and firm profitability

By Shaun Jardine, founder, Big Yellow Penguin

The death of the billable hour has been mooted for some time. Fixed pricing is clearly now fairly well-engrained. However, the concept of so-called "value-based pricing" – explicitly setting fees based on an understanding of the value to the individual client – seems to be becoming more recognized as an option. In this chapter, I will draw on research carried out in 2022 on law firm profitability, which demonstrates how different pricing approaches affect (professional service) firm profitability.[1] The chapter looks at the opportunities to generate more value for professional service firms and their clients, and to create a better work–life balance for employees.

> *"No single management lever available to you can boost profitability more quickly than even a slight improvement in average price levels."*
> *The Price Advantage* – Michael Marn, Eric Roegner, and Craig Zawada (Wiley, 2004)

Read that quote again: "No single management lever…". Pricing is important. I hope I can convince you to look carefully at how you price and consider changing how you do it, if required.

Some history. In 2022, I commissioned a thought leadership and pricing confidence survey[2] for a virtual conference I organized for a group called the Legal Iconoclasts. I was delighted to receive responses from 63 law firms located all over the world.

The first question the survey asked was:

On average, what has happened to your firm's total profit over the last three years?

- An increase of over 30 percent per annum.
- An increase of ten to 30 percent per annum.
- An increase of five to ten percent per annum.

- An increase of less than five percent per annum.
- Static profitability.
- Decline in profitability.

The second question asked was:

If you made no change, what would you expect to happen to the firm's profitability in the next three years?

- 18 percent of respondents said profitability would decline.
- 24 percent said profitability would be static.
- Ten percent said an increase of less than five percent per annum.
- 22 percent said an increase of five to ten percent per annum.
- 19 percent said an increase of ten to 30 percent per annum.
- Seven percent said an increase of over 30 percent per annum.

What was interesting about the answers to this question was that a number of firms were predicting to grow by ten percent or more and *not change anything*. I call these firms the *ten-percenters*.

When I examined the data further, I found the *ten-percenters* had the following characteristics:

- 21 percent were charging by billable hour.
- 48 percent gave a fixed fee.
- Seven percent were a hybrid of the billable hour and a fixed fee.
- 24 percent priced based on the known value to the client.

Crucially, other features of answers given by the *ten-percenters* were:

- 81 percent asked clients what success looks like on their cases.
- 85 percent had a clear business development and positioning strategy.
- 77 percent had a clear pricing strategy and vision.
- 62 percent asked the client about service expectations.
- 75 percent asked what business or personal outcome they want to achieve.
- 69 percent agreed clear service standards with the client.

- 62 percent empowered their people to decide not to work with a client if they were of the view that the client's value was low.
- 75 percent had strong management and capable champions who could implement change.

They have systems and processes. They have questions they ask.

A further question in the Legal Iconoclasts survey was:

Which of these statements is closest to the truth?

- We have a strategy and pricing policy that is consistently applied.
- Individual matters are priced on a best-efforts basis.

The answers were split – 43 percent to the former and 57 percent to the latter.

I have continued to ask this question of numerous firms at conferences and at partner retreats that I have conducted, and the answer to this question always comes out broadly 60/40.

What is alarming about this 60/40 split is it indicates most law firms leave their pricing strategies and policies to their individual lawyers to design and implement. This is a bit like a supermarket leaving it to the shop floor staff to work out what products should be priced at, as they stack the shelves. We know this does not happen in retail. Why does it happen in legal?

It gets worse. I have asked over 300 law firms the following questions:

When someone new joins your firm, how is pricing training undertaken?
The predominant answer is: "It's not!"

How are your pricing policies currently documented?
Predominantly the answer is: "They are not." Very few firms say they have a practice area-specific policy document.

How is pricing set and reviewed at your firm?
The most popular answer is: "I have no idea."

We have a situation in the legal profession in which the majority of law firms have no real pricing policies, no real training, and quite frankly no idea when it comes to pricing. Many rely on time recording and the billable hour.

Can it get any worse? Sadly, the answer is yes.
I have asked hundreds of lawyers the following question:

True or false: My colleagues and I know who the most profitable and strategically important clients are in our firm.

Generally, no more than 12 percent of respondents answer in the affirmative.

Do you believe that some of the clients your firm acts for should be dismissed as they are too painful and/or unprofitable to act for?

The answer is always a majority of "yes", with a range between 53 and 96 percent.

Our lawyers know who the poor clients are, and they continue to act for them, in most cases because there is no oversight or mechanism to look at clients and work out who should be "deselected". The vast majority of lawyers who I survey have no idea who the best clients are.

So, what can be done? Let's look again at the *ten-percenters'* answers, which I regard as best practice, and let's consider how you may be able to emulate them.

I have grouped the *ten-percenters'* answers into four themes.

1. Business development, clients, and positioning strategy

- 85 percent have a clear business development and positioning strategy.
- 62 percent empower their people to decide not to work with a client if they are of the view that the client's value is low.

2. Understanding clients

- 81 percent ask clients what success looks like on their cases.
- 62 percent ask the client about service expectations.
- 75 percent ask what business or personal outcome they want to achieve.
- 69 percent agree clear service standards with the client.

3. Create a pricing strategy and vision

- 77 percent have a clear pricing strategy and vision.

4. Lead the change

- 75 percent have strong management and capable champions who can implement change.

Business development, clients, and positioning strategy

In my view, there are some relatively quick wins. However, it will take some thought to formulate your policies and strategy. In the space allocated to me in this chapter I cannot deal with strategy and positioning in great detail. However, here are a few pointers to consider.

What work do you do at your business?

It's a serious question. Do you know all the work types your firm delivers? I guarantee that all of your staff don't. How often do clients go elsewhere because they did not know you offered a service they wanted? Why don't clients know what you do? In short, it's because they were not told, and no one took enough interest in their affairs to find out what they may need in the future. You must make sure your clients know what you do. It is not the client's job to find out.

What do your clients buy from your lawyers?

Again, you may think it's an odd question. When I ask lawyers what clients buy from them, I routinely get answers that include, "knowledge, expertise, time". It is only after a minute or so that someone will mention "outcomes and results". Clients want outcomes.

Clients visit lawyers for two reasons. They are either in pain, or have something to gain.

Pain can be being sued, needing a divorce, wanting probate dealt with quickly so granny can have access to her late husband's bank account, having access to children, obtaining compensation for a life-changing accident, or help to support a failing business.

A gain can be wanting to purchase a dream home and be in before the new school term starts, having peace of mind that a will is drafted so there will be no issues on death, fulfilling an ambition to own a business or sell a business and retire. All of these are outcomes. Clients don't care about the lawyer inputs required to get these results. No client has ever felt that a will was so well drafted they read it again for entertainment purposes!

Clients do not really care who delivers their work, as long as they get the outcome they want. They don't care how long your firm has been in business. They don't even care that much if you are qualified to do the work. They will assume you are, as you work at an organization that describes itself as a law firm. They will assume that you are competent to deliver a quality and compliant legal service. In 36 years of practicing law, no one ever asked me to show them my qualifications. I suspect you never ask to see your dentist's qualifications either. Competence is table stakes, not a differentiator.

Have you the right people in your business who can satisfy client pains and gains? I suspect you have. Do these lawyers fully understand what clients really want? I suspect they don't. They need to know, and they also need to be trained if they don't. This may require a change of thinking.

Client selection and deselection

You have to get rid of poor clients.

Let's start this section with a few myths that need to be dispelled. They are:

- All clients are good clients.
- All clients are the same and should be treated the same.
- You cannot give a fixed price as you don't know what is going to happen.
- Clients are ringing around.
- Our competitors charge less so we should drop our prices.
- There is a "going market rate" for the job.
- Clients won't pay more.
- Clients are not interested in value-based pricing.

We know many of our lawyers think we act for clients who should be deselected. You should act on this information to improve your profitability.

I recommend that you undertake a project and grade your clients A-D, where D stands for Ditch. The clients that should be gently persuaded to leave the business. The characteristics of such D clients are easy to identify:

- Someone who is unprofitable.
- Someone who doesn't pay their bills promptly or at all.

- Someone who doesn't accept or respect the advice that your lawyers give.
- Someone who doesn't respond to requests for information until the last minute.
- Someone who is disrespectful to your staff, is a bully, and makes them feel physically ill. (I am being serious. Ask them.)
- Someone that contributes to lawyer burnout and sickness absences.
- Someone who negotiates lower rates on the basis of giving increased volumes of work that never materializes.

In 2023, I facilitated a partner away day for a large UK regional law firm. There were 26 partners of the law firm present. One of the exercises I led was to ask them to write down three clients that they would like to fire. When I asked the first person to list the three clients on his list, he gave the name of a large, well-known, international blue-chip company. There was a lot of laughing. I asked how many other people had got the name of this blue-chip company on their list and five hands went up. The partner responsible for this client didn't really know that this client was disliked by many of his partners. When we drilled into the numbers, the client was not worth a significant amount of fees in any event and clearly was using other firms for more profitable work.

Work out who your ideal clients are

Some of the criteria of category A clients could be:

- They create profitable revenue for your business.
- They complement the categories of work you do and are strategically important.
- They are in a niche sector you operate in and want to exploit.
- They have growth potential and cross-selling opportunities.
- They provide you with kudos.
- The individuals concerned have considerable financial net worth.
- You enjoy working with them.
- They appreciate the work that you do for them.
- The work is simple for you to do.

I have read articles where commentators refer to the wrong types of clients as BMWs (Bitches, Moaners, and Whiners) and PIAs (pains in the ass). However, I think that is misconceived, rude, and quite frankly disrespectful for a number of reasons:

- Your lawyers choose the clients you currently act for.
- Your lawyers set the pricing they charge.
- Your lawyers choose to deliver work out of scope and do more than they envisaged.
- Your lawyers drafted the bill (even if it wrote off WIP they didn't want to ask to be included in the bill).
- Your lawyers took the client's money when they paid.
- Your lawyers decided to ignore and avoid difficult conversations with clients when bills became overdue.
- Your lawyers decided to take no action when matters went out of scope or put matters on stop until clients paid.
- Your lawyers moan about the clients to colleagues when they put the phone down after having a conversation with them but do nothing to make the situation better.
- Your lawyers stop credit control chasing the client for payment as *"they are a good client and will pay… eventually"*.
- Your lawyers take on the next matter from the same client without addressing any of the points above.

> *"Be sure you've done everything within your power to turn a low value customer into a high value customer. The fact of the matter is that your customers are not going to get better until you do."*
> Ron Baker, *Pricing on Purpose.*

The ten-percenters empower their people to decide not to work with a client if they are of the view that the client's value is low. Follow their lead.

I believe bad clients also drive out good lawyers. Do something about your client base. It will help with lawyer retention.

Understanding clients

We know the *ten-percenters* do the following:

- Ask the client what success looks like on their cases.
- Ask the client about service expectations.
- Ask what business or personal outcome they want to achieve.
- Agree clear service standards with the client.

These are all relatively simple things but, in most cases, they don't get addressed. Lawyers often assume they know what the clients want and don't always check in to make sure they are on the same page.

A research study by Lexis Nexis in 2016[3] surveyed the legal landscape and interviewed 122 law firms and 108 clients. It contained a section dealing with client perceptions and what clients wanted from lawyers. One of the highlights in the report was a list of 14 features that lawyers were asked to list in order of importance to clients. The researchers also asked clients to rank the same 14 features, identifying what was most important to them. Guess what? They were dramatically different. The report adds:

> *"Lawyers also seem to have a skewed sense of what their clients actually care about when it comes to service. When we asked lawyers what their clients value most, they put 'clear cost/fixed fees' at the top of the list. But when we asked clients, they put 'a clear understanding of my particular needs' above everything else."*

We must have value conversations with clients to find out what they want, what their needs are, and what outcomes they are seeking to achieve. We then have to demonstrate that we understand their pain and/or gain. These questions are part of a value conversation. It's important the conversation happens as we don't know what a client values until we speak to them. A value conversation is not responding with an email or – even worse – have our websites create prices for legal services without speaking to clients at all!

It's a shame to say that, for some lawyers, actively listening and showing empathy during a conversation are not skills that come easily. We have all experienced doctors with poor bedside manners. Sadly, some lawyers are the same. I once came across an individual working in a law firm, who, when taking enquiries on probate matters, never said *"I'm sorry to hear about your loss"*. When I asked the person concerned why she didn't ever mention this, she told me, *"They know their mother has died as that is why they are calling us to deal with the probate"*. Nothing wrong with her logic, just an appalling bedside manner on a human level.

You may be surprised to learn that clients have very low expectations of the way they are going to be dealt with when they meet a lawyer. The 2015 *Lexis Nexis Bellwether Report*[4] does not pull its punches when it comes to outlining a client's expectations.

> *"Most clients aren't exactly excited about the prospect of having to find a good lawyer. Though they may respect lawyers' knowledge, clients are less flattering about their human qualities. Clients don't tend to expect a high degree of rapport when they enter into the relationship. As one client put it, 'Lawyers are not people people. They talk more than they listen, which is a big turn-off. I judge them based on the questions they ask'."*

The balance of power in the client/lawyer relationship is shifting. The report explores how independent law firms and sole practitioners are responding to a new breed of client.

So, let's start asking good questions; let's find out what clients want, what success looks like, and how they would like to work with us. Once we have asked the questions, we must listen empathetically to the answers given.

As part of the creation of a value-based pricing process, I recommend your teams discuss which value-based questions should be asked when meeting a client and discussing a new matter. What are the questions that should be asked to find out about them and their issues? What keeps these clients awake at night when thinking about the issue? Your lawyers should discuss them, write them down, hone them, work out which are the best ones, create a list and put them into whatever departmental practice manuals/processes they have. Start creating a system.

I have listed a few value-based questions to consider. When I work with law firms, individual practice areas can quite quickly create at least 30 probing questions.

1. If money were no object, how would you like us to work with you? (The important thing about this question is it can give you an idea of the service levels they want and whether you can deliver them. It can identify boundaries and guidelines for working with clients who respect and value your services.)
2. What are your objectives and what does success look like for you?

3. Why are you instructing us now?
4. What is the current problem?
5. What is the solution you are hoping for?
6. What do you think the biggest threat to a successful outcome is?
7. What precise aspects are most troubling you about the case?
8. What is keeping you awake at night?
9. What is a good outcome for you?
10. What is a bad outcome?
11. What does success look like for you in terms of this case?
12. How involved do you want to be in the case? What can you do? What are you prepared to do?

I am not for one moment suggesting that 30+ questions should be asked of every client/prospect. Your lawyers can and should select some that they are comfortable asking and monitor the responses they receive.

Asking good questions to find out the problem will reassure the client that you can help them solve their problem. Good questions make clients feel at ease. It's important the lawyer is seeking to understand the problem and demonstrate that they understand their circumstances.

Create a pricing strategy and vision

We have to consider how can we emulate the 77 percent of the *ten-percenters* that have clear pricing strategy and vision and price with value in mind.

You probably know the joke about a retired mechanical engineer who gets called out to fix a mission-critical machine that has broken down at the factory and caused production to grind to a halt, causing huge losses each day the machine is not running. The old engineer arrives on site. He is taken to the machine. He puts his ear on the machine and listens intently. He then puts his hand into a tool bag and brings out a hammer. He taps the machine gently and it starts to run. He is in and out of the plant in 15 minutes. The engineer sends an invoice for £1,000. The owner is upset when he gets the bill and demands a detailed breakdown. He receives an amended invoice from the engineer, which reads: "£5 for the cost of the hammer. £995 for knowing where to tap." The joke is value-based pricing in action!

My definition of VBP is "agreeing a price that is fair to both the client and the law firm, a price that reflects value for both parties". It's not a time-based measure. Put another way, it's not the six minutes it takes me to tell you the answer to a problem. It's six minutes plus the 36 years of experience that allows me to know the answer and convey it in six minutes.

Before you can devise a strategy for the future, you have to look at what you do now.

The billable hour

As lawyers we have got used to the billable hour. It's easy to calculate a lawyer's profitability. Most firms will use an equation along the lines of one-third salary, one-third overheads, one-third profit. If a lawyer's salary cost is £60,000, set a target of £180,000. It's easy to explain to a client that the lawyer's rate is £X per hour. It's easy for lawyers to record and bill their time. Except it ISN'T!

When clients are told that an hourly rate is £360, their immediate concern is naturally, "Wow, that sounds a lot… £360 per hour… How long is this going to take?" The lawyer's fallback position is usually, "We don't know as we haven't done the work yet , but we will charge an hourly rate and book the time and tell you as we go along".

I have asked hundreds of lawyers if they would willingly engage a builder to build an extension to their home and be charged a day rate by the builder. I have yet to find one lawyer who says yes. So why do lawyers expect clients to do the same with their law firm? Yet it happens every day.

Time recording is not accurate and never has been

- Not all lawyers time record the work undertaken on a matter accurately. Some will leave their time recording for days or weeks. One of my old partners, 15 years ago, used to leave it months before filling in time sheets. People forget what they have done.
- Can you say that your firm's time recording policy is adhered to by all your staff? Do you even have a coherent detailed written policy? Not all firms do.
- Not all time recorded is genuine.
- Not all lawyers use their technology effectively.
- Some lawyers don't believe they are actually worth their own hourly rate and as a result discount what they do.
- Some lawyers who give fixed fees and estimates will stop time

recording once the estimated fee level is reached, as a WIP write off may result in a difficult conversation with a partner that they will seek to avoid.

How are fixed prices currently calculated at your firm?

The chances are that in some way, shape, or form your fixed prices are linked to the billable hour.

- A lawyer might estimate how long a piece of work will take and multiply it by their hourly rate.
- It might be made up on the fly / gut feel / best endeavors (delete as appropriate).
- It could be following what your competitors do.
- It could be relying on what the lawyer learned at their previous firm and letting them carry on doing that at yours.
- Allowing lawyers to learn from each other via trial and error, and osmosis.
- Relying on the time recording data booked to a similar matter.

When you think about the way we buy anything, most buyers of anything (including those who buy legal services) want:

- Price transparency;
- Certainty;
- Results;
- No extras; and
- Value.

It's that last bullet point – *value* – that is hard to get our heads around, for the simple reason that everybody is different and so are their needs. We won't know what a client's needs are until we speak to them.

Getting to grips with value is not easy. I guarantee that you and I have different tastes in wine, watches, music, cars, houses, and holidays, to name a few matters. A car might be very important to you; it's not to me.

Value is subjective

Because we are all different, it is important to understand that it's the customer's perception that matters. Value is subjective, and our own personal histories impact the way we look at value. Jewelry and watches may be important to some. Clothing and designer brands may be important to others. We are all different and we all have different buying habits.

Value is not rational

I only want a car to get from A to B. I don't care what I drive. It surprises me that some people will pay ten times the amount that I will pay for a car. I think that it's not rational to do that.

Why do people buy Apple products? When you speak to IT people, they always tell you that androids are better, have more functionality, and are cheaper. My IT guy Kevin told me this when I started my consulting business Big Yellow Penguin. I ignored him and ordered an Apple iPhone. Why? Because I know how an iPhone works and couldn't be bothered to learn how another cheaper, better phone may operate. Not rational – according to Kevin.

Value is contextual

Value changes depending on where you are.

Let's take the most abundant product on the planet: water. The amount you pay for water varies according to your location and circumstances. You will pay next to nothing for a glass of water in your home. You will pay more when you pick up a bottle of water from the garage. You will pay even more when you order a bottle of mineral water in a high-end restaurant. You would probably pay a huge sum if you were emerging from the desert, having been stranded without water and were offered a drink by an unscrupulous vendor. Context and circumstances impact price.

If you were on a long car journey with a quarter tank of petrol and you came across the last garage for 250 miles, you would buy the petrol and pay the price on the pump. You would probably pay more than you would have had you stopped 20 miles earlier in the journey. It's just the way things are. Your situation, the context you were in, allowed the garage to charge and receive the higher price.

We need to try and acknowledge that value is a feeling and factor this into account when we are selling legal services. Are we even aware of the emotions that our clients may be feeling whilst engaging with us as lawyers? Do we acknowledge them? Are we putting ourselves in their shoes? Do we see and understand why something might be so important to them? Do we know how they feel? Probably not. Do we care how they feel? I suspect yes, but we must have a conversation and ask them questions to understand their feelings.

Pricing is important

We know pricing is the number one profit lever if used correctly. Yet in most law firms it is totally neglected, and I know this because lawyers tell me so. Multiplying an hourly rate by a ledger of hours at the end of the matter is not pricing, it's billing. Pricing is what you do before you have lifted a finger.

To help explain pricing in greater detail, let's get some expert opinion on pricing from an advertising and marketing genius, David Ogilvy, and Mark Ritson, a marketing specialist and former professor from the London Business School.

> *"Pricing is guesswork. It is usually assumed that marketers use scientific methods to determine the price of their products. Nothing could be further from the truth."*
> David Ogilvy, *Ogilvy on Advertising*

> *"Pricing is the worst managed of all marketing areas. How prices are decided is often a mixture of voodoo and bingo."*
> Mark Ritson, London Business School

Ah, Houston we have a problem! I don't know any voodoo; it was not on the syllabus at the College of Law I attended. And that is the problem. Lawyers don't understand pricing because we have never been taught how to do it.

> *"Lawyers must learn to accept no one has a silver bullet perfect solution that many committees seem to be waiting for. Many firms that wait for the proven perfect solution could go out of business before it arrives."*
> Jim Hassett, *Client Value and Law Firm Profitability*

Jim Hassett is now happily retired. He wrote his book in 2014. How many law firms have gone bust in the intervening years?

The sad thing is Mark Ritson is not wrong. In the numerous surveys I have undertaken with law firms, many lawyers tell me there is very little ownership and oversight when it comes to the pricing of their services. But we know that pricing is the number one profit lever if used correctly. So, what is going on?

What currently happens in many law firms is a combination of:

- Hourly rate setting and time recording.
- Standard fixed prices set for services such as conveyancing, simple will drafting, lasting powers of attorney, and low-priced fixed fee matrimonial products.
- Debt recovery litigation with fixed prices for letters before action and fixed cost recovery from courts.
- Fixed prices for other work looked at on a case-by-case basis if the lawyer can be cajoled into giving a fixed price.

In each of the cases outlined above, the price setting process within teams is pretty much left to the lawyers, partners, or team leaders with little or no oversight and input from the management team as to how those prices are set, communicated, and reviewed. There is no structure and no discipline. There is precious little attempt to capture some of the value created by the lawyers. Why? Because we don't know how.

Consider this:

- What procedures can be put in place in your firm for communicating and approving pricing?
- How can you exchange information about pricing and ensure teams know what is going on in the department?
- How can you train your people to understand more about pricing?
- How can you create departmental policies, procedures, and templates that all lawyers can refer to and contribute to?

This can be done. But it takes work. If pricing is not making it on to any agenda of your management team, hopefully this will encourage you to add it.

Give customers a choice

If we accept that value is complicated and determined by the customer, then it should make it easier for you to agree that presenting clients with choices and price options is a logical step.

We all like choices in our daily lives. We choose our car wash menus. We choose what cars we drive. We choose what clothes we wear. We choose the wine we drink with dinner in a restaurant.

A detailed look at how you go about creating options for legal services is outside the scope of this chapter. However, when working with law firms I suggest they look to create options for clients. Think of Gold, Silver, and Bronze options, with different service levels and price points. Lawyers in your organization will tell you it can't be done, as their work area is special. They are wrong. Your lawyers need to be trained to create and explain the options.

If retailers can create different price points for water, then you can do it for legal services.

The legal profession can and must move on from a choice of take it or leave it, which is often the only choice that is presented when an hourly rate is an option, and seek to capture some of the value lawyers create that is left on the table in many transactions.

There are many benefits of implementing value-based pricing.

- You focus on what customers want – results, outcomes, and solutions. Customers are not interested in time and inputs.
- You won't treat all clients equally, simply because not all clients are the same. We know some are prepared to pay for a better service level than others and those that pay more should receive a better service level.
- You will work for customers who really value what you do.
- Your numbers of customer complaints should fall. How many current complaints relate to fees and clients not being updated regarding costs?
- Your customers will become a referral source.
- Your cash flow will improve.
- Aged debt will reduce.
- You will stop doing work for free.
- Your administration costs will reduce.
- Your lawyers will work smarter, not harder.
- Your lawyers will have a better work–life balance.
- Your business will become more profitable as you will dispense with an artificial cap on its income earning potential (hourly rates x annual chargeable hours = lawyer target).
- You may even choose to free yourself from the tyranny of time recording completely. The only time our clients are interested in is how long it takes to get the result.

Pricing is not something you do once and then ignore for the next 12 months. Pricing is an ongoing transformative process. To implement a pricing process, you need to first design the framework, design documentation to utilize within the structure, communicate rules, create boundaries, and then train people how to use it all.

At present, in most law firms, there is not a clearly defined and regulated pricing process – and there needs to be. The *ten-percenters* have one.

It is interesting / depressing (delete as appropriate) that pricing seldom features in a law firm's vision and strategic planning process. When was the last time (if ever) the management team of your business looked at the pricing policies and procedures of individual practice areas, other than talking about raising hourly rates in those teams?

Lead the change

You will recall the *ten-percenters* reported that 75 percent of their firms felt they had a strong management team and capable champions who could implement change.

Have you got the leadership required to change?

If you are serious about looking at pricing and profitability, you need to make it a strategic objective. It is not, as many law firm leaders think, a "Jean Luc Picard" instruction where the CEO says to another member of staff, *"Make it so"* with no strategy or support provided. You will fail.

There are many reasons why I believe law firms should look seriously at implementing value-based pricing and strategically look at their pricing models. Let's take a look at some of the likely ones:

- No one owns pricing at your firm and your price setting policies are flawed.
- The current practice of law firm setting budgets is illogical and frustrating.
- Your business is not making enough money, or you think it has the potential to make more revenue or a better margin.
- You are not capturing the value you create.
- You have succession planning issues and need to make your business more attractive to encourage lawyers to remain with the business.
- You want to improve your relationships with clients or get new ones.
- You may feel that the billable hours days are numbered and would like to get ahead of the curve.

- You may feel that Generative Artificial Intelligence is going to steal your lunch! (I personally believe GenAI is the final nail in the coffin of the billable hour. Lawyers have to work out quickly what value they can add to GenAI created documentation.)

The *ten-percenters* have pricing under control.

Law firm leaders have to take control of pricing in their businesses and stop what in many firms is a complete free for all, where lawyers continue to do what they've always done, completely unchallenged. This can include lawyers who have recently joined your firm.

Implementing value-based pricing is a change management program. I have devised what I call an Eight P Point Plan™, which can be followed to implement value-based pricing.

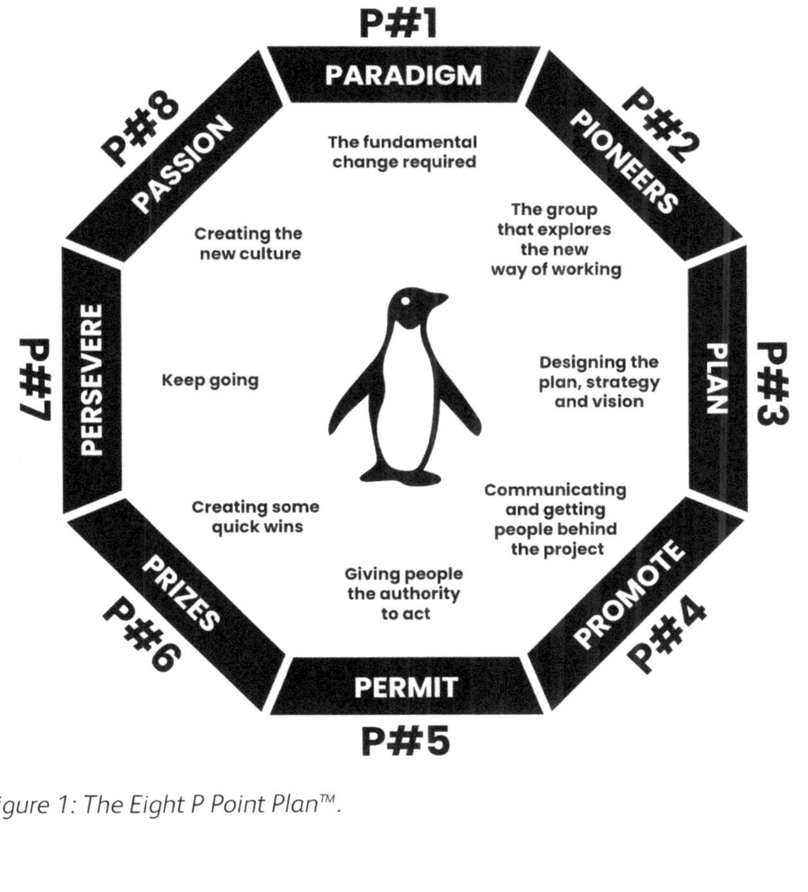

Figure 1: The Eight P Point Plan™.

Successful implementation requires:

- P1. A Paradigm shift. A desire and will to change.
- P2. Pioneers within your organization to research what is happening currently and help deliver change.
- P3. A Plan, strategy, and vision.
- P4. Promotion of and communicating the plan.
- P5. Permitting people to act and make changes. Also permitting them to fail.
- P6. Prizes will need to be awarded to support and make people enthusiastic about the change.
- P7. Persevering with the change is crucial. Keep the pedal to the metal.
- P8. Passion. Be passionate about the changes you implement and the change of culture that follows.

You have chosen to buy and read this book because you are concerned about profit. You know that pricing is one of the easiest ways to impact profit. You need to take back control and ownership of your pricing – and soon.

References

1 In his chapter, Shaun Jardine, author of *Ditch The Billable Hour! Implementing Value-Based Pricing in a Law Firm*, draws on research carried out in 2022 on law firm profitability, which demonstrated how different pricing approaches affect (professional service) firm profitability.

2 Pricing approaches and firm profitability, Study findings Autumn 2022. Provided by The Thriving Company, September 2022. For access to a full copy of the results of the Legal Iconoclasts survey and to read more about the ten-percenters, please contact Shaun at shaun@bigyellowpenguin.co.uk

3 www.lexisnexis.co.uk/bellwether/assets/pdfs/Lexis-nexis-report-2016_interactive%20version03.pdf

4 www.lexisnexis.co.uk/bellwether/assets/pdfs/bellwether-report-2015-age-of-the-client.pdf

Chapter 6:
The roadmap to £1,000,000 extra profit in three years

By John McCarthy, profit coach, Summit Business

Introduction

As an experienced lawyer, I'm sure you follow structure, principles, or precedents that have been well thought out, are evidence-based, and even tested in a court of law to try and achieve the best outcome possible for your client.

Would it make sense to follow a similar approach when you're building your law firm?

The challenge is finding such a system. Especially one that is tried and tested, proven to work, and easy to implement.

The intention of this chapter is to introduce you to six initiatives:

1. The world-class P.R.O.F.I.T.[1] business building system that ticks all the above boxes;
2. The Business Blueprint, which will help you know exactly where to prioritize your time when growing and managing your business;
3. The five cash flow levers that will show you how to immediately boost your cash flow;
4. The profit maximiser, which will show you the easiest way to dramatically increase your profits;
5. Real-life examples of how law firms have implemented these elements and achieved incredible results; and
6. Exercises that will give you the inspiration and focus to put more money in your bank account in the next three months and the potential to massively increase your profits in the next 12 months and beyond.

The P.R.O.F.I.T. system

The P.R.O.F.I.T. system was developed by a team of over 100 world-class P.R.O.F.I.T. coaches, all members of the Business Coaching Academy.[2]

By combining decades of training, education, and experience, they have collated the world's best business practices and put them together to form a highly effective business-building system.

This system has enabled thousands of businesses around the world to generate higher revenues, greater profit, and allow the owners to reduce their working hours and stress levels.

It is by far the best system I have found anywhere in the world (and yes, I have looked!).

It is unique because it not only sets out a structured process to build a highly profitable and valuable business that can run without you needing to be there; it also sets out the order in which you should work on your business so that you get maximum bang for your buck, i.e., achieve more with less work and in a shorter time period.

By following the P.R.O.F.I.T. system and utilizing the appropriate business resources, a client of mine was able to:

1. Reduce his working hours by 50 percent in the first year;
2. Within two years take a two-month vacation to the other side of the world without needing to answer his phone or emails;
3. Increase his profits by £1 million within three years;
4. Increase the value of his business from very little to between £10 million and £100 million (with apologies for not being permitted to disclose the exact number); and
5. Achieve an amazing lifestyle he could not even dream of before he started his journey.

Many other clients have achieved similar successes by following the P.R.O.F.I.T. system.

In this chapter, I am going to share stories from a selection of clients to provide ideas and inspiration to achieve similar success in your business.

The nine-step roadmap

The P.R.O.F.I.T. system comprises three parts:

1. Five levels of business ownership:

Moves you from Overwhelmed and Overworked through Organized and Overseer to becoming a true business Owner.

2. Three business pillars:

Building the three critical business pillars – Vision, Velocity, and Value – that are required to move up the five levels and build a highly profitable, sustainable, and valuable business.

3. Nine-step roadmap:

The step-by-step process that provides the structure, resources, and training to help you build your three business pillars and create your ideal business.

Figure 1: The nine-step roadmap.

When implemented correctly, you will create an extremely profitable and highly valuable business that gives you the time and financial freedom to enjoy your ideal lifestyle.

Step 1: Alignment accelerator

This is about aligning your business goals with your personal goals. Rather than building a business and just hoping it is going to provide you with what you want on exit, it is far better to plan your personal goals and then work out what your business needs to achieve to deliver it. Set your ten-, five-, three-, and one-year personal goals, and then align your business goals with these personal goals.

Step 2: Driving growth (a detailed strategy)

Once you have your business goals, you need to do a *complete* business audit to understand exactly where you are right now. This will identify your strengths and where your gaps are.

With this information, you can make a high-quality, comprehensive business plan to help you get from where you are now to where you want to be.

Doing this step helps you avoid short-term, knee-jerk goals and tactics, and ensures you constantly move toward your long-term goals.

Step 3: Dynamic planning

Now you have your starting point (from Step 2) and your business goals (from Step 1) you can create your plans:

- Three-year vision orbit.
- 12-month business plan.
- 90-day action plan.

The 90-day action plan ensures you work on the most important tasks every week and don't get distracted or sidetracked by "non-important but urgent" things.

Ideally, everyone in your business will have their own 90-day action plan so that your whole team is working towards your business goals.

Step 4: Profit and cash

Your priorities should be increasing profits and managing cash flow – not marketing. That comes later, because if your margins are low and/or your cash flow is not controlled, increased marketing will damage your business.

Attracting low-value clients into an inefficient business with poor cash flow will increase your workload as you will have to work harder and harder to fix the inevitable financial problems. Maximize your efficiency and profitability and improve your cash flow management before focusing on marketing.

Step 5: Marketing and revenue

Good marketing will attract A-grade clients who are willing to pay you handsomely for your expertise and are fun to work with. And when you get it right, it is free! That is right, *free* clients! When you have developed your marketing properly you will get a brilliant return on investment (ROI) because every client is a profitable client.

Step 6: Operations and systems

As your business grows, you will need improved systems and processes. Without good *business* systems (to compliment your client-facing *legal* systems), your customer service levels will drop as the team gets busier, and you will be working harder to fix the problems.

Systems should run the business and people should run the systems. It is your job, as the business owner, to manage and lead the people. With good systems, training, and people in place you will have the confidence that your business can grow whilst you reduce your working hours.

Step 7: Financials and KPIs

Just like an aircraft pilot needs flight instruments in his cockpit, you need financial information and KPIs in your business so you can make good decisions. Without good business data, you are flying blind. Your KPIs should relate to your 12-month and 90-day plans so you can measure progress and correct course as necessary.

Step 8: Innovation and leadership

You have probably heard of Kaizen, meaning "continuous improvement". Innovation does not necessarily mean big, impressive initiatives. The best innovation in your business will come from consistent small changes that culminate in huge improvements – the principle of marginal gains. When your team members are highly engaged, taking ownership, and demonstrating self-leadership, they will identify and implement these improvements for you.

Step 9: Team and culture

Developing a world-class team and culture will enable you to step back from the day-to-day running of the business. You will be able to focus on the strategic direction and have the confidence that you have people even better than you who are running their departments. At this level, you have the income and the time to do what you want, when you want, with whom you want – complete freedom!

Implementing the P.R.O.F.I.T. system

When I first met these two business owners, they were working very long hours, which was causing them a lot of stress and sleepless nights. They were not getting the quality time they wanted with their families. Despite working very long hours, the business was not very profitable and they could not achieve the growth they hoped for.

By working through the nine steps in a structured manner, in the subsequent four years their turnover increased from £300,000 to £3.5 million, their staff increased from eight to 120, and they were able to purchase £1 million in assets.

Along the journey, the business owners moved away from carrying out client-facing work to purely a management role, and they are now acting as the leaders with a management team running the business.

They have created a business that provides them with the lifestyle and quality time they want with their young families and gives them the opportunity to work in non-executive director (NED) roles for other expanding businesses.

The business blueprint

Rather than going through the whole P.R.O.F.I.T. system in detail, this chapter focuses on one of the fundamental principles behind it – the business blueprint. Let's explore why following a blueprint is so important and what the consequences are if you don't.

Not many business owners realize that focusing on the wrong areas, or the right areas in the wrong order, can damage their business.

Effective marketing and business development are the life blood of any business; however, if you focus on these before getting a tight grip on cash flow and profitability, you are likely to be damaging your business.

Imagine if you focused on marketing and you suddenly had double, triple, or even quadruple the amount of work coming in. What would happen?

Despite what people say, it is not a nice problem to have. Your business would, most likely, be under a lot of stress because it is not set up to grow at that *velocity*:

- Your team may not be able to deal with all the leads or work effectively;
- Your systems would start to break down, and you may become less efficient; and
- The quality of your service might become sub-optimal due to overload.

As a result, you might:

- Need to work longer hours firefighting and dealing with team issues on top of your own increased casework;

- Suffer a reduction in profits because your systems are not designed to cope with the increased capacity, and so your business becomes less efficient; and
- Struggle with cash flow as you may need to employ additional staff. Your team may struggle to stay on top of invoicing and debt collection, as well as their increased workload.

Not exactly what you hoped for when you implemented that growth strategy!

> *"The people who win in the game of business are those who have the business skills and the tools."* Keith Cunningham

Not following the business blueprint

The managing partner of a law firm reached out to me because he realized the traditional model was not serving them well anymore. Their 23 fee earners were working hard, and the partners were busy delivering client work and running the business. No matter how hard they worked, cash flow was often difficult and there never seemed to be enough profit.

The partners felt frustrated because they were not receiving the rewards they deserved for all their hard work. They could not work any more hours. They knew they had to do something differently.

The problem was not a lack of experienced fee earners, or client work, or even revenue. The challenge was that the focus was on driving revenue and billable hours without enough focus on profit margins and cash flow.

They were good at being lawyers, but their traditional *business model* did not work for them anymore, financially or personally.

How will you benefit from following a blueprint?

Building a business is a bit like building a house. If you are building a house, you need to have blueprints for plumbing, heating, electrical wiring, and flooring. Everything needs to be mapped out so you know where everything is going and the order in which the work needs to be done.

Building a house without following these blueprints or plans correctly is likely to result in a badly built, unsafe, and unsustainable building – you probably would not want to live in it!

You would not start to build a house without any plans, but a lot of people start a business or try to grow their businesses without having a good plan or even understanding how all the elements of their business are interrelated.

When you are building a business, you should have a business plan, finance plan, marketing plan, operational processes, team development strategy, and effective management and leadership. As you grow your business, all these elements must be considered in your planning process because they are all connected. Growing one element of your business, e.g., marketing, will have an impact on other elements, e.g. operations and finance.

You could be forgiven for thinking that all this planning would take a lot of work and time, and often, these plans will just get stored in a drawer, lost on a hard drive, or simply forgotten about.

Writing these plans is not the main challenge. In reality, there are plenty of consultants, coaches, mentors, and agencies out there who can help you do this. The challenge is knowing where to start and how to implement all these elements in a coordinated manner.

Having a tried and tested, proven blueprint to follow gives you structure so that you know where to focus to gain maximum effect. It will save you months or even years of effort and enable you to achieve far more than you ever could if you tried to build your business without it.

Following the business blueprint

In November 2019, I started working with three partners of a law firm who had all been shareholders in the firm for over 12 years. They had a good business – revenue, profit, and cash flow were all ok. But they wanted to take their business to the next level. They wanted to feel more in control of the firm, receive higher personal income, develop a business that gave them greater financial security (an exit plan), and be able to enjoy more personal time with their young families, doing fun stuff along the journey.

Like most law firms, things were good but could be a lot better. They did not have a business model to follow to ensure they achieved their business and personal goals.

Over the next five months, we started to follow the business blueprint with a focus on cash flow and profitability.

Unfortunately, in March 2020, the UK went into lockdown due to the COVID-19 pandemic. As you know, it was a worrying and uncertain time for all business owners (unless they were selling toilet rolls or hand sanitizer).

However, because we had spent five months focusing on cash flow and profit, they understood how a *business* needs to work. They had significantly improved their profit margins already, had a 90-day cash flow forecast in place, and had good control of the financial numbers in their business.

The result was they were able to focus on transitioning to home working with minimal impact on their team or finances and were able to reconfigure their business so that their profits continued to grow throughout 2020 and beyond.

If we had not done the work prior to lockdown, they would have struggled throughout the pandemic because they would not have understood which areas of their firm were profitable and which areas were not and would not have had the relevant information to make good, business savvy, data-based decisions.

The business blueprint explained

The business blueprint was developed by Keith Cunningham and published in his book, *The Ultimate Blueprint for an Insanely Successful Business*.[3] Understanding and implementing the business blueprint will ensure you can grow your business in a structured way, meaning greater cash flow and far greater profitability whilst working fewer hours and enjoying more control of your business.

It follows the principle that the purpose of a business is to generate cash from its assets. In this model, we recognize an asset as anything with an economic value, for example, your fee earners, your website, your reputation, marketing resources, and databases.

Cunningham emphasizes "*cash* not *profit*, and definitely not *revenue*!". Cash is the most important of the three because without it, businesses struggle, and with it, the business owners have more choices about how they utilize it.

As shown in Figure 2, there are three main ways that cash can be used:

1. Paying the directors;
2. Paying down debts; and
3. Reinvesting back into the business.

The key to utilizing the blueprint effectively is realizing that you cannot generate cash directly from your assets. There are three stages that must be understood and managed well to maximize cash flow from the business assets:

1. You need to be as *effective* as possible at generating revenue from your firm's assets.

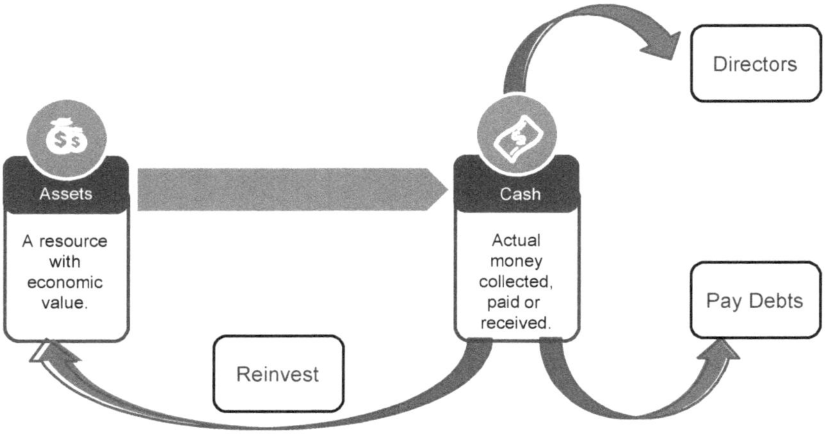

Figure 2: The three uses of cash.

2. You need to run your firm as *efficiently* as possible to generate maximum profits from your revenue.
3. You must be as *productive* as possible so that you maximize cash flow in your business.

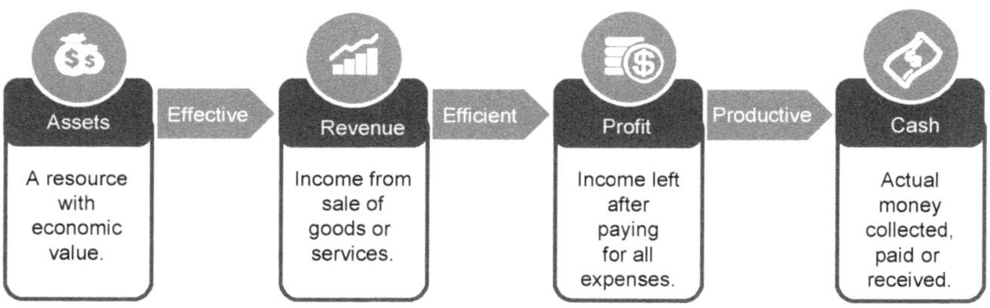

Figure 3: The business blueprint.

As the saying goes, "Revenue is vanity, profit is sanity, cash flow is reality".

How to implement the business blueprint

You should *understand* the the business blueprint (see Figure 3) from left to right but *implement* it from right to left. The order in which you need to work on your business is:

1. Cash is critical to running a business so your priority must be to manage your cash flow effectively (productivity).
2. Profit is obviously important; without it, your business is going to suffer, so you must maximize your profit margins and efficiency (efficiency).

3. Revenue – ensure you maximize your business development opportunities and derive as much revenue as possible from your assets (effectiveness).

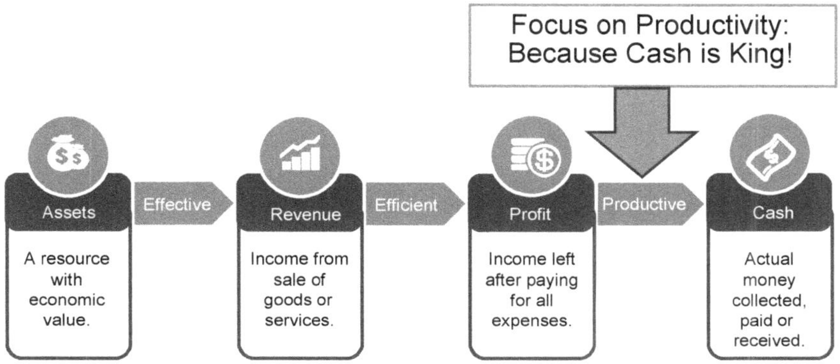

Figure 4: Be productive; cash is king.

Have you ever had a meeting with your accountant, and they congratulated you on how much profit you have made, but you cannot understand why the profit is not in your bank account?

If so, you are not alone. Many business owners struggle with the concept that profit is not cash. It is an important distinction to understand. In fact, it is critical to understand the difference between them so you can make key decisions regarding your business' performance and financial health:

- Profit is defined as income less all the expenses of a business in a certain period.
- Cash flow is the actual movement of money in and out of a company.

How poor cash flow almost sank a law firm

The partners of a law firm confided in me that they were unable to pay their upcoming VAT bill and were about to put their own savings into the firm to keep it afloat. I knew cash *should* be available because the whole team had been working incredibly hard all year – so where was it?

I told them I wasn't going to let them use their own cash to subsidize the business and asked the partners to investigate:

- Invoices that had been sent out but payment had not yet been received;

- Work that had been done but had not yet been invoiced for; and
- Cases that could be closed down and invoiced for in the next four weeks.

The result was over £110,000 of cash identified that could be made available within the next three months. This is why it is critical to manage your cash flow proactively.

Would you be willing to consider selling a stake in your business to external investors?

A survey commissioned by litigation funder Harbour revealed that 149 of the 200 law firm partners surveyed said their firm would consider external ownership.[4] One of the main reasons for this was due to cash flow challenges. The firms surveyed had revenues of between £5 million and £100 million or more, so revenue wasn't the issue – it was profit and cash flow. If firms do not manage their cash flow effectively whilst they are growing, they can be building bigger problems further down the line.

To avoid this happening, do not chase revenue targets. Focus instead on managing cash flow and maximizing profits. Once you start to do this in your practice, it will run more smoothly, you will feel more in control. You will be able to work fewer hours and be able to earn more personal income.

The five cash flow levers

It's not as difficult as you think to improve cash flow in your law firm – you just need to know how to utilize the five cash flow levers.

Cash flow lever #1: Reducing expenses

For example:

- Reduce costs of goods and services bought (replace or renegotiate with suppliers).
- Stop or reduce spending on ineffective marketing.
- Cut costs in general and administrative expenses.
- Reduce interest paid on loans.
- Reduce tax bills.

Cash flow lever #2: Increasing revenue
For example:

- Increase fees.
- Attract more clients and higher paying clients.
- Retain clients longer (repeat business).
- Increase conversion rates.
- Cross sales/refer more business between departments.
- More accurately estimate the value of cases.
- Clarify the scope of work and set expectations with clients.
- Charge when going over the initially agreed scope.
- Consider charging more for urgent work.
- Improve time recording/charge for all billable hours.
- Improve your billing process and ensure your team follows it correctly.
- Charge incurred costs and interest.
- Stop or reduce discounting.
- Improve efficiency (complete cases more quickly).
- Consider how you could improve your billing cycle – could you bill more frequently?
- Stop working for clients who do not pay.

Cash flow lever #3: Reducing receivable days (the time clients take to pay you)
For example:

- Set expectations/agreements with clients.
- Payment upfront – monies on account in advance.
- Shorter payment agreement.
- Invoice immediately.
- Credit control/manage debtors.
- Reduce debtor days.
- Fire customers who do not honor payment agreements.
- Enforce agreement (you get what you tolerate).

- Proactively follow up (squeaky wheel gets the oil).
- Be front of mind by building a relationship with the person who pays the invoices at the supplier company.

Cash flow lever #4: Increasing payable days (time your take to pay your bills)
For example:

- Place smaller inventory orders but more often.
- Negotiate on hidden costs, e.g. shipping and handling.
- Negotiate longer payment terms with suppliers.
- Find new suppliers with preferential terms (reduction in costs or longer credit).
- Create some competition between suppliers or form a buyer's partnership.
- Stretch all payments to the last day (but not late).
- Negotiate longer payment terms with suppliers.
- Always avoid late charges.

Cash flow lever #5: Reducing inventory days (time delay from completing work to invoicing for it)
For example:

- Set up systems and management systems to review the progress of cases.
- Train and monitor your team to ensure cases progress efficiently.
- Close cases quicker.
- Invoice quicker.

If you implement just a few of these strategies in your law firm, your cash flow will increase considerably. This means your business will be a lot less stressful and far more fun to run.

Putting it into practice

How much could each of these five cash flow levers improve your cash flow in the next three months? Pick three easy-to-implement strategies and implement one per month for the next three months. See how your cash flow improves.

The five cash flow levers being implemented

When I first started working with this firm, the owner was about to borrow £30,000 from the bank to fund growth for marketing and staffing costs. Within a month of implementing the cash flow levers he had found over £30,000 that was hidden inside his own business. The cash flow had improved so much that he no longer needed to borrow the money.

Within the next few years, all business loans were repaid, cash flow was never an issue, even during year-on-year growth, and the company went on to achieve a six-figure profit.

Figure 5: Focus on efficiency; profit is sanity.

Most business owners want to generate more profit in their businesses, and they think the best way to achieve this is by increasing revenue. Often, focusing on revenue growth is not the best way to increase profits. In fact, it can damage your business.

Once you have improved your cash flow, you should move on to improving your profitability. Then, and only then, should you focus on growing your revenue.

When aeronautical engineers want to redesign a plane to make it go faster, they do not just put a bigger engine on it. The first thing they do is reduce the drag, because this will increase its speed without the need for extra power. Once they have maximized the aerodynamics, they then upgrade the engine.

It's the same in business. If you want more profit, do not just make a bigger engine (e.g., increase your marketing) to increase your revenue. Instead, reduce the drag of expenses first because this instantly boosts your profit. Below is an example of how this works.

Profitability and efficiency first, marketing second

Consider two businesses – Business A and Business B (Figure 6).

Both have a revenue of 100 units and have costs of 90 units, giving a profit of ten units (ten percent).

As an example, this could be:

Revenue: £1 million
Expenditure: £900,000
Profit: £100,000.

They both want to increase profit by 30 percent.

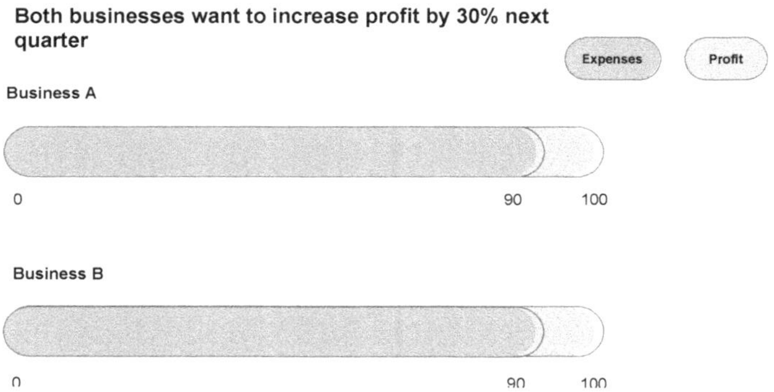

Figure 6: Businesses A and B want to increase profit by 30 percent.

Business A: Increases revenue by 30 percent

Business A does what most businesses try and do, and increases revenue by 30 percent (Figure 7).

Revenue +30 percent = £1 million × 1.3 = £1.3 million.
We can assume expenditure also increases by 30 percent.
Expenditure +30% = £900,000 × 1.3 = £1,170,000.
Profit = £1.3 million - £1,170,000 = £130,000.
(Equates to 30 percent growth in profit.)

It sounds logical, but just think how difficult it will be to grow your business by 30 percent. It is expensive and takes a long time.

Imagine how much extra work your team would need to do or how many extra staff you would need to employ if your workload increased by 30 percent.

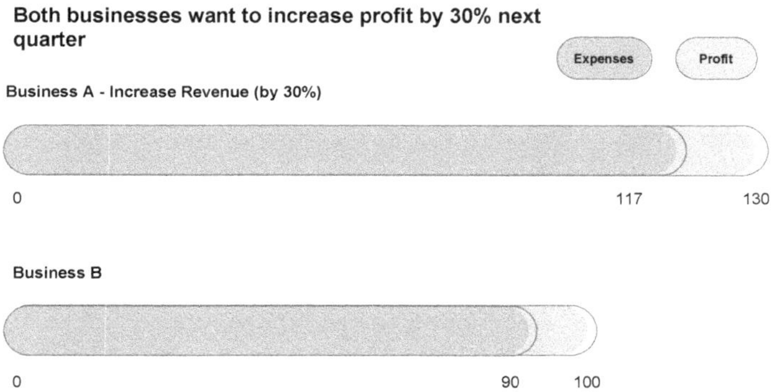

Figure 7: Business A increases revenue by 30 percent.

Business B: Decreases expenditure by 3.33 percent

Instead of increasing revenue, Business B decides to reduce its expenditure by just 3.33 percent (£3,330), which achieves the same increase in profits (Figure 8).

Revenue = £1 million.
Expenditure -3.33 percent = £900,000 × 96.67 percent = £870,030.
Profit = £1,000,000 - £870,030 = £129,970.
(Equates to 30 percent growth in profit.)
Ok, so there is £30 difference, but you get my point.

Just think how much easier and quicker it is to reduce expenditure by 3.33 percent compared to growing revenue by 30 percent.

This equates to the same profit outcome but it can be achieved much easier and much faster.

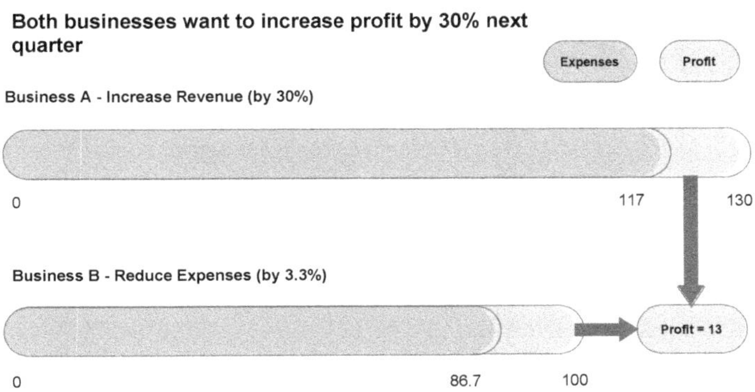

Figure 8: Business B reduces expenditure by 3.33 percent.

You can decrease your costs in several ways:

- Reduce overheads (expenditure you have regardless of whether you carry out any work).
- Reduce costs of sales (fees incurred only when you are actually doing work).
- Improve efficiencies (do more in less time/use fewer resources).

If Business B now increases revenue by 30 percent, it will achieve an overall increase in profit of 70 percent!

Business B has already increased profit by 30 percent without actually increasing its revenue. It can now invest this additional profit in marketing to increase revenue. It is important to note that it is now growing a more profitable business.

If we follow the above example and assume it then grows revenue by 30 percent:

Revenue = £1 million × 1.3 = £1.3 million.
We can assume expenditure also increases by 30 percent.
Expenditure + 30 percent = £870,030 × 1.3 = £1,131,039.
Profit = £1.3 million - £1,131,039 = £168,961.

This is £68,961 additional profit from the original starting profit of £100,000 – almost 70 percent growth in profits (Figure 9).

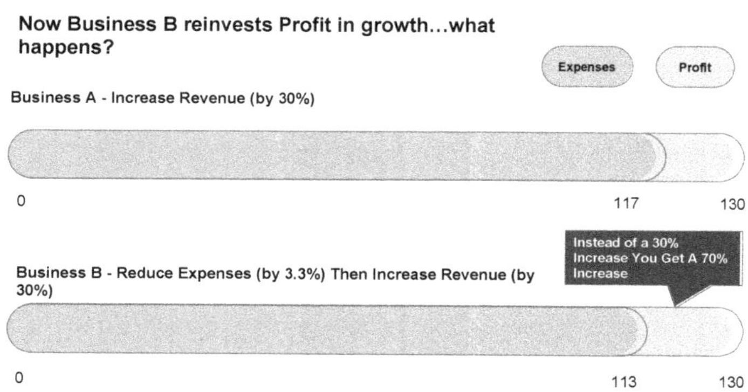

Figure 9: 70 percent growth in profit.

Profit exercise

Let's make the assumption that you would be interested in growing your profits by at least 30 percent in the next 12 months without having to increase your workload.

Make a start and complete the exercise below to see how much extra profit you can generate in the next 12 months. You may need to look at your profit and loss statement from your accounting software or from your accountant.

1. Find out your current revenue, expenditure, and net profit. Your net profit is your revenue minus your total expenditure. Put your numbers into boxes 1, 2, and 3 in Figure 10.
2. Estimate what you could reduce your annual expenditure to in the next 12 months by reducing overheads and incurred costs and improving internal efficiencies. Put your new expenditure number into box 4 in Figure 11.
3. Estimate what you could increase your revenues to in the next 12 months. Put your new revenue number into box 5 in Figure 11.
4. Calculate your new net profit – box 5 minus box 4. Put your new profit number into box 6 in Figure 11.
5. Lastly, calculate how much extra profit you would make by subtracting box 3 from box 6, and input it into Figure 12.

1. What is my current:

Revenue: £.................................. per annum (box 1)

Total expenditure: £.................................. per annum (box 2)

Net profit: £.................................. per annum (box 3)

(Note: Expenditure = box 1 minus box 3)

Current

Current revenue: £ (1)

Current total expenditure: £ (2) Net Profit: £ (3)

Figure 10: Current financials.

2. What could I reduce my annual expenditure to?
   (reduce overheads/incurred costs, improve internal efficiencies)

   £…………..………………….. per annum (box 4)

3. What could I increase my revenue to per year?
   (marketing, grade A clients, internal referrals, improved billing)

   £…………..………………….. per annum (box 5)

Target

Total expenditure target: £ (4)

Revenue target: £ (5)

New net profit: £ (6)

Figure 11: Potential financials.

4. What is my new net profit (box 6)? £…………..…….. per annum

5. How much extra profit can I make? £…………..…….. per annum (box 6 minus box 3)

Figure 12: How much extra profit could you generate?

What was your new profit number and how did it make you feel? Excited? Nervous? Run the calculations again with some different numbers in boxes 5 and 6 just for fun; explore the "art of the possible".

If you have been brave and you have got some big numbers, you are probably wondering, "Can I do it? Is it this simple?"

The answer to those questions is yes, you probably can, and it is not that complicated once you understand and implement the business blueprint.

I have worked with many business owners who have grown their business profits by more than 1,000 percent in just a few years. They did it by following the above steps – controlling cash flow, maximizing efficiency and profitability, and then growing the business.

They did these steps whilst always ensuring that their team and their clients were valued, respected, and looked after. Cash and profit should not be maximized at the expense of your clients or your staff.

Implementing the profit maximizer

This is a great example of how quick and easy it is to increase your profits.

The owner of this firm completely understood the profit maximiser principle and got started immediately. He looked at every detail in his business to identify areas to reduce expenditure and improve efficiencies. He worked very closely with his team to identify where financial savings and efficiency improvements could be made.

Some financial savings were simple; for example, not leasing unnecessary or unused office equipment (including the plants), reviewing office space usage, and getting a closer grip on discretionary spend. Some efficiency improvements were simple – for example, staff suggested that if they had two computer screens each, rather than one, they would save a lot of time switching from one application to another.

The most significant efficiency improvement required investment in bespoke software that reduced client enquiry/onboarding time from 20 minutes to one minute. With 2,000 enquiries per month, that was a saving of over 600 hours per month. With the time saved, the business was able to take on more clients with no increase in costs.

The business became so efficient and profitable that its employees had their working hours reduced by two hours per week but retained their full salary, and a percentage of profit was distributed to staff in a discretionary bonus scheme. Over the next three years, profit increased by over 400 percent.

Don't do what many other law firms do

I speak with many owners of law firms who want to "grow" their businesses. Understandably, they want to focus on improving their marketing to get more clients and increase revenue. As you can see from the business blueprint, by focusing on "getting more clients or increasing revenue" they are likely to be building an unprofitable, cash-eating monster because they will have missed the two most vital elements in the business – cash flow and profit.

This is why there are so many owners of law firms out there who are working hard but not receiving the benefits they deserve. Do not do what they do. Maximize your cash flow (productivity) first, then your profitability (efficiency), then focus on your effectiveness (business development).

Focusing on effectiveness

When I first met this business owner, he was working 80-90 hours per week and making minimal profit. The first area we focused on was ensuring billing was accurate and invoices were sent in a timely manner. This improved cash flow and reduced a lot of stress for the business owner.

The next step was to identify the profit margins in each of the departments. It transpired that 80 percent of the work was unprofitable. They immediately increased the prices in these unprofitable departments and focused marketing efforts on the more profitable departments.

Within the next three years the business achieved 900 percent growth in revenue and profits, and the business owner was able to reduce his working hours by 50 percent. The business owner is now enjoying running a profitable business and is able to spend quality time with his partner and young family, and have time for himself to regain his own physical fitness.

Putting this into practice

There is so much information out there, it is easy to get stuck in overwhelm, not knowing where to start. As a result, people procrastinate. I hope that you are finding this chapter easy to read, simple to understand, and straightforward to put into action.

- Are you going to take action?
- Have you completed the above exercises?
- If you did, was it just in your head, or did you write it down? Your chances of success are far greater if you have written it down in a suitable place.
- Have you thought about a few actions you can take right now that will improve your cash flow and/or increase your profitability?
- When are you going to commit to start doing them?

It would make sense to set time aside in your diary to review your notes and commit to taking action and/or delegating these actions to someone else to ensure they are completed.

We are all busy – in fact, I have rarely met a successful business owner who is not working long hours. Most of my clients consistently worked 80 or more hours a week, every week. They did not have piles of cash to invest, or hours spare to spend working on their business. They were stressed out, overworked, and underpaid.

They didn't let their current situation prevent them from creating a much better future. We followed the nine-step roadmap, focusing on a few key areas in a specific order to ensure they gained traction and momentum. This structured approach enabled them to progress, step-by-step, towards their goals, whilst reducing their working hours.

If you look at the nine-step roadmap in Figure 1, you will notice that this chapter has focused on step four – Profit and cash. After developing your goals and building your plans (steps one to three), this is your starting point for growing a highly successful and profitable business.

Closing thoughts

Can you gain an extra £1 million profit in the next three years?

It is impossible for me to answer that question.

Maybe you can, maybe you cannot, maybe you are not interested in generating that level of wealth. As a business owner, it is your choice.

However, I am certain you could achieve the most amazing results in your business in just a few years if you follow a proven, tried, and tested business system and focus on the business. This chapter has given you enough to get started.

I am hoping the real-life examples I have shared resonate with you and have given you some ideas you can implement in your business, and the confidence that you can achieve your goals. Many other owners of law firms who were in situations just like yours have built brilliant businesses, giving them the personal finances and time to enjoy their lives on their terms. They have achieved this with only a few years of focused work, and so can you.

I do not want you to just read this chapter and then move on to the next without implementing something that will move you towards your goals.

So, if you have not done so already, take a few minutes and review your notes. Put some thought into *exactly what* you are going to do and *specifically when* you are going to commit to doing it. A few minutes or hours spent now will pay you back many times over.

I want you to take action. Now! Good luck and have fun on the journey.

References

1 P.R.O.F.I.T. is an acronym for steps four to nine in the nine-step roadmap:

P: Profit and Cash

R: Marketing and Revenue

O: Operations and Systems
F: Financials and KPIs
I: Innovation and Leadership
T: Team and Culture

2 https://businesscoachacademy.com/

3 *The Ultimate Blueprint for an Insanely Successful Business*. Keith Cunningham. Key to the Vault, 2012.

4 www.legalfutures.co.uk/latest-news/most-law-firms-willing-to-consider-selling-stake-to-external-investor

Chapter 7:

How a sound matter pricing strategy can elevate law firm profitability

By Jack Kingston, account manager, BigHand

In my 20 or more years of working with the legal industry and supporting its financial leadership, no subject has come to light more often than elevating profitability. Firms are looking for advanced data to better understand their business and how they can make their firms more profitable. Advanced BI and software programs are coming to the forefront to help firms digitize their data and reporting initiatives, resulting in better use of time through advanced data visualization. Getting this data to the stakeholders is important to the leaders in the finance function, in terms of data enablement and preserving their sanity by not being asked to create ad-hoc reports. One can only measure what one can see, and firms seek to enable their stakeholders with data to make sound business decisions. Firms continue to evaluate profits based on client, department, fee earner, and practice group levels, using various methods of proper profit calculation (like FTEs or just hard costs). This is a direction of travel and forward-thinking firms are already there, but a lot of firms are still focused on vanity metrics like billable hours/revenue, whereas profit is much more important.

One highly used analogy is that revenue is vanity and profit is sanity. There is no right or wrong way to automate a profitability journey, it just must be defensible and make sense to the firm. The hard costs of a resource are quite simple to quantify, like salary, 401K, and benefits calculation. Where firms struggle is when considering if they look at profit as a combined firm or if they'd like to do it by office location. Considering the cost of real estate is much higher in a major US market like New York or San Francisco vs an office in Nashville or even Boise, Idaho, there is much to consider. Would the Boise office exist without the national presence in New York? Or should Boise be treated as a true satellite office without consideration of the larger costs of the New York flagship office? You can see a case for either scenario, but firms must be diligent about their understanding of the profit metrics. These are just a couple of high-level examples of what law firm leadership is looking at when considering their profit calculations.

One major blind spot – is the work you are doing making you money?

No other area of the business of law has seen more attention to profitability metrics than at the matter level, where firms are looking at staffing and rate structure costs. Oddly, a pricing strategy within legal is a relatively new phenomenon, despite sounding like a very logical starting point when onboarding a new piece of work. Gone are the days when a lawyer or legal assistant would price a piece of work in a vacuum or provide a low rate "just because" or for legacy reasons. Firms need to get in touch with their data to maintain a sound culture of profitability as they move forward in their journey. Legal clients are shopping for services, so why should the firm not consider making a rate that is attractive to its bottom line?

Firms are now looking for experienced pricing professionals who are supported by technology to dig into the data. These professionals are also digging into the rates to see if they have been raised, and if they remain competitive in the market in which they play. Many larger and even mid-market law firms are hiring entire teams dedicated to both pricing and legal project management. There has also been a cultural shift at many of these mid-sized and large law firms to a keener eye toward financial awareness. Lawyers are being compensated on profits more than ever before, taking some attention off the billable hour, all this despite more firms increasing the targets for billable hours in 2023. Never has getting the full rate set been more important to the bottom line of both the firm and the partner.

Bringing in the best matters for your firm

All pieces of legal work are not created equal, and firms need to understand the underlying metrics to be intelligent about the work they are bringing to the firm. There might be a very good reason for bringing on a lower margin piece of work for reasons like client attraction or retention; however, all work cannot be loss leaders. Firms need to understand what areas of business are contributing to their bottom line and what areas of work are easily repeatable with good profit metrics. Firms need to consider what types of matters they wish to bring into the fold and what clients are truly driving profits forward. Lawyers of today are not just practicing law, they need to be better business people and understand why their efforts support the firm from a financial perspective. These decisions will impact the health of their firm, and in turn their compensation.

Leveraging past data to make sound business decisions has become an enabler throughout the industry. Having the proper technology stack to support sound business decisions and save valuable time with pricing and project planning is seen as critical. Areas of importance within the technology stack are proper real-time consistent reporting, supported by easy-to-understand visuals and exportable data sources to ensure ongoing client communication. In the past, firms have been doing these tasks via legacy tools like Excel. While Excel is a powerful and useful tool, it cannot navigate to a practice management system to consider exception rates that may exist for a particular client. Excel can also frustrate users with broken formulas or not enable users with previous versions of budgets, which exist in most modern technology stacks. Answering RFPs is an arduous task and using automation to solve this has been critical. Firms can use the data to understand if the piece of work is worth bidding on and how they should quote the work to the customer.

The industry is seeing that most major firms require all new matters to start with a top-end budget, which Excel just could not solve in a meaningful way. Enter a tool for automating the process where graphs can be leveraged to understand the matter at a first glance, but also to provide the data as pricing leaders dig deeper into all phases of the matter. Ensuring that data is coded the proper way plays a large role in leveraging historical data for use in future budgets. To quote a too often used cliché, "garbage in, garbage out" – the coding of the proper phase and task is gaining traction for use on future work and budgets. Lawyers are using phases like the L100 UTMBS code (discovery) as a dumping ground, which does not bode well for leveraging data for future use or from the client billing perspective. The industry is seeing a push towards artificial intelligence to read these narratives and code the work properly. This is done using things like narratives to ensure the work is properly coded and one area of business is not having the dumping ground situation referenced above. The benefit of a situation like this is two-fold in that the data is there for future use and fewer e-bills get rejected by the purchasers of legal services. This is especially true for firms with a large insurance practice where e-bills and proper coding are paramount. A rejected e-bill can add to the work-to-cash cycle and negatively affect the collections effort, which leads to a negative impact on the firm's realization percentage and possibly affects bonuses and the financial wellbeing of the firm. For every period a firm waits on its collections, the likelihood of collecting all the outstanding amounts lowers, making this an area of profit leakage.

Differing approaches for payment of legal services

Purchasers of legal services are asking for alternative fee arrangements (AFAs) or flat rates for legal services. For example, a client might request that a piece of work be done for 100K, leaving the firm with a blind spot on how to price the work. By using technology, the firm can put in a top-level amount and begin to put resources in place to complete the work. This activity will tell the firm how profitable the work will be based on who is doing the work (either specific people or levels, like an associate or partner, for example). Technology will also enable the firm to do "what if" scenarios, moving their resource around to see what the best staffing model should be. They can then use that data to price future pieces of work by creating a template or versions of said templates. In addition to special fee arrangements, clients are also asking for special rates or rate exceptions. Moreover, they are also asking for more scope and shadow billing of said AFAs to keep on top of what they are paying for their legal services. Unlike in years past, these clients are becoming savvier and shopping around for better rates or scopes of work. Past loyalty models and staying with just one firm are largely a thing of the past. Things like reduced demand, staffing challenges, and economic headwinds are also having an impact on loyalty and client retention. Recently, I sat in a focus group of financial leaders from law firms who said they use several firms for differing scopes of work. This differs greatly from having one sole provider for your enterprise of legal services, meaning firms must be more flexible and adaptable when pricing or answering client RFPs.

An industry-leading technology company specializing in legal productivity, BigHand ran a survey, titled "Improving client engagement to safeguard profitability",[1] gathering 800 responses from senior legal finance roles, CEOs, managing partners, FP&A, and finance systems roles from law firms of 100+ lawyers in the UK and North America. The survey produced some eye-opening statistics about client and firm perspectives, including:

- Half of the firms report their clients demanding real-time financial updates (yet less than four percent of these firms are providing these updates).
- 44 percent of firms globally are producing matter budgets.
- Almost all firms are reporting increased billing realization when a budget is assigned to a matter.

To stay competitive and profitable with happy and engaged clients, law firms must understand the impact of taking on an AFA and produce the staffing model that makes the most sense. When pricing by the hour (bottom up, in industry speak), allocating the right number of hours to the right resource or resource level is seen as best practice. Giving the right work to the right person at the right rate will help firms stay competitive in a challenging market. This will also help firms retain talent by giving the proper work to the proper people and helping partners with their leverage percentages. Firms should also be asking themselves questions like, "Are we giving the right rate to our customers", "What are we going to collect" and "What can we do to reduce write-offs or write-downs". Having the proper technology stack can help these pricing professionals answer these critical questions. It will also help firms conduct a "write-off" review process to ensure future matters are modeled most profitably, or "what if scenarios" on each of their matters by moving resources in or out of the projects. In the same report mentioned earlier, it was noted that:

- 70 percent of firms globally have seen an increase in write-offs over the previous year (more than half have seen these write-offs increase by ten percent).
- 69 percent of firms plan to invest in legal pricing solutions.

This matter-level data will enable firms to make sound business decisions, which will result in less profit leakage. Having technology in place is a great safeguard to prevent leakage and increase profits across the enterprise of mid- to large-sized law firms. Pricing professionals are not cheap resources, with most making more than 200K per year. Enabling these costly resources with technology will enable them to do their jobs better and help firms leverage the human capital investment made in these pricing professionals. These pricing professionals are also helping the partnership with client communication by speaking with the clients directly. Having data at their fingertips from an automated system that provides the data will greatly help these professionals with messaging valued clients. The cost of the average pricing and planning tool is a fraction of the cost of a single pricing body, making automation software and solutions a virtual no-brainer. Simply put, automation can help a firm save on the cost of adding more data analysts or pricing professionals.

Matter-level discounts are yet another area of leakage of profit and a large blind spot for law firms. In the past, a partner or firm would provide an overall discount to a client simply because it was the norm. The firm had no true understanding of how the discount would impact the bottom line. A pricing tool – which many leading software companies offer their clients – can show the firm the KPIs and how a discount truly affects the bottom line. By arming the firm with this simple data point, the firm can decide if the discount is worth the impact on the bottom line or if a new rate needs to be negotiated. The software solutions sold to law firms help the firm service their client while understanding the benefit a new matter will bring to the table.

Another benefit to properly pricing and planning matters would be to drive collections. As law firms increased their rates with big law rising by record highs in 2023, scoping legal services is critical. These rate raises were seen as a break from the norm of basic economics due to the decrease in demand in 2023. Clients are pushing back on scope overruns but generally are agreeable to paying the increased rates, even if said rate increases were not desirable. If a firm wants to keep its realization percentages high, it needs to ensure they are delivering proper scope and staying out in front of changes and overruns. Leveraging an alert system as part of the technology stack will also enable pricing directors and matter-responsible lawyers to stay aware of their projects by providing clarity when a phase or task reaches a certain threshold of completion. This way, the pricing directors or relationship-owning lawyers can communicate the potential overrun and still manage to keep their collections efforts high. Increasing visibility will keep the stakeholders informed and allow them to take proper action to keep their collections levels high and help reduce lock-up in the firm.

Yet another market shift in the past 18 months has been that purchasers of legal services are demanding more diversity from their legal services providers. Firms can leverage technology not only to plan and price matters for profits but also to measure DEI statistics. It is not only important for people of diverse backgrounds to receive the work, but to ensure people of diverse backgrounds are getting career-advancing work. Not only will these metrics satisfy the clients of law firms, they will also help firms retain the talent they have. When a major manufacturing or insurance client is asking a law firm for DEI information, a firm should be able to access this quickly and, more importantly, accurately. A quick search on Glassdoor reveals that the average salary of a legal associate in a major market like New York is close to 200K, often more. Retaining these associates is critical to the bottom line since onboarding and ongoing training are costly to the firm. Having technology help enable retention remains a hot-button subject in the business of law and pricing and DEI is a natural progression to advanced reporting metrics. Firms are also going towards being "Mansfield Certified",[2] which is a structured certification process to ensure that all talent at a law firm has a fair and equal chance at advancing to leadership. The rule focuses on broadening the talent pool for consideration, including those historically underrepresented in the legal profession, and is a major driver to doing business with a firm. Having an equal share of both the volume and the quality of the work remains critical.

In conclusion, leverage technology to help you and to bridge the gap. It will help bring better value to your clients and increase profits and compensation. By understanding the impact, your firm can make wise business decisions, prevent leakage, and grow organically with your clients.

References

1 www.bighand.com/en-us/resources/whitepapers/improving-client-engagement-to-safeguard-profitability
2 www.diversitylab.com/pilot-projects/mansfield-overview/

Chapter 8:
Questioning the value of law firm rack rates

By Richard Brzakala, senior director, Global External Legal Services

Background

For decades now, it has become common practice for many law firms in North America to offer up "discounted" hourly rates to their corporate clients in exchange for potential legal work. The discounted rates are typically benchmarked against what many in the legal industry refer to as a law firm's "rack rates", which are almost always some of the highest rates a firm will charge clients. I refer to this law firm practice as *rack rate benchmarking* or RRB, which has become entrenched with many firms as a mechanism by which law firms can maintain rate predictability and increase profitability for themselves while also providing the optics of trading off "discounts" in exchange for potential legal work from some of their clients.

Nothing sounds better to a corporate legal department (CLD), especially in an inflationary business cycle, than hearing from their panel firm that they have been offered the benefit of double-digit discounts off a firm's rack rates or what the firm charges its other clients. Typically, RRB discounts are provided to those clients that have either specialist (i.e. expensive) legal work, large volumes of work, or the client has some tenure or history with the firm. Increasingly, firms are starting to utilize their RRB discounts to attract new clients and portfolios of legal work.

RRB incorporates various empirical market factors such as cost of living allowance or rate of inflation, market benchmarking data, administrative overhead, employee retention costs, infrastructure, leasehold and technology, and insurance costs. In addition, law firms may also include other factors such as a firm's profitability margins, forecasting estimates as regards market demand in specific practice areas, and resource availability. Many of the latter factors, it can be argued, may end up being based on projections. However, in the end, all if not some of these factors get baked into the establishment of a firm's rack rate.

It is against a firm's rack rates that a firm makes a determination as to whether or not to afford a new or existing client a discount to its hourly rates.

Regardless of the discount, most firms are incentivized to ensure that the RRB is increased every year so that the higher the increase on the annual rack rate, the greater the opportunity and margin for law firm profitability and ultimately employee bonuses.

With increased competitiveness in today's marketplace, most firms will try to entice new clients with some sort of discount against the firm's rack rate. On the surface, a discount proposal of any kind that promises to save a client money is especially welcome to those existing and prospective CLDs who are looking to save costs in an inflationary environment.

But is this in fact true? Is the client coming out ahead and getting the benefit of cost savings by accepting discounts based on an RRB approach? If not, what can CLDs do to ensure they receive the best possible (truly discounted) rates? And as for law firms, what can they do to win clients over to accept their rack rate proposals? These are just some of the questions I will look to answer in this chapter.

Why RRB discounts are so attractive to CLDs

RRB discounts have for years been attractive and popular with many CLDs because RRB discounts don't require a lot of data analysis and work. RRB discounts offer CLDs a very easy, uncomplicated opportunity to simply accept what is put in front of them without having to do any independent analysis or time-consuming negotiation.

For those CLDs that may not have dedicated resources to manage external counsel or finite resources to manage a multitude of responsibilities and/or projects, RRB discounts offer at least the optics of receiving some level of discount without the fuss of having to negotiate or undertake a data mining exercise. In order for a CLD to negotiate rates, they must first have a good understanding of what they want to achieve in terms of cost savings or discounts. That level of understanding begins with some level of data analysis on the part of the client in order to establish a base line against which potential cost savings can be measured.

In order for many CLDs – even those with mature and established Legal Ops teams – to develop a reliable and accurate data set and analysis, an experienced and dedicated data or legal operations resource is required – something that may not always be readily available within most CLDs.

Firms know all of this and are only too happy to offer up some type of discount to busy CLDs that want to make a quick decision without having to do a lot of work. Firms deliberately position their RRB discounts in the form of future cost savings by making statements like, "If you continue to bill our firm at last year's level of legal spend, the discounts we offer you will save you X$ in the coming year".

If CLDs are stretched thin in regard to data analysis resources, or existing resources have competing priorities, RRB discounts offer CLDs a quick and expedient way of demonstrating some level of cost savings to their general counsel or senior executives. Therefore, it's not surprising to see why a law firm's proposal, almost by default, has historically been the more attractive option for many CLDs in terms of simplicity, convenience, and expedience.

Yet, despite the appearance of a benefit to the client, firms are under no obligation to offer RRB discounts to all of their clients. In fact, many firms will tell you that a large percentage of their work is billed using rack rates without the benefit of any discount. The perception of exclusivity is perhaps another reason why some clients are attracted to accept RRB discounts. Offering up some type of discount helps reinforce the belief (especially for a new potential client) that a firm considers the client a "preferred client" and to back that up the firm is willing to make what appears to be a pricing concession in order for the firm to win new work from the client.

The credibility of cost savings based on RRB data

Many CLDs and their general counsels have increasingly come under pressure to cut costs and implement greater fiscal responsibility around their legal spend. With that added responsibility has come the accountability to create and report reliable cost savings data. Consequently, more and more CLDs are questioning the integrity of the RRB practice as they look for greater pricing transparency in order to generate reliable cost savings.

As CLDs become increasingly more sophisticated in the management and the analysis of their legal spend data, and have resources to better understand their spend data, they have grown increasingly skeptical of the data that firms utilize to arrive at their pricing proposals and the proposed discounts they offer to their clients.

For mature CLDs, it's no longer an option to automatically accept an RRB proposal that is significantly weighted in favor of a law firm. Inflationary market pressures are incentivizing increasing numbers of CLDs to pay greater attention to cost savings data and proposals from either law firms or alternative legal service providers (ALSPs).

Moreover, general counsel have taken on the responsibility of implementing, tracking, and reporting on cost savings initiatives to their respective boards and CEOs. Therefore, it is crucial that the integrity of any cost savings data be accurate and reliable and that any cost saving proposals received from a law firm should be validated internally by a CLD in order to make a final determination as to the value and benefit of the proposed cost savings to the client. Relying on a law firm to tell a CLD what they have supposedly saved puts a CLD's credibility at risk in terms of reporting biased, perhaps questionable, cost savings data to their executives.

The utilization of supplementary fees

The credibility of cost savings based on RRB data is further exacerbated by firms billing a supplementary fee for work that appears on invoices in the form of a percentage multiplied by the sum total of fees billed to the client. Firms position the supplementary fee as a necessary cost of doing business to cover off such internal expenses as investments in technology, administrative overhead, leaseholds, premise costs, or insurance expenses.

These types of supplementary fees may be valid and make sense from an operational and business perspective, but ironically, some of these expenses are often already baked into the methodology a firm uses to develop its rack rates. Consequently, it is not uncommon for some firms to include the cost for their internal expenses as part of their supplementary fee and also as part of their rack rate calculation, which would result in creating a cost savings disadvantage for the client and the appearance of double-counting the same expenses.

In addition, CLDs focused on cost savings often overlook the impact that a supplementary fee may have against the potential cost savings a firm promotes as part of its RRB savings promotion. For example, if a firm is proposing a ten percent discount off its rack rates and bills a supplementary fee of four percent on the total value of fees being billed on every invoice, the client may in fact only be receiving a discount of six percent or less.

All too often, clients only discover the supplementary fee during an invoice review or as part of their engagement process when a firm asks the client to sign an engagement letter. Regardless of the justification for charging supplementary fees, they detract from any proposed rack rate discounts and ultimately diminish a CLD's ability to generate real cost savings.

Zero negotiation strategy

As we move beyond a global pandemic, the legal market is in a stalemate of sorts where CLDs want to limit and cut expenses while the law firms want to increase profitability using strategies like RRB and supplementary fees. Neither side has much margin to make any concessions, but undeniably both sides must find a middle ground.

Unfortunately, CLDs are increasingly finding some of their panel firms adopting a very rigid posture when it comes to their rate proposals. I refer to this as a zero negotiation strategy, which reflects a growing belief amongst some firms that their work product – the services they provide, the experts that they employ – delivers exceptional value and consequently they will not negotiate their rack rates or make any type of pricing concessions. Their rates are the rates they bill and there is zero room for negotiation.

Any risk (or fear) of losing clients (or market share) to less expensive firms or ALSPs is a risk that more and more firms are willing to take, especially in highly sought after practice areas where specialized and experienced legal professionals are in high demand. As a consequence, rates for high demand specialties like, for example, regulatory and securities law, privacy, cyber security, and litigation defense work, have skyrocketed to the point that some firms refuse altogether to give any of their clients discounts and charge their clients rack rates with no room for negotiation. In the end, some clients are faced with either having to accept zero negotiation and higher rack rates or look elsewhere for other less expensive options.

In fact, very few CLDs are seeing their panel firms backing away from perennial increases for the sake of their long-standing "relationship". All of this has led to rack rates increasing to such stratospheric levels that one wonders if such expensive levels are sustainable and, if not, how long before strategies such as zero negotiation will have an adverse impact on established relationships.

What are CLDs looking for?

In today's cost conscious environment, in which almost all CLDs are struggling to achieve measurable cost savings, CLDs want and require more from their firms. If firms are going to propose cost savings based on RRB, then how a firm approaches its pricing proposals needs to change and go beyond the allure of cost saving enticements tied to inflated rack rates.

For those law firms lucky enough to have been part of a client's panel, this may mean taking a more bilateral – even consensual – approach that affords the client an opportunity to provide feedback to a firm's proposal. Sometimes, how a message is delivered and its context is just as important as the message itself.

Taking a more pre-emptive approach prior to finalizing and delivering a firm's rate increase announcement should first involve asking a CLD for such things as candid real world feedback, understanding if a client has any significant budget constraints, asking whether the client has any cost saving targets to achieve, and how will a proposed rate increase impact those goals, and what expectations the client has in regard to future legal work. These types of questions (and more) play into gaining valuable insights into how rack rate increases will impact a client and ultimately the relationship between a firm and the client. Understanding a client's perspective on rate increases is a more palatable and welcome approach for both parties and helps mitigate against mistrust, misunderstandings, and any potential adverse impacts on the relationship.

Unfortunately, that is not always the case. Over the years, many firms have gotten used to issuing ubiquitous rate increase announcements with zero tolerance for any discussion or negotiation with their clients. From a client's perspective, many CLDs have come to view this type of law firm behavior as a risk to established relationships as it demonstrates apathy and an indifference to the client's needs. Some CLDs have characterized this type of approach as being tone deaf to the needs of the client and contradictory to how CLDs in a post-COVID marketplace expect legal services to be delivered – two good reasons for any law firm to pause and reexamine their approach in a highly competitive marketplace.

CLDs have come to expect a lot more from their firms than just excellent legal advice at reasonable prices. There is an expectation amongst CLDs that, if a firm is on a client's panel, the firm will understand the importance of service delivery and how critical a component it is in the business of law and the relationship firms enjoy with their client. Firms are expected to understand how clients run their businesses and if the client has cost savings targets, to try and help their clients achieve those targets.

Clients, on the other hand, must balance their cost savings and efficiency targets with law firm demands to remain profitable. Most CLDs understand that profitability is a good thing and many would not deny their firms the opportunity to increase margins. But if that profitability is a result of zero negotiations and at the expense of clients having to absorb dramatic rate hikes based on RRB that may have serious repercussions on a client's business, then the firm owes it to its client, and itself, to have a pre-emptive discussion in order to try and mitigate the impact of its rate increases.

For those firms committed to building long-term relationships, the investment in making the time to have meaningful discussions with a client is just as important as selling time and services to a client. One cannot exist without the other.

How firms manage their rate strategy and work with their clients to find ways to mitigate against any adverse impacts resulting from a firm's necessary increases will always play a determining factor in the longevity of many new and existing relationships. Unfortunately, when the well runs dry and the work stops flowing to a law firm, more times than not, the issue is around a lack of communication and affordability. Both those issues can trace their origins to service delivery and to a firm's RRB pricing strategy.

Law firm reliance on pricing specialists and business intelligence tools

Most firms' RRB pricing strategy relies on a variety of data analysis tools. Amongst those tools and resources, internal and external pricing specialists, generic rate reports, and business intelligence and objective AI tools can help firms respond to client concerns about pricing, formulate responses to RFPs, and assist a firm with their RRB processes in order to try to gain market share and maintain or grow profits. Firms will try and use any means in order to gain a competitive advantage over their peers and to ensure that their firm remains competitively priced.

The outflow from utilizing such pricing resources has inevitably resulted in annual increases to a firm's rack rate and, as a consequence, the rates firms charge many of their clients. Not surprisingly, this has resulted in a follow-the-herd mentality, with many firms across a multitude of metropolitan markets in North America and beyond.

The race for increased market share and profitability often sidelines, if not in some instances downplays, the relevance and value of a historical relationship and all of the value indicators that are baked into what constitutes a successful relationship.

Value indicators such as honesty, transparency, communication, reciprocity, loyalty, tenure, exclusivity, risk sharing, and pre-emptive knowledge of how a law firm's unilateral rate increases might impact a client and their relationship with their service providers all seem to take a back seat to the importance of empirical pricing data.

Undeniably, there is value in market rate reports and the output that is generated by professionals working to understand and predict forecasting trends. However, more firms might be better served if they were to encompass a more holistic approach and look beyond just the empirical data or market rate reports, worry less about how competitively priced they are, and look more towards how to maintain and grow the needs of their existing or new clients. Often times, all of this begins with engaging clients and having a constructive dialogue. Perhaps not with every client, but firms are savvy enough to understand which clients matter the most or impact their margins the greatest.

The marginalization of value indicators in favor of increasing profit margins ultimately produces less than optimal results and undermines the longevity of lasting relationships. Consequently, for CLDs looking for value-driven relationships, this has become a highly desirable area of change with their legal service providers.

Profitability, employee retention costs, and administrative overhead are examples of empirical factors that almost always supersede the repercussive implications and impact of increases on the client and the overall relationship. Many institutional clients have grown weary and will no longer tolerate what they see as dismissive behavior and a growing market apathy to what, if any, impact a firm's rate increases may have on the client's business. Dismissing the relationship components around rate discussions and adopting a zero negotiation posture is increasingly being viewed by the buyers of legal services as adversarial, and risks undermining a client's business and its relationship with firms.

In fact, zero negotiation has also inadvertently fueled the common misconception amongst some firms that the larger the client (in terms of market capital, revenues, and profitability), the less concern there should be around how, or if, the client is able to absorb a rate increase. The thinking being that if a client is profitable, it should have no problem absorbing what a firm proposes in the way of increases.

Regardless of the size of a client's company or profitability, firms would do well to re-evaluate their overall approach to how they attain profitability and their processes, including RRB, while retaining their longstanding clients. Being prepared with the proper rationale and, more importantly, how a firm expects to mitigate the impact of rate hikes on a relationship, are two things that should be baked into all firms' rate proposal strategies.

What CLDs want to see from firms utilizing a RRB strategy

Perhaps the most meaningful way law firms can provide greater transparency around how they establish their pricing structures is to proactively communicate to their clients their approach to RRB and to have a meaningful dialogue, well in advance of implementing any increases, on why, how, and what variables are at play in the RRB process and how that process is fair and reasonable to both parties.

Historically, this type of approach – and with it law firm transparency – has unfortunately been more of the exception rather than the norm in the legal marketplace. Law firms are extremely guarded about proprietary intelligence that is considered a competitive advantage. But as the legal marketplace tightens up in a recessionary environment, firms are beginning to become more aware and receptive to how important it is to provide their clients with the right type of information in order for the client to make better and informed decisions.

Approaching clients pre-emptively in order to explain a firm's rate strategy and invite a dialogue around a proposed rate increase is a far better approach than one that takes a unilateral proclamation without the benefit of any client input or discussion.

For those firms that have managed to achieve a true partnership built on trust, reliability, transparency, and communication (i.e., a strategic partnership), those value indicators are the standard and help serve both parties in reaching a fair and reasonable middle ground in terms of pricing acceptance.

As one GC told me years ago, proper dialogue and communication helps mitigate against surprises and the unknown – even if it involves RRB, the discussion with a client is much more meaningful and more often results in positive outcomes for both partners. Firms that understand and live by this rule understand what is important to the client and the overall relationship and enjoy the benefits of their relationship much more than those firms that act unilaterally, issue rate hike proclamations, and view clients as nothing more than monetary transactions.

Firms would be wise to reexamine their approach to their largest and most strategic clients and not make assumptions that their relationship is fail-safe. Having expectations of entitlement around legal work can be a risky venture in a highly competitive marketplace. This is especially risky for those firms that have embraced zero negotiation and assume that just because they are on a panel or have a historical relationship, the client will value their services more if the firm increases its rates. Unfortunately, price and value are two separate things and just because the price increases, doesn't necessarily mean that the purchaser values the goods or services more. All that it means to the client is that the goods and services are more expensive and may ultimately incentivize a client to look at other legal providers that are more reasonably priced or affordable.

Despite increased scrutinization, validation, and transparency taking place around RRB with many firms, most clients want their firms to remain profitable. However, CLDs also want a better understanding of what that road and strategy to profitability looks like. CLDs want an assurance that law firm profitability doesn't solely rely on the perennial exercise of one-sided automatic rate hikes. Moreover, CLDs want to understand the firm's value proposition and efficiency model – things that show a client that a firm is thinking strategically beyond just RRB and hourly rates to maintain margins and increase profitability.

To that end, GCs in many CLDs have for decades now become responsible for creating and developing cost-saving initiatives in order to manage, control, and reduce internal as well as external expenses. Increasingly, CLDs are looking to their legal service providers to become more fiscally prudent and cost efficient and to look for internal opportunities by which a firm can balance maximizing revenues with minimizing costs as opposed to simply relying on the RRB strategy and charging clients a higher hourly rate.

Internally, firms can focus on such things as business optimization, reducing overhead and administrative costs, deferring technology investments or automating processes (only if there is a guarantee of cost savings), reviewing the need for expensive office space, or reviewing technology redundancies and business processes with a view to making things more efficient and effective. All of these can have a positive impact on a firm's profitability and take the pressure off having to increase rack rates, thereby creating cost savings for a firm's clients.

For years, I have heard firms justify their RRB increases with comments like, "It's the market that is setting the new rate", "We need to stay competitively priced", or "That's where the market is", to try to justify their increases. Sophisticated CLDs have developed a somewhat skeptical viewpoint when it comes to these types of statements. They view such statements as hollow rationalizations attempting to justify knee jerk increases, all at the expense of the client and without any regard to what impact or how detrimental a rate increase may be on a client's business or even the relationship.

If a firm is going to utilize RRB as the basis for its increases, it should also be proactive and consider providing its clients with supporting data and information on what type of data the firm utilizes in the establishment of its RRB exercise in order to arrive at its increases. Coupling the data with pre-emptive and constructive rate discussions can help a firm gain greater insight and understanding into how a firm's proposed rate increases will play out for the client, as well as reinforce the firm's commitment to partner, provide transparency, and ultimately to build trust in the relationship.

The importance and value of transparency

For clients looking to track real cost savings, understanding the basis from which benchmarking data has been composed is perhaps one of the best ways to help CLDs manage their external spend, tracking, and reporting of cost savings to their GCs and leadership teams.

If CLDs are beginning to question the integrity of the RRB process, the onus rests on law firms to provide the necessary assurance in whatever processes a firm may use to establish its benchmarks.

Firms need to understand that in the new post-COVID legal marketplace, it is no longer just about providing great legal advice and mitigating risk for the client. It is also about great service delivery, transparency, and helping the client achieve its cost saving goals. Failure to provide transparency and assurance to the client will only reinforce the belief that how a law firm calculates its discounts has more to do with maintaining profitability and less about growing a relationship and providing the client with a real opportunity to create cost savings.

Getting a law firm to be forthcoming about any of its inner-operations or business strategy around rack rate pricing can be an uphill battle as most firms will be extremely guarded about anything they may consider to be an advantage over their competition. This is why having a regular and meaningful dialogue between both parties is critical to understanding and achieving expectations around such things as cost saving goals, business needs, risk appetite, service delivery, strategic planning, business transformation, and budgets. Having an open and candid discussion on these topics will allow both parties to understand each other's position and, if required, an opportunity to make accommodations in the interest of the relationship. Trying to manage pricing with unilateral decrees is myopic and risky and may backfire for any firm, regardless of size, tenure, or expertise.

Providing CLDs with greater transparency as to why a firm is increasing its rates will also help add credibility and validity to a firm's proposal while allowing the client to make a better informed determination as to whether a proposal has merit and is reasonably priced, given market conditions.

Without an adequate level of transparency, clients may reject the proposed rates and select another service provider or ALSP. Also, offering up greater transparency around RRB pricing increases may be counterintuitive, but may ironically become a competitive advantage for firms looking to distinguish themselves from their peers and establish long-lasting, honest relationships that go beyond ad hoc transactional work.

In terms of transparency, CLDs may want to ask their firm(s) some of the following questions if approached with a rate increase proposal:

- Rate hikes should be the last resort and not an annual ritual. What cost control measures has the firm put into place to help offset the need for rate hikes?
- How has the firm invested in new technology, processes, or people to make its service delivery more efficient and effective?
- How has that cost of investment impacted the firm's bottom line and translated into cost savings that reduce the need to increase rates?

- Has the firm saved money through its technology changes? If not, can it explain whether or not the client is having to pay for those tech investments?
- Are any technology investments being passed onto the client? If so, why?
- What other administrative overhead or infrastructure costs are being incorporated into the rack rate?
- Can the firm provide a list of areas where operational costs have increased and are now being passed onto the client in the form of rate hikes?
- Can the firm provide a list of exceptional circumstances to rationalize a basis for an increase?
- If merit is being used as a criterion for increases, only those timekeepers who have added value to a client's matters (in the past 12 months) should be considered for a rate increase. What percentage of a rate hike relates to merit?
- If a firm is looking for across the board (i.e., across a specific class of professionals) rate hikes, can it explain the rationale behind this and why it benefits the client?
- Can the firm provide examples of what it is doing to manage its internal costs better?
- Are there internal cost saving initiatives, with targets, to create cost savings? If so, how are those cost savings impacting profitability targets and how are those targets offsetting pressure on a firm to increase its rates?
- What is the firm doing to save money for its clients?
- Can the firm break down and list the different criteria used to determine a rate hike?
- Can the firm provide a numerical percentage for each criteria used to calculate the firm's RRB?
- What is the firm doing to move away from RRB?
- What is the firm doing to implement a greater focus on building value in how it delivers its legal services?

What CLDs don't want to see as part of any RRB exercise, or rate increase announcement, is:

- Generic, unilateral proclamations of increases with zero negotiation or client discussions.
- Lack of pre-emptive communication.
- Lack of transparency.
- No real meaningful explanation or supporting rationale for increases.
- A notification that increases are retroactive.
- Market verbiage that tries to rationalize increases (e.g., "We are not competitively priced or underpriced relative to our peers", "The market is setting the benchmark, we have to stay profitable", "Our margins have increased, our professionals are in high demand").
- Across-the-board increases.
- Non-negotiable increases.
- Double-counting the criteria used in the formula for rate hikes and including them a second time in a firm's supplementary administration fee.
- A false assumption that legal services are automatically worth a perennial increase based on a calendar.

Utilizing a tailored approach that helps the client achieve meaningful cost savings, especially those with budgetary challenges, may help win client loyalty. Providing reliable, unbiased data along with a realistic pricing proposal that provides the client with a clear understanding of pricing changes, coupled with a clear understanding of value and how a firm can manage a client's matters to save money, would be a more welcome approach than a ubiquitous RRB strategy that is heavily weighted in favor of the law firm's interest to generate profits and less about the client's interest in generating cost savings. Finding a middle ground would serve both parties well.

Conclusion

In the end, firms need to sell their value beyond simple hourly rates and start thinking in terms of a more inclusive approach that weighs less on the numbers and math and favors the client's interests and a commitment to being long-term and strategic partners, vested in the client's business operations. This includes being part of the solution and not the problem when it comes to predictable cost control.

If a firm is going to expend its energy, resources, and capital on trying to win work and drive sustainable profitability, it also needs to focus on its client retention strategy, which should include rethinking how it approaches the practice of RRB – focusing more attention on the overall value of the relationship and how the client values a firm's work.

Firms need to ensure that their path to profitability includes strategies that focus more on creating internal operational efficiencies and less reliance on utilizing rack rates as their primary mechanism for generating profitability. However, if a firm continues to utilize RRB as part of its strategy then coupled to RRB should be the intangible value indicators such as transparency, communication, and a commitment to properly rationalize why increases are needed to grow the relationship.

Mutual trust has to be established between both parties in order for there to be real progress towards a symbiotic relationship that depends on each other and both parties benefit from the value of the relationship, services delivered, and strategic advice that empowers the client, yet provides respectable profits for the law firm.

Richard Brzakala has extensive experience in the legal operations field and is based in Toronto. He contributed this chapter in his personal capacity. The views expressed are his own.

Chapter 9:

The next frontier in pricing strategy – capturing value from legal technology

By Stuart Dodds, principal, Positive Pricing

A quick glance at legal press headlines or at the wealth of end-of-year law firm surveys continues to highlight the inexorable rise of legal technology and Generative AI. Much of the supporting commentary is focused on the strong capabilities these solutions will provide to law firm and client alike, and how this will ultimately support the delivery of more effective and cost-efficient solutions for both parties. However, current commentary has yet to focus on what this *actually means* to those who are tasked with pricing within a law firm, their need to manage internal (partner) and external expectations, and how to appropriately incorporate pricing legal technology as an integral part of their firm's pricing strategy.

As many law firms continue to develop and enhance their existing legal technology platforms to drive both greater internal efficiency and address client demands, this has introduced a new dimension when pricing legal work for clients. Namely, how do we best capture the value of this technology when it is often relatively unproven and not clearly understood; how does this impact more traditional (primarily time-based) pricing approaches typically adopted; and does this change the very role of those supporting pricing within a law firm?

This chapter seeks to redress that imbalance and is based on a wide range of conversations held with key legal pricing professionals on this very theme over the late summer and autumn of 2023.[1]

But first, some context. A survey published by the Law Society in February 2019[2] included a quote from a senior law firm executive who said that legal tech start-ups are not necessarily reinventing the wheel but looking to provide a "shinier new wheel". Indeed, this is one of the challenges that many legal tech firms are currently facing, with current technology promising lots of capability but still sometimes struggling to deliver against the promise.

Recent reports don't help either. A report by Goldman Sachs,[3] published in March 2023, estimated that up to 44 percent of tasks conducted within the legal sector could be automated by AI in the US and Europe (compared with an average of 25 percent across all industries reviewed). Although there has since been some discussion about what the 44 percent actually represented (for example, did this refer to legal tasks, work, positions, or a combination of all three?) there is no getting away from the fact that a fundamental change is happening, and future expectations are being set – intentionally or not.

When discussing this theme at a number of legal pricing roundtables conducted by Positive Pricing between 2019 and 2023, and as part of other legal industry events, we took the view that we needed to approach this topic from three different perspectives, recognizing that each provided their own inherent challenges and opportunities. Our three perspectives were from the law firm partner's perspective, the client's perspective, and, finally, the pricing professional's perspective.

However, before looking at each in turn, let's quickly define what we mean by legal technology for the purposes of this chapter, to help establish our context.

Making sense of the legal technology landscape

The legal technology landscape can be both daunting and confusing to the uninitiated, given the wide plethora of tools now available and the constant coverage in the legal press and as legal conference sponsors.

As of mid-2023, it was estimated that there were approximately 7,500 firms active in developing legal technology-based solutions (with estimated funding of over $13bn),[4] and that number probably excludes many of the law firm-driven internal initiatives in place.

But what is it? One helpful definition, provided by the Law Society,[5] is that it encompasses technologies that "aim to support, supplement, or replace traditional methods for delivering legal services, or that improve the way the justice system operates". As such, it covers a very wide range of potential tools and supporting processes – for example, those that support document automation, practice management tools, knowledge management and legal research capabilities, and also predictive artificial intelligence (something even more prevalent today with the rise of Generative AI). If one adopts this definition, the 7,500 firms mentioned above suddenly becomes much more plausible.

Thankfully, *there are* a number of logical groupings that emerge when reviewing different segmentation approaches. Whilst there are many ways to segment the legal technology landscape, there are primarily four main areas, namely:

1. Those solutions focused on legal knowledge or education. This would include well known firms and products such as Bloomberg Law, Thomson Reuters' Westlaw, IBM Watson, and Lexis Nexis, and their respective solutions in this space.
2. Those solutions focused on the presentation and delivery of data. This would include those firms that support data visualization such as Tableau, Structure Flow, or Jigsaw.
3. Those solutions that have strong search and find capabilities. This category is sometimes further broken out into those solutions that focus on eDiscovery (such as Relativity, Nuix, and Brainspace), legal analytics (such as Brightflag), or even more practice-specific solutions (such as contract due diligence tools such as eBrevia, Kira, and Luminence).
4. Those solutions that are more focused on task automation and workflow. This would include those such as Contract Express, Contract Intelligence, Della, and Neota Logic.

Schema developed by others may also include solutions that support the so-called "liquid workforce" of contract lawyers or alternative legal service providers (this including firms such as Lawyers on Demand and Axiom, amongst others).

Each of these solutions and segments support the observation made by Richard Susskind that, "machines and systems will work alongside tomorrow's professionals as partners. *The challenge here is to allocate tasks, as between human beings and machines, according to their relative strengths*"[6] (emphasis added).

To that observation I would add one further consideration. Each of these solutions and segments provide *different levels of value to a potential client* – for example, while efficiencies may be greatly improved by adopting task automation tools (and therefore potentially reducing overall cost), the insights delivered by some of the legal analytics tools may be ultimately of much greater value. It is important that those involved in pricing these solutions are able to make these distinctions when developing and shaping internal and external value propositions.

But why I am telling you all this? For the following reason(s) – it's complex, can be confusing, and it's a lot to understand on top of what we need to do during a "normal working day". It can be equally confusing for *all* the key stakeholders involved – so let's now dive into it to see what this means from the three perspectives identified earlier – those of the law firm partner, the client, and finally the pricing professional.

The partner's perspective

For most partners, the need to be responsive to client concerns and opportunities is paramount. In today's legal landscape this can often include offering to develop or provide legal technology platforms to their clients. However, as well-known legal commentator Bill Henderson identified in a *Legal Evolution* blog post[7] around the same time as our first roundtable on this theme back in 2019, "The driver is the preservation of multi-million-dollar relationships – relationships that are difficult to replace. *This approach is fundamentally reactive*" (emphasis added).

Often the main drivers for conversations with clients are either at the client's instigation, driven by the fear of what the competition are doing, coupled with the surrounding hype and publicity that many of these legal tech solutions have generated. There is also often the need to be seen as being more innovative than the legal market, or at the very least, not lagging behind the competition.

But a number of additional challenges also exist. The desire to please clients often leads to investments and pricing decisions being made at a *client-specific level* rather than being considered more fully from a *firm-wide* perspective, creating a lack of consistency in how these solutions are developed, deployed, priced, and managed going forward. Still too few law firms are proactively managing the investment in these solutions and reviewing the subsequent return on investment (even at a very rudimentary level, such as the value of time saved divided by the license fee).

Another challenge often cited by those supporting these initiatives in law firms is that partners (and other involved fee earners) often approach these types of opportunities in the same way that they would approach managing a more traditional legal matter. Given the more iterative nature of technology implementations, this can often prove less successful and more frustrating to those involved. There may not be a "perfect solution" out of the box and dealing with ambiguity often can be challenging in this context.

A final consideration is that many partners are now being exposed to new and unfamiliar stakeholders, both internally within their own organization (for example those working within IT, legal technologists, or indeed pricing) and externally (where this is likely to include a group much wider than the traditional business stakeholder contacts).

For many, what maybe seemed a good idea at the time in terms of introducing legal technology into their client conversations quickly becomes much more time-consuming and frustrating than first thought.

The client's perspective

When looking at this from the client's perspective, there are also several considerations that we need to keep front of mind.

The first of these is what the client's expectations may be around the products and capabilities, given how these products are being marketed compared to the actual ease of implementation. What may be marketed as a relatively simple implementation may in reality be significantly longer and challenging.

We then move into some more traditional pricing-related challenges. The first is the recognition that the *value delivered* by many of these legal technology products is very different to the normal, more traditional approaches to the delivery of legal work. Therefore, there needs to be much greater emphasis placed on articulating the value of how these products will help the client achieve their objectives, for example by being quicker, faster, and more efficient through automation or by mitigating risk by reducing complexity or ambiguity. The second is around the price point itself. For many of these products, clients have no real reference point as to what the appropriate price should be, unlike more traditional legal services where they are able to more easily compare one law firm's proposed fee to another. How does a client therefore know whether their adoption of this technology represents to them "fair value"? It is perhaps unsurprising that many clients are now questioning whether the fees being charged are "fair" and even are beginning to request a share of the resultant "savings".[8]

The final consideration we need to be aware of is that around budget. Often the level of investment budget required by the client is either not available or is not fully understood, where the greatest challenge for general counsel when it comes to legal technology has often been making the case for budget. When budget has been found, there is also then the associated challenge of what solutions to actually invest *in*. Again, many clients are looking to their law firm partners to help guide them through the legal technology landscape as it applies to *them*, with a number of leading law firms having quickly taken up the request – for relationship (and sometimes "consulting" revenue) opportunities.

Given the challenges outlined above, many law firms still provide legal technology solutions to clients for free or building this in as a "cost of doing business" – a solution that serves neither party well, as the law firm continues to invest in a product that maybe has much greater potential for both revenue creation and client retention, and a client not appreciating the value it is being provided as it has been given away for free.

When it comes to legal technology solutions, what is becoming crystal clear is that there is a need to shift the general counsel/client dialogue from one that evaluated fairness of price in a cost-plus environment to one that is much more focus around value creation. It is becoming increasingly important to be comfortable in having that conversation – many, yet, are not. Which leads us to the third and final perspective – that of the pricing professional and how they can support these conversations.

The pricing professional's perspective

The evolution of legal technology products provides a wonderful opportunity for many in pricing roles today, and although there may be a number of potential obstacles during the early stages, these can easily be addressed with planning. These may be grouped as driving greater visibility and engagement; the changing internal role; the need for different skills; the current lack of real data and measurement; and managing expectations. Let's take a closer look at each.

Greater visibility and engagement

As law firms are more proactively engaging clients in using these products in the delivery of matters, this offers the pricing professional much greater visibility and engagement within their internal organization. It enables them to be much more client-facing (if not already) by having a key role to play in the communication of value and the pricing of the legal solution being offered. There is also, in speaking with several senior pricing professionals who are already further down the path of this journey, the opportunity to be involved in the actual product development teams themselves or – at a more macro-level – the innovation steering groups or committees within their respective law firm.

Changing roles

One thing those in pricing positions need to quickly recognize is that their role begins to change. First, there is a much greater need to test the value of the product being proposed *with* the client. This can become an iterative process, and one that involves much greater client contact and engagement than as part of a normal or more traditional client engagement. Not all law firm partners will necessarily be as comfortable with this – either driven by a desire to "own" the client relationship completely or the potential ambiguity around how the eventual solution may work.

Second, the role that they take internally is also going to change. In speaking with those actively involved in this area, what many have found is that they also now have the challenge of maintaining and corralling the entrepreneurial spirit within their law firm to make sure that the firm takes *firm-wide* investment decisions when it comes to legal technology solutions, rather than partner-driven, client-specific requests, whilst not losing the enthusiasm that the partners may have to explore these exciting new avenues. How they approach this challenge can be critical as it can have the unintended consequence of making a law pricing function appear to be a blocker to innovation rather than the helpful conduit it should be.

This therefore puts much greater emphasis and focus on change management. Although many in pricing currently recognize that this is already a key skill required in the successful execution of the role, nowhere is this perhaps more evident today than here.

The final impact on the changing internal role is probably the most predictable – that of time. Those currently supporting both the pricing of matters and client relationships and also now the pricing of legal technology solutions understand the much greater demands now being placed on their time and the associated impact on resourcing. A number of senior pricing professionals I spoke to mentioned that their firms had actually hired a number of additional resources within the pricing team to focus solely on this area and I am sure there will be many more instances of this.

Changing skills

Not only will the legal pricing professional's role change, but they may also need to change their existing *skill* set. Perhaps ironically, the role now becomes much more similar to non-legal professional service pricing roles.

The pricing of legal technology requires more of an *iterative* pricing strategy, which focuses on the ability to launch a product then test it, refine it, and validate it in the light of customer feedback (in many respects similar to both software products and consumer products). There needs to be much greater focus on identifying the value proposition to the client and then the associated price level and price structure (for example, is this a monthly subscription, per user, or built into an overall fixed fee for the matter?).

It requires an awareness of the concept already extensively adopted within software development of the "minimal viable product" – in other words, what is enough to address the client's *immediate* requirement rather than developing the perfect solution from the off. It encourages law firms to have much greater segmentation of the services and product lines that they will offer their clients. And it will require more frequent conversations with clients to assess the value of the product and refine it, going forward.

It's also important that those involved in pricing or who are part of pricing functions have a much greater understanding of the legal technology products and landscape and how these products will help support the legal matters and benefit both the firm and the firm's clients. Linked to this theme, they are likely to have a much more significant role in helping educate those within their own firm and their firm's clients on the benefits and the value of the proposed legal technology approach versus the costs of the solution, moving in many respects into more of a commercial or sales-focused role.

The lack of real data and measurement

Another challenge faced by those in pricing roles is the lack of real data and measurement criteria available currently. As any good pricing professional knows, it is important to be able to quantify the benefits that your product or service delivers, to help you develop broader internal and external business cases. If you are able to do so, the benefits can be significant. For example, Luminance, a well-known AI platform for the legal profession, identified that (post-set up) a document review task that had previously taken 15 hours[9] was able to be done in ten percent of the previous time when using its platform. A number of other AI providers point to similar benefits. Law firms have so far been slower to capture and quantify how this can help them and their clients using real life situations.

Perhaps as a consequence, few law firms have been able to draw a direct line from implementing pricing legal technology services to firm revenue. Many firms are yet to assess the impact that this technology will have on law firm profits (more on that theme later), and few monitor the return on their investment of these technology purchases. This can make the development of a compelling business, internally and externally, extremely difficult.

Managing expectations

The final challenge is around managing expectations. Those involved in pricing discussions within their firm know that a key component of the role is to help manage expectations of what is feasible and what represents "fair value" for both the law firm and the clients they serve. They also know that the hardest conversations can often be those internally – nowhere more so than when it comes to profitability (whether at a firm, client, or matter level). And it is here that the harder conversations are going to need to happen as legal technology (and its newer sibling, Generative AI) take hold. I already alluded to the impact these types of tools can have above, and most legal commentators acknowledge that *time*-based savings of 50 percent are not unrealistic and may even be conservative in nature.

Law firms are going to need to increasingly adopt legal technology (and especially Generative AI) into their processes and workflow, both to serve client demands and to eliminate more administrative and laborious activities. And this comes at a cost – the cost of these solutions (for example, license fees or internal development), the costs of set-up and ongoing maintenance, and *critically the cost of lost billable time.*

Those more familiar with law firm profitability know that the "engines" of profitability within most firms are the associate (especially senior associate) ranks, where the hourly rate charged provides a healthy margin once respective costs are deducted. But what happens if these technology-based solutions we are discussing remove the ability to charge time? Not only that, but charge time where the majority of margin is generated for the firm? It is here that the pricing professional's role in managing internal expectations around profitability will be essential.

A quick review conducted by Toby Brown and his fellow "Three Geeks" – Greg Lambert and Ryan McClead – in a series of blog posts during July and August 2023 highlights the potential impact.[10] Using genericized e-billing data provided by CounselLink for the purposes of the review, Toby and team identified that for a representative M&A matter (and based on the sample data provided) where 40 percent of the effort was conducted by partners and 60 percent by other fee earners, even a situation in which five percent of partner work could now be replaced by legal technology and 20 percent for the fee earners, the number of hours reduced would be approximately 14 percent, revenues reduced by 13 percent, and profit by over 11 percent. In a worst-case scenario, where 20 percent of the partner effort could be replaced and 40 percent of the fee earners, the numbers (unsurprisingly) were even more dramatic, with a 32 percent reduction in hours billed, billed revenue down by over 38 percent, and profit reduced by a similar amount. This is *before* the scenarios modelled needed to factor in the associated cost of the solutions themselves.

Each scenario summarized above is – in all likelihood – conservative, especially once these tools and solutions become more widespread and integral to current matter workflows and there is a greater degree in the confidence of "client-ready" output. Certainly, the impact will vary depending on the type of work being performed, with higher value work perhaps being less susceptible to such a change. Even then, many parts of a matter will be conducted using these types of tools. The key questions that pricing professionals need to be asking themselves (and others within their firm) *now* – before it is too late – are the following:

- What work will legal technology and AI best suit?
- Who is (typically) doing the work?
- What does this mean for underlying law firm profitability at a matter, client, and firm-wide level?

Although the majority of (UK-based) law firms "believe that (Generative AI) will have a positive impact on revenue and margins",[11] those in pricing roles need to start doing profitability analysis to model the broader impact of legal technology in specific practice areas, across their client portfolio and ultimately the firm, so that the "right conversations" can begin to happen, expectations be *proactively* managed, and appropriate pricing strategies be developed and implemented. Now is the time to understand the impact to the firm's bottom line.

Pricing approaches adopted to date

So, what are the typical pricing approaches developed for legal technology pricing? When asking a number of pricing professionals and also (for good measure) a number of software providers, there were five approaches commonly adopted. Four of these I would recommend and one I would not.

The first, and also in some respects the easiest, is where the fee is built into the overall cost of the deal. This of course assumes that the cost of the legal technology has been accurately scoped and that some element of margin has been captured, if possible.

The second is one that is favored by many software providers and where there is a "pay to play" type model, either by transaction or by volumes of data processed. This can help in significantly lowering associated barriers and costs of adoption with a very clear rationale of how pricing has been developed. It is also a model that many are familiar with more generally, and also specifically within legal (for example, if you consider some of the discovery solutions available on the market).

The third, and closely aligned to the above model, is one that is more subscription-based – again one that many in law are familiar with.

The fourth and final model *recommended* is one where there is a one-off fee. Although this can significantly increase the sales cycle due to the initial upfront investment required from the client, it is then in the client's own hands how much they use – and benefit from – the technology acquired.

Which brings me to the fifth model and one that I do not recommend. Unfortunately, this model is today the prevalent one – where the legal technology solution is given away effectively for free. This is driven by a number of factors including client partner reluctance to ask for a fee (as they themselves may not be completely sure how this would help the client, and which comes back to the need for a strong value proposition) and the lack of client budget. Not only does giving it away for free remove potential profit (or at least the ability to recover cost) on the specific matter (or matters), it also sets a very dangerous reference point for any future conversations around legal technology with this client.

As increasing pressure is put on billable hours through the adoption of these solutions, many firms need to start (if not already) their move towards increased adoption of fixed fees. Not only does this mean that the "inputs" to a matter in terms of time are less relevant, it encourages greater rigor around *where and how* technology can support matter delivery. Very importantly, it also encourages a much more systematic review of what the matter is "worth" and in *collaborative* value discovery with the firm's clients, allowing the law firm to ensure their price is "fair" to both parties – this being driven by what it enables the client to achieve (for example, helping them to drive increased revenues, improve cashflow, or managing and mitigating risk).

It is in *these* discussions that pricing professionals have a critical role to play.

Key considerations

Many barriers exist at the firm-wide level to making the adoption of legal technology solutions swifter and many of are these fundamental to the industry – including risks around compliance, the law firm partnership model, and continued use of billable hours as the main revenue generation tool.

Other considerations that need to now be factored in by client teams and law firm management much earlier in the legal technology development process (as these relate to pricing) include those such as:

- Who leads the client discussion and who is best placed to represent the firm? No longer may this be the sole role of the client relationship partner, but now include those pricing, legal project management and/or legal technology roles.
- Who is best placed to help develop the value proposition? This may not now only reside with a practice group marketing team or proposals group, but again may need to be much wider in coverage to capture different perspectives and insights across the firm.
- Does the law firm risk driving a commoditization of their services and

what are their key points of differentiation that they need to defend and articulate? Closely aligned to this; is the law firm in danger of cannibalizing its own revenues? (As an illustration, document automation solutions can sometimes eliminate 60-80 percent of the billable hour costs and associated revenues).

- Who is responsible for the development and ongoing maintenance of these solutions once implemented with a client? Have these additional elements of cost been considered both at the initial product pricing stage and thereafter?

Once again, it is in these discussions that pricing professionals have a critical role to play.

What we can learn from the early adopters

Legal technology, whilst still in an early stage of its development, is one with limitless potential. But what pricing tips can we learn from those firms that have been testing, developing, and implementing this for a while?

In summary, five key themes stand out.

1. Pricing legal technology is likely to be much more resource-intensive than "normal" law firm pricing, especially in terms of time and skills required.
2. There is a greater need for those in pricing to explore and educate internally on these new tools, as they seek to identify which practice areas and matters can pivot towards fixed fees.
3. It is important that those with pricing responsibilities avoid partners making unilateral pricing promises to their clients re legal tech. These are *firm-wide* investments and should be managed accordingly.
4. It can be helpful to approach this much as a venture capitalist would when assessing where to invest firm resources and when reviewing progress. If it isn't making money or significantly helping your clients, it is time to move on.
5. Some firms have found that having a separate P&L to measure the impact of these initiatives within the law firm helps bring greater focus, rigor, and success.

This technology is clearly going to become one of the key methods of delivering superior client value when delivering legal services in the years to come. As one commentator remarked a few years ago, "It may even be considered legal malpractice not to use AI one day... It would be analogous to a lawyer in the late 20th century still doing everything by hand when this person could use a computer."[12]

Those involved in helping client teams successfully deliver legal technology solutions to their clients and helping ensure appropriate firm-wide investments and profits are being made need to be acutely aware of the pricing pitfalls that may occur at the early stages of this journey. For many, this may mean dusting off the pricing textbooks and remembering how other industries (such as consumer products and manufacturing companies) need to approach their pricing challenges.

To quote Jordan Furlong, a respected legal commentator who has been tracking developments in this area for a while, "If there was ever an issue that qualified as 'important but not urgent', this is it",[13] as someone somewhere has already started getting their house in order.

We still undoubtedly have much to learn, but it this instance, fortune really does favor the brave.

References

1 Many of the themes discussed in this chapter feature in the author's book, *Smarter Pricing, Smarter Profit*, American Bar Association (2019).

2 The Law Society, *LawTech Adoption Research: February 2019* (2019).

3 Briggs/Kodnani, *Potentially Large Effects of Artificial Intelligence on Economic Growth*, Goldman Sachs (26 March 2023).

4 Tracxn.com.

5 The Law Society, *Introduction to LawTech: A practical guide to legal technology* (2019).

6 Richard Susskind and Daniel Susskind, *The Future of the Professions: How Technology Will Transform the Work of Human Experts*, Oxford University Press (2015).

7 Bill Henderson, Legal Evolution, *Special Post: A+ team being assembled at Baker McKenzie* (27 January 2019).

8 The Lawyer, *"Give Us Some of the Upside": Clients demand benefit from AI cost-savings* (10 October 2023).

9 Based on sample scenarios outlined in Luminance, *Building a Business Case for AI* (2019).

10 3 Geeks and a Law Blog, *"AI-Pocalypse: The Shocking Impact on Law Firm Profitability"* (3 August 2023).

11 As identified in the PwC Law Firms' Survey 2023, *Overview and Key Themes* (October 2023).

12 Tom Giraldi, as quoted in Neil Sahota's *Will A.I. Put Lawyers Out of Business?* Forbes (9 February 2019).

13 Jordan Furlong, *This is how the billable hour dies* (16 August 2023).

Chapter 10:
Harvey Specter – the ghost of a law firm reality yet to come

By Phil Nixon, senior sales executive, Elite Technology

We are standing on the precipice of an unprecedented change in legal service delivery. GenAI has captured the imaginations of the general public across the world with the latest release of Large Language Models (LLMs) such as ChatGPT, and there is specific interest in the partnerships between leading firms and legal AI tool Harvey. But how will this new dawn in technology affect law firms and their underlying profitability?

What does the law firm of tomorrow look like, and just how far can AI and technology go in changing the fundamentals of law firm service delivery and operations? How can a law firm embrace this change when the technological foundations of the firm are often undervalued?

"I fear you more than any specter I have seen"

Figure 1: Part man, part machine. Harvey Specter is a lead character from the TV series, Suits, about a law firm. Harvey is a generative AI company backed by OpenAI's start-up fund. With credit also to Dickens.

This chapter focuses on the potential impacts of GenAI on law firm operations, cashflow, and profitability – both as an internal and external use case. It also encourages law firms to embrace technological change across the board, providing a roadmap of areas to consider, ensuring your firm has the correct foundations in place to best face and embrace the coming wave.

The number one topic on the minds of futurists and legal technologists right now seems to be clear – Artificial Intelligence. Not a day goes by without another new product or feature enhancement being released that includes AI – an arms race of sorts being carried out between vendors. The perception is that if your product does not utilize some level of Artificial Intelligence, it is not worth having. This has led to often underwhelming "innovations" being released and rebranded as a means of keeping up with the Joneses.

But what is happening more broadly is equally spectacular as it is frightening. Artificial Intelligence models have accomplished some incredible feats, such as outperforming scientific experts by over eight times in solving "one of the toughest problems in science"[1] in predicting protein folds, and comprehensively beating the world's best players of the amazingly complex game "Go" using a move no human had ever comprehended.[2] AI tools have designed more effective vaccines[3] and found new use for an existing medication as "arguably one of the more powerful antibiotics that has been discovered".[4] Looking forward, AI could help usher in a new wave of "synthetic biology" – we're even now in the realms of scientists creating synthetic brains in a petri-dish, which have managed to master basic games such as Pong.[5] For those interested in this subject, I highly recommend reading *The Coming Wave*.[6]

It's easy to be lost in the hype and the frenzy of Artificial Intelligence, and it's also just as easy to be an ostrich and bury our heads in the sand. "Thanks, not for me."

This has been the default response to legal technology from law firms for decades. Often, law firm leaders will invest only in technology when a gun is held to their heads. A new system is purchased when the prior system has been sunsetted or is no longer compatible with modern software, and even then, this decision is often left until the last second.

For too long, it's been seen purely as a cost, a "nice to have" rather than a necessity. We've had law firms since 1570,[7] and nothing has ever changed the model we still work with today, so why fix something that isn't broken?

The difference with GenAI is that this is something wholly different to anything we've seen before. As a species, we are at the top of the food chain due to our knowledge and the power of our brains – enabling us to have mastery of all other species despite inferior physical capabilities. Now, this truth is under threat. What happens to our species if we create something that is so powerful that we become subservient?

These questions are existentially broader than what we can deal with as a legal industry. It will require a collective effort, across borders, to understand how best to deal with this threat.[8] The duality of AI is that it is both the biggest threat, and the biggest opportunity, that we face.

What is available and how will this impact legal services?

It is unfair to categorize all law firms as ostriches, of course. Allen & Overy, and now Macfarlanes, have been at the forefront of working with the much discussed "Harvey", and Travers Smith has worked to build a legal layer on top of ChatGPT, known as YCNBot[9] (which is open source for other firms to take advantage of). These solutions are taking advantage of the investment and expertise of the team at Open.AI and "training" the system to understand legal data.

Harvey can combine data from your own firm and amalgamate that with publicly available information on the internet to help with drafting, researching, and reviewing.[10] Whilst it has incredible potential, it's not the only tool aiming to help in this regard. Thomson Reuters is heavily invested in AI, utilizing the wealth of data it has with regards to case law and legal guidance[11] and allowing users to bring this data and suggestions into their live documents. Similarly, LexisNexis has recently announced the availability of its Lexis+ AI platform to US customers,[12] with the ability for conversational search, help on document drafting, as well as quick case and document summarization.

Other forward-looking firms are also now starting to implement AI technology – looking to establish real-world use cases for where this can help speed up legal service delivery. At a recent LawtechUK event in Manchester,[13] an innovation manager for a leading firm was sharing how their firm has built use cases across almost all the departments at the firm, and how they have trained their model for their competition and regulatory compliance team. They have trained a model to look for and highlight any potential anti-competitive covenants on land sales of supermarkets, which would usually restrict future supermarket builds. The model understands that clauses such as "cannot have refrigeration onsite", or "cannot have lorries delivering goods between X and Y" would prohibit the opening of a future superstore in this location and is therefore anti-competitive, and it can also carry out pre-checking for anti-competitive clauses prior to completion of a land transaction. This team has also implemented the technology to review associated documents and provide commentary – something that would have taken a lawyer hours previously.

Microsoft's sizeable investment into Open.AI is a clear indication that it sees this as the future of its platform. Microsoft's usage is ubiquitous in legal, an extremely trusted provider by firms of all size. Now it is rolling out access to its latest creation, Copilot. Copilot will sit within the Office suite and across all applications will allow the end user to communicate via natural language to get the desired end results, and faster. Within Microsoft's wider platform, AI is now being used to allow users to design Power Apps and automation workflows, specifically for their business, via natural language. This is a whole new level of empowerment for law firms and lawyers themselves.

But the biggest driver of change is, of course, external factors. Prospective clients currently bring a problem to a lawyer and ask them to resolve it. This involves complexity, and therefore cost. With the release of public Large Language Models (LLMs) such as ChatGPT, Bing, and Bard, clients are starting to be able to self-serve – and use lawyers as a point of clarification rather than knowledge creation. How will law firms adapt to clients asking them to proofread a pre-populated NDA or other legal document, taking only a matter of minutes rather than hours?

This brings us back to a conversation that has been debated by legal commentariat for many years – the end of the billable hour. Yet until now, nothing has realistically changed. Lawyers still are, broadly, targeted on billable hour delivery, law firms are still charging by the hour, and clients are still expecting a bill broken down in this manner. But if we continue to stay warm under this safety blanket, this method of charging will hit law firms where it hurts – in their pockets. Firstly, due to the cost to acquire the AI solutions,[14] which clients will expect to be table stakes, and secondly, in the race to the bottom brought about by trying to retrofit an hourly charging model against a tool capable of completing thousands of complex calculations in a fraction of a second. Instead, law firms will need to quickly understand the value of their services to their clients, and charge accordingly. Value-based pricing, not simply time-based AFAs, will need to become as commonplace as it is within other industries for law firms to continue to thrive.[15]

If you think that this is not reality – think again. At the aforementioned LawtechUK summit, a large corporate was asked if, due to the widespread availability of AI solutions and the impact they have, they would be putting pricing pressure onto their legal suppliers to deliver for much less cost. The answer? An assured "Yes".

Will you take the blue pill, or the red pill?

"Take the red pill – you stay in Wonderland and I show you how deep the rabbit hole goes."
Morpheus to Neo, The Matrix

The challenge described above is one that will be a huge consideration for lawyers in the years to come. Technology continues to advance, and AI and other tools will only become more prevalent and powerful. For an industry that trades itself on knowledge and words, it's a harrowing thought to see a machine already outperform humans and be able to achieve things such as passing the American BAR exam in the 90th percentile.[16]

But this challenge is also one that may serve as a distraction for the here and now, and the challenge that law firms have today in ensuring that their foundations are laid correctly to embrace this change, as and when it occurs.

Building the foundations for technological success

Talking about how GenAI will revolutionize the legal industry is met with much skepticism, and it's easy to see why. We've had multiple false dawns previously, and nothing has fundamentally changed in terms of the technology that lawyers use day-to-day.

One problem with many law firms and technology is, as mentioned, that law firm leaders often leave making decisions about moving their foundational platforms until there is a gun held to their heads. Rather than embracing change and looking at adopting new ways of working and new technology, many law firms have persevered with the same legacy software that has often been utilized for 15-20 years, be that case or practice management. They do so through a fear of the unknown, and a misunderstanding of the value in which more modern systems are able to drastically improve the performance of both individuals, and the firm as a whole.

It is hard for leaders to hear about the impact of LLMs, AI, quantum computing, or whatever else comes next when they are still running programs designed in the mid-90s to run their firm on. Making it even more difficult is that vested interests will often advise reasons as to why their hybrid deployment is actually the right deployment for your firm, and is not holding you back (aka, "We are unsure as to how to develop our solution quick enough"). How can technology built when a phone was just a phone work in a world of constant evolution and change?

One of the biggest "gun to the head" moments was of course the

COVID-19 pandemic. This led to a divide – some firms had prepared by having cloud-based systems, providing laptops for employees and so on, whereas some firms ground to a halt overnight. Compounded with an end-of-life notice for Windows XP and Server 2008, as well as production being halted in East Asia, it was a perfect storm of problems when it came to trying to quickly adapt to changing circumstances with aged technology. The pandemic shone a light on the "cloud", and how firms can no longer simply prefer to say that they would rather have their data in a box in a corner so they "know where it is".

The "cloud", however, is more than just putting an aged system in a datacenter and ticking a box. It's a completely different way of working, of developing, and is inherently far more secure than having a local legacy application. This has inspired a raft of acquisitions, leading to private equity companies taking ownership of legal technology providers and implementing a strategy of consolidation of older technologies into their one chosen "cloud" solution. There is nothing like a situation filled with uncertainty to force the heads of the ostriches back down their holes.

Cloud solutions enable quick utilization of new technologies and allow for advancements in development to be deployed much quicker to customers. It allows for law firms to focus on what makes them great rather than spending time keeping the lights on. But it requires a new way of thinking about budgeting. Cloud solutions, on paper, seem more expensive than what many leaders may feel comfortable with.

In the spectrum of profitability, it is vitally important that your firm looks to establish the right foundational platform for success. Embracing a true cloud solution now will enable you to better take advantage of the upcoming wave of advancements, and allow you to spend more time understanding how best to deal with the undoubted pressures that will be presented to your margins as we move into a world where legal work and engagements are potentially flipped on their head.

Can technology actually help us become more profitable?

Technology alone is not an answer, but it is an incredible tool to help.

Every law firm will have slightly different challenges and inefficiencies. The first task is how to understand where those challenges and inefficiencies lie. Taking a fresh view of these, and being the annoying wasp at the picnic, is key. The question of "why" cannot be overused. Once documented, engage your IT teams, start your research online, engage with vendors, and if required, use a reputable independent consultant to help you.

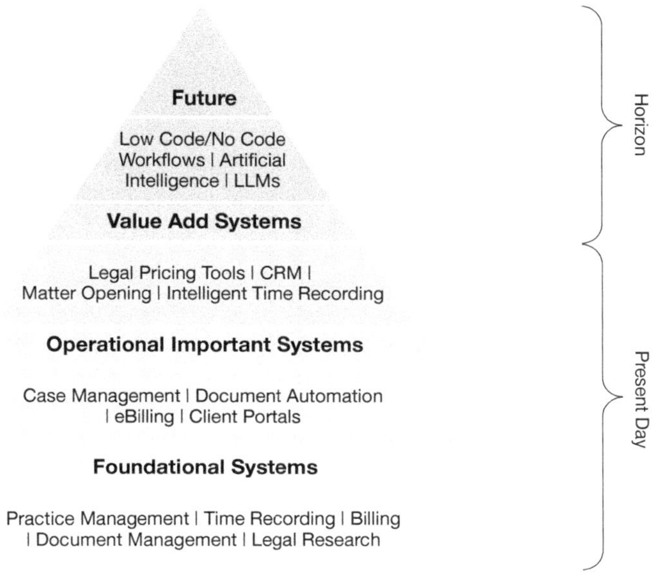

Figure 2: The hierarchy of technology for legal practice.

The two strands of conversation I am often involved in are improving profitability and improving cashflow, through the use of technology and automation. With regards to profitability, information and efficiency are the two keys.

With regards to information, law firms need to best understand their people and their data. Many law firms struggle to use their practice management solutions to provide useable and up-to-date reports on key performance indicators, leading to a "sticking plaster" approach of often tagging on a third-party reporting tool. Through the use of technology, firms should be easily able to understand the leverage associated with any given matter, and have tools to understand and easily keep on top of the rates assigned with them. Many firms will have myriad rates across the firm with nuanced bespoke rules associated with them; understanding what these are and offering a simplified "menu" option helps the firm become more efficient.

Regarding efficiency, technology can clearly make individuals more efficient. Electronic workflow has been a classic example for many years, with use cases such as providing automation for lawyers who are needing to better control bottlenecks within transactions, or a digital workflow for finance team members to speed up authorization processes. This will only proliferate over the coming years as technology continues to become more widely available, and open, allowing law firms to create bespoke process flows throughout the whole firm via platforms such as Microsoft's Power-Automate.

Low-code and no-code automation platforms are becoming more widely available, but perhaps there are none more permeating than Microsoft's Power Platform. The Power Platform is an often-underused tool. Microsoft has continued a strategy to include more and more applications within its standard Office 365 licensing mechanisms, and at times, it has been difficult to keep up with everything being released.

PowerAutomate, and PowerApps, allow law firms to design their own process workflows and applications for their own specific use cases without the need to be a full developer. Online courses are widely available, as are YouTube videos, meaning information on how to use this platform is freely available for everyone. Microsoft has also introduced AI-guided design tools, so that end users can simply describe the workflow or application that they want to be built, with the platform then suggesting and building the flow or app back to the end user.

This is democratizing access to software for law firms, allowing firms that do not have extensive development resources to start to improve efficiencies across the firm, without needing to engage external providers. It also allows for lawyers to start to think more about the "art of the possible", and to document and work through all those "wouldn't it be great if" ideas.

Utilizing these platforms and no-code automation tools, however, doesn't preclude the need for other specialized software providers. There are still areas of huge complexity that a lawyer or an IT developer alone cannot address. Practice and financial management solutions are necessary for firms to run alongside other tools due to the sheer complexity and risk associated with getting this wrong. However, being able to have a solution that can easily integrate via modern APIs (Application Programming Interfaces) with these tools will be extremely valuable in the months and years to come, allowing you to focus on the legal work safe in the knowledge that you have, yet again, a strong foundational layer of software underpinning the business.

Using tools such as PowerAutomate, and modern cloud foundational software, law firms can also look at ways and means to increase their work-to-cash cycle and get paid faster. The average lock-up for UK law firms stands at 140 days, according to The Law Society's financial benchmarking report from 2022;[17] this is an awfully long time for a firm to go without getting paid. In a time of higher interest rates and inflation, a cost-of-living crisis, and an ever-increasing cost of retaining and attracting talent, ensuring that cash is brought into the firm as quickly as possible is pivotal to the ongoing success of the firm – and this benchmarking survey doesn't account for any of this.[18]

So how can this be done via technology today and in the future?

Improving profitability and WIP to cash with technology available today

The first thing firms should be looking at improving is the initial client experience and onboarding solution. Having a tool that makes it easy for both you and the client to onboard improves the likelihood of them signing up and of repeated business. There are many tools now which are available off the shelf and can be integrated into many of your existing practice management solutions.

When the engagement letter is received, there may often be bespoke agreements as part of this. For example, there may be a specific agreement that, for one client, you are not able to recover "travel time". However, many systems do not easily allow for these restrictions to be recorded and will often lead to the firm either sending out bills in error (requiring partial credit notes to then be issued), or having to get finance team members to write down WIP on bills, leading to a poorer realization rate across the firm. If you can capture these requirements and agreements at the outset, then you can stop this becoming an issue further down the line. Some systems in the market allow for these rules to be captured and translated into the client and matter records, so that when a lawyer records time against a prohibited action, they are warned at the point of time entry. This saves time, prevents write downs, and leads to fewer bills sent in error/rejected by the client, ultimately saving potentially weeks of turnaround time in the work-to-cash cycle.

Whilst we've spoken about the rise of value-based pricing, and the potential death of the billable hour, for now it is still here and going strong. As a result, it is worth considering this area for improvement via one of the multiple solutions in the market – some inbuilt and some standalone – that allow for better time recording. Whilst some systems still require manual inputs, table stakes in the time recording world now should be set at having intelligent time recording. This is where the system passively listens for activities being carried out and suggests these to lawyers. Whilst the level of time taken to complete transactions may not be any quicker as a result of implementing these solutions, there will undoubtedly be more accuracy around the actual time spent on the activities through the matter, and less opportunity for "forgotten" time. In 2023, we shouldn't be weighing a file in our hand and sticking a number on it.

Electronic workflows for billing should be easy for lawyers to use and initiate. It should allow for bills to be dealt with via exception, automating where possible, and should absolutely automatically send these bills to clients. There are still many firms that allow lawyers to maintain control of this communication channel, and those individuals will figuratively, and literally, stick the invoice in their drawer and not ask for payment due to "awkwardness" around doing so. This is an engrained issue for lawyers – after all, they haven't been trained to be debt collectors or salespeople.

Eliminating this step and implementing a credit control workflow will shave crucial days off the WIP to cash cycle. Automating chasers and providing reminders for phone calls, whilst allowing for differences in collections procedures, should be actively encouraged (or mandated).

eBilling is a growing area of concern for law firms, and a significant area of slowdown, and many firms have still not embraced a specialized solution to deal with the requirements that are being imposed on them by their clients. Since the pandemic, firms are seeing increases in the requirement for eBilling, and the amount of outside counsel guidelines (OCGs) and solutions they need to comply with are ever proliferating. There are solutions in the market that can integrate with your existing practice and financial management solutions to automate the process of eBilling through to your client's chosen solution(s) and in the specific format you require, allowing for sense checking of time entries versus agreements and rules. This allows for law firms to understand the likelihood of an eBill to be rejected before it is even submitted, and provide insight as to why. Getting this process right first time will eliminate an excuse for your client to delay payment into the following month's run of payments, and significantly help to speed up the work-to-cash cycle for these engagements.

Improving profitability and WIP to cash with one eye on the future

The above guidance is all delivered by solutions available today. This is a great starting point, going back to the prior point of "foundational" platforms, and if your firm is not already considering implementing policies and solutions to help in this regard, it should.

But this is not to say that this is the way that things need to continue to work. Ultimately, if AI tools have the capabilities of uncovering the secret regulatory code of our DNA,[19] then why can't they learn the internal operations of a law firm?

Imagine where an AI model, or models, can work in conjunction across the law firm in different areas. Having separate models could still tick the box in terms of the segregation of duties, whilst allowing for automation through the whole administrative process of finance.

At the point of matter inception, an LLM could consume the client agreement, and work with your existing foundational technology's APIs to automatically set-up the client file, the matter file, and carry out any conflict checks against the entirety of your client database – flagging where necessary any conflicts that need to be investigated. It could set up specific rate agreements within your solution, including exceptions and prohibited narrative. As an LLM, it could interact via natural language with the lawyers and could consume and understand the policies of the law firm, applying these against the data it knows and understands.

So, if the policy of the firm is that when WIP hits a threshold of £5,000, a bill is automatically raised and sent via email to the matter payer, then an AI tool could implement this. It could potentially be used client-facing so that the client can have a chatbot-like communication with the LLM to answer any queries they may have about this bill.

It could be able to respond to prompts from lawyers: "Can you raise a bill for client XYZ for £10,000, and apportion this accordingly across all fee earners associated with the matter?" No problem, and no need for a lawyer or an administrator to understand how to actually do this in the software either.

As the model(s) would have access to a wealth of information instantaneously and could potentially integrate with external benchmarking tools and data, partners could simply ask the AI for a projection of cashflow, or for what/if analysis, on the fly.

Month-end reporting? "Hey AI, run my month-end reporting pack."

I'm not saying that, right now, we can eradicate all forms of data entry or manual administration, and there are probably hundreds of reasons you would not want to do this today; but this is the trajectory for AI across industries. Technology has always been geared towards allowing people to "move up the stack" in terms of focusing more on high-value tasks and less on manual labor. The real question is how far does this go, and what impact does this have on society and the legal industry as a whole? If we automate the tasks that our junior lawyers, administration, or finance staff do today, how will we train our next generation of partners and leaders? Will we need a next generation of partners, or will GenAI become the lawyers and arbitrators[20] of the future?

A technology roadmap – getting your house in order

#	To-do Items	
1	Be a "wasp at a picnic": a. Identify team members who are the drivers. b. Engage individuals within teams in a project to map out processes, understand bottlenecks and areas of double keying (i.e. bank websites/PMS systems). c. Build out a process map and understand the slowdown. d. Understand intricately the common reasons for write downs, write offs, rejections etc. and brainstorm how these can be alleviated if technology was not an issue.	☐ ☐ ☐ ☐
2	Review existing solutions: a. Engage with vendors – understand their technology roadmap. i. Is this product true cloud, is there a concrete plan to get there? ii. What are you considering with regards to AI enhancements in your product? iii. What areas of your solution are we not using right now that could be helpful to us? iv. Can you provide us with a roadmap for integration capabilities? How agnostic will the system be? v. Do you have an alternative piece of technology that is likely to replace our tool?	☐ ☐ ☐ ☐ ☐ ☐
3	Internally discuss responses and assess the confidence in responses, the timelines given, and what the impact of this is.	☐
4	Engage with alternative vendors. Assess the market and maintain good communication with all organizations in the legal industry – it's always a good idea to understand what others are working on so you are ahead of the curve.	☐
5	Work with reputable external consultants where required. Whether that is to better understand the technology market, or to help with training your team members around negotiations, this is usually money well spent.	☐
6	Work on implementing new processes to address those areas you have identified.	☐
7	Look at integration opportunities for areas where your technology cannot help right now.	☐

#	To-do Items	
8	Understand what the future looks like for your foundational technology and what the lifespan is of this – there has been a lot of consolidation in the past five years, which has caused significant concern for thousands of firms in the UK.	☐
9	Empower your IT teams to skill up where necessary in areas such as Power Platform development, and API and AI capabilities.	☐
10	Build an AI strategy for your firm (and use tools like Travers Smith's YCNBot layer for ChatGPT to ensure no comingling of data)[21] – people will continue to use AI whether you ban the website or not, so it's better to control than prevent.	☐
	a. Can we trust the solution will not bring issues concerning confidentiality of data and ensures no comingling?	☐
	b. Can we trust the information it provides us?	☐
	c. Document use cases for your firm, and prioritize areas where the highest efficiency gains can be achieved (and involve your lawyers!).	☐
	d. Ensure that the firm has communicated a clear policy as to what can and cannot be entered into your chosen AI tool.	☐

References

1 Ian Sample, 'Google's DeepMind predicts 3D shapes of proteins' (*The Guardian*, 2 Dec 2018) www.theguardian.com/science/2018/dec/02/google-deepminds-ai-program-alphafold-predicts-3d-shapes-of-proteins.

2 Cade Metz, 'In Two Moves, AlphaGo and Lee Sedol Redefined the Future' (Wired, 16 March 2016) www.wired.com/2016/03/two-moves-alphago-lee-sedol-redefined-future/.

3 Elie Dolgin, ''Remarkable' AI tool designs mRNA vaccines that are more potent and stable' (Nature.com, 2 May 2023) www.nature.com/articles/d41586-023-01487-y.

4 Anne Trafton, 'Artificial Intelligence Yields Powerful New Antibiotic' (MIT News, 20 February 2020) https://news.mit.edu/2020/artificial-intelligence-identifies-new-antibiotic-0220.

5 'Human Brain Cells in a Dish Learn to Play "Pong"' (Genetic Engineering & Biotechnology News, 13 October 2022) www.genengnews.com/news/human-brain-cells-in-a-dish-learn-to-play-pong/.

6 Mustafa Suleyman & Michael Bhaskar, *The Coming Wave: AI, Power and the 21st Century's Greatest Dilemma* (2023, Penguin).

7 Thomson Snell & Passmore, 'Oldest law firm in operation celebrates its 450th

anniversary' (22 July 2020) www.ts-p.co.uk/news/oldest-law-firm-in-operation-celebrates-its-450th-anniversary/.

8 Dan Milmo & Kiran Stacey, 'Five takeaways from UK's AI Safety summit at Bletchley Park' (*The Guardian*, 2 November 2023) www.theguardian.com/technology/2023/nov/02/five-takeaways-uk-ai-safety-summit-bletchley-park-rishi-sunak.

9 Travers Smith, 'Travers Smith launches innovative open sourced YCNBot' (24 May 2023) www.traverssmith.com/knowledge/knowledge-container/travers-smith-launches-innovative-open-sourced-ycnbot/.

10 Stephanie Wilkins, 'A&O on Harvey and AI: 'The Lawyers Would Like it to Stick Around for a While'' (Law.com, 6 June 2023) www.law.com/legaltechnews/2023/06/06/ao-on-harvey-and-ai-the-lawyers-would-like-it-to-stick-around-for-a-while/.

11 Thomson Reuters, 'Generative AI is coming to Westlaw Precision' (2023) https://legal.thomsonreuters.com/en/c/westlaw/generative-artificial-intelligence-upgrade.

12 Bob Ambrogi, 'LexisNexis Rolls Out Lexis+ AI for General Availability, Promising Hallucination-Free Answers to Legal Questions' (LawSites, 25 October 2023) www.lawnext.com/2023/10/lexisnexis-rolls-out-lexis-ai-for-general-availability-promising-hallucination-free-answers-to-legal-questions.html.

13 LawtechUK in Manchester – 1 November 2023 https://lawtechuk.io/events/lawtechuk-in-manchester/

14 "$30 per user per month cost"; Richard Speed, 'Microsoft 365 Copilot 'generally available' – if you can afford 300 seats' (The Register, 3 November 2023) www.theregister.com/2023/11/03/microsoft_365_copilot/.

15 "We anticipate that alongside the rising popularity of time-based AFAs, value based AFAs will receive greater attention in the coming years, and will become a tool in the toolbox of CLDs that are willing to experiment with the psychological shift toward paying for value received rather than effort expended." Mark Ross, Jack Diggle & John Walker, 'Value-Based Pricing: Aligning the Cost and Value of Legal Services' (Deloitte 2021) www2.deloitte.com/content/dam/Deloitte/us/Documents/Tax/us-tax-value-based-pricing-aligning-the-cost-and-value-of-legal-services.pdf.

16 Karen Sloan, 'Bar exam score shows AI can keep up with 'human lawyers,' researchers say' (Reuters, 15 March 2023) www.reuters.com/technology/bar-exam-score-shows-ai-can-keep-up-with-human-lawyers-researchers-say-2023-03-15/.

17 The Law Society, 'The Law Society's Leadership & Management Section: Financial Benchmarking Survey 2023' (10 March 2023).

18 *Ibid.*, p9 "Our findings do not reflect many of the challenges currently facing firms, including record high inflation, increased bank base rates, record energy prices and high wages growth."

19 Stowers Institute for Medical Research, 'Explainable AI for decoding genome biology:

Opening the black box to uncover the rules of the genome's regulatory code' (ScienceDaily, 18 February 2021) www.sciencedaily.com/releases/2021/02/210218151102.htm.

20 "The decision is mine—ChatGPT backs up my decision" Columbian Judge on use of ChatGPT to help decide the fate of a court case: Charles Lew, 'The AI Judge: Should Code Decide Your Fate?' (Forbes, 22 Aug 2023) www.forbes.com/sites/forbesbusinesscouncil/2023/08/22/the-ai-judge-should-code-decide-your-fate/?sh=796a57614597.

21 Travers Smith, 'Travers Smith launches innovative open sourced YCNBot' (24 May 2023) www.traverssmith.com/knowledge/knowledge-container/travers-smith-launches-innovative-open-sourced-ycnbot/.

Chapter 11:
AI and what it means for law firm profitability

By Wayne Hassay, managing partner, Maguire Schneider Hassay

There exists a palpable objection among lawyers in firms of all sizes about integrating Artificial Intelligence (AI) into their practice. In fact, in the current environment, the objections seem to have taken on mythical proportions, like a boogeyman. Granted, all industries and professions are struggling with how AI will change the world. The common struggle is rooted in ethical concerns. This is a comfortable posture for the legal profession because ethical grounds are generally the objection when the legal profession has been faced with change.

The open source information revolution of AI has the unprecedented potential to quickly marginalize lawyers and therefore do the public more harm than good – a worthy basis for an ethical objection. In the past, ethical objections have supported the status quo of how the profession works with the public. This time, the status quo cannot be maintained. The AI revolution is just that, a revolution. The profession has always been able to keep its grip on the one core thing that lawyers use to be in control and that is information. This time, lawyers will lose their leverage.

Just like nearly everyone facing the AI conundrum, lawyers unquestionably fear something that appears as if it could significantly marginalize them, as some of their work product becomes more accessible, and more easily produced. Regardless of the trepidation, the marketplace will drive the needle.

How the overall risks of AI are managed may make the difference between success and catastrophe for society in general. The legal profession, while infamously risk averse, must face the existential threat head-on. Lawyers must be candid with themselves and the public and stand firm on the true value of their services. Responsibly managed, AI is not here to disbar or replace lawyers, but rather will empower them to be more successful and help the public that they serve.

The ethics objection

The vague ethics objection is basically AI could lead to incorrect outcomes, thus hurt clients, and therefore get lawyers in trouble.

AI systems are based on historical data. It must be acknowledged that the data analysis will assuredly have biases and flat-out mistakes. Notably, however, law clerks, paralegals, lawyers, and judges also "sometimes" have biases and make mistakes. And "sometimes" means always. Meanwhile, as AI learns from the historical data, it is merely learning from the previous precedents, with all its biases and flaws, that the legal profession has created and relied upon for centuries. Now envision an experienced lawyer, with biases and flaws, billing the tenth hour of the day, poring over law journals. How perfect is that lawyer? Further, keep in mind those law journals were long ago amalgamated by electronic research services. But now seemingly overnight that has evolved, given the moniker AI, and the clamor of objections is loud. Where is the inherent reliability in any of this, other than one's own confidence or even arrogance in one's own abilities?

AI at all levels (i.e., open and closed) is being programmed by thousands of resolute, intelligent, but imperfect humans who will work painstakingly to obviate mistakes and biases. AI naysayers claim there are bad actors producing AI. That is alarmist and to the extent it might be accurate, the marketplace will soon destroy those bad actors. Certainly, the imperfect lawyer practicing on Main Street cannot be suggesting they might do the job better on their own. Is the supposition that a human bestowed a law license undoubtedly parses information better than technology? Even if this is an understandable yet perhaps short-sighted, self-interested suggestion, lawyers having more information invariably leads to more accurate and better decision-making. Lawyers cannot overlook AI's self-evident strengths in the name of potential flaws when the current process is fraught with similar flaws.

From the invention of the wheel to AI, it is disingenuous to argue human ability is superior to technology when it comes to brute tasks. The first stone wheels had some limitations, but progress did not stop. The problems with open AI are obvious. Open AI's hallucination of case law is cited daily by those who claim the ethical high ground. Those electronic research companies that lawyers have trusted for decades, however, are investing billions into developing, and selling to lawyers, AI that lawyers trust. AI will soon be able to parse the entire written history of any legal issue in seconds. In fact, the ethics issue will dissipate when more lawyers deem the AI they use to be trustworthy. That investment of billions of dollars tells lawyers everything they need to know. AI is here to stay and will affect their practice one way or another.

As for actual governance, nothing much has changed. Model ethics rules that apply include competency, communication, and confidentiality. But it is an understatement to say these are vague when staring down the AI revolution. Most lawyers are notorious for not wading into gray ethical areas for fear of being disbarred. The fact is, regulation and compliance always lag behind the functioning world. Amid rapid change, there is flexibility. The rules and regulations give lawyers the leeway they need to do what must be done to remain viable businesses that are essential to the public. Of course, it would be helpful if regulatory bodies supplied direction. For instance, in early 2023, the European Union enacted the AI Act declaring "legal interpretation" AI as a high-risk category requiring more stringent requirements before being placed on the market. Even so, the passage and implementation of any regulation is also fraught with issues.

The bottom line is, a lawyer's duty is to work effectively for clients and employ the best decision-making. Thus, while never to be trusted blindly, reasonable, thoughtful, and careful lawyer engagement of AI technology is the only real choice.

The fear of change

The real objection may be fear of change. The overstated fear is that AI will replace lawyers. The realistic threat is that AI will change some jobs, success, and profit. Indeed, AI will automate certain tasks, i.e., document review. The fear seems to be a tacit admission that in the AI age many legal services cannot carry the traditional price tag.

Lawyers are complacent, charging a certain price for rote and mundane tasks. Ask most lawyers why their hourly fee is their hourly fee, and why things take so long, the answer will likely be because the job is hard, time-consuming, and expensive. There is little analysis of the component parts of client costs, such as salaries and rent. Fees are set because that is the fee the lawyer down the street charges. While lawyers will set prices as they employ AI, the non-lawyers in the marketplace will disrupt lawyers' age-old model. Lastly, overlooking the AI revolution, there is little sense in charging traditional fees when few can afford those fees and therefore lawyers often do not realize accounts receivable or even find paying clients at all.

Moreover, the marketplace will drive the needle. Entrepreneurs and venture capital will bring AI technology to willing lawyers – or without willing lawyers – to the public at large. Undoubtedly consumers will use AI, when AI delivers more services with purported quality at a better price.

In the AI age, lawyers must reconsider the true value of their services. A focus must be on what can be done faster, better, more efficiently, and less expensively for clients, using AI or any modern methods. The focus must be on the highest level of strategic thinking and client relationships. Revenue that is lost because of automation must be gained in client acquisition, volume, and retention. Clearly, AI will make for an even more competitive legal marketplace. Yes, AI will replace *some lawyers*; those who fear it or even those who merely shy away from it.

The risks and emerging power of AI

What should a lawyer do to effectively manage risks and embrace the power of AI? The following is an exercise that has been done before. It merits repeated presentation. What does AI itself say about this very issue? The following is taken directly from the ChatGPT3.5 inquiry: "Write an article about the risks of law firms using AI".

Title: Navigating the Risks: AI in Law Firms

Introduction
Artificial Intelligence (AI) has been rapidly transforming various industries, and the legal sector is no exception. Law firms are increasingly turning to AI-powered tools to enhance efficiency, accuracy, and client service. While these advancements offer significant benefits, they also come with their fair share of risks and challenges. In this article, we'll explore the potential pitfalls that law firms may encounter when implementing AI solutions.

Ethical dilemmas
One of the primary concerns surrounding AI in law firms is the potential for ethical dilemmas. AI systems, while powerful, lack the ability to understand context, empathy, or human intuition. This can lead to decisions based solely on data, potentially overlooking critical nuances in legal cases. For instance, an AI tool might fail to consider the emotional state of a client, leading to suboptimal legal advice.

Data privacy and security
Law firms deal with highly sensitive information, making them prime targets for cyberattacks. When implementing AI, firms must consider the risks associated with storing and processing vast amounts of confidential data. Inadequate security measures or vulnerabilities in AI systems could lead to breaches, resulting in compromised client information and reputational damage.

Bias and fairness

AI models are only as good as the data they are trained on. If the training data contains biases, the AI system may inadvertently perpetuate and even amplify them. In the legal context, this could lead to biased outcomes in decisions, potentially affecting marginalized communities disproportionately. Ensuring fairness and impartiality in AI algorithms is a critical challenge for law firms.

Overreliance on technology

Relying too heavily on AI systems can lead to a complacency that may erode the skills and critical thinking of legal professionals. Lawyers may become overly dependent on AI tools for research, document analysis, or even case strategy, potentially neglecting their own expertise and intuition.

Liability and accountability

Determining liability in cases involving AI-generated decisions can be a complex legal issue. If an AI tool provides incorrect advice or outputs, who bears responsibility: the developer, the law firm, or the AI system itself? Clear lines of accountability must be established to address potential legal implications.

Transparency and explainability

AI models often operate as "black boxes", meaning their decision-making processes can be difficult to understand. This lack of transparency can be problematic, especially in the legal field where transparency and accountability are paramount. Lawyers and clients alike may struggle to trust AI-generated insights without a clear understanding of how they are derived.

Regulatory compliance

Legal systems around the world are grappling with how to regulate the use of AI in various industries, including law. Compliance with evolving legal frameworks, such as GDPR in Europe or CCPA in California, is essential. Failure to navigate these regulations could lead to legal penalties and reputational damage for law firms.

Conclusion

While AI offers tremendous potential for revolutionizing the legal industry, it is not without its risks. Law firms must approach AI implementation with careful consideration, ensuring that ethical, privacy, fairness, and accountability concerns are addressed. Striking a balance between leveraging the power of AI and maintaining the human touch that is integral to legal practice is crucial in navigating these challenges. By doing so, law firms can harness the benefits of AI while mitigating its associated risks.

Unsurprisingly, this AI-generated article strictly answers the question, focusing almost exclusively on defining what could lead to problems and liability for lawyers. There is nothing incorrect in the answer. However, exactly what to do is left an open question. Please especially note, careful consideration, context, empathy, intuition, and human touch are left to humans. Again, strictly answering the question, like a coached deponent.

The demonstrated limitations may ease some concerns. However, there will be a vast difference between the large language models of AI and what will quickly emerge – more advanced, Generative AI. Generative AI will create more advanced data, predict, and answer the next logical question, produce images, and even video, all of which will mimic the characteristics of humans, such as context, empathy, and intuition. The arguments will rage if this is advancement or a world without rules. Regardless, consumers will use it!

Indeed, most articles written by those in the legal profession regarding AI are about lawyers. They focus on ethics, false case citations, and effects on work product/billable hours. All of that is very lawyer-centric. What does that say about lawyers? The profession is too much in its own box, concerned about precedent and the status quo of its business. AI will soon drive how consumers answer their simple legal questions. Those answers will drive how consumers then find their lawyers. AI will have set the consumer's expectation of the time, efficiency, and cost of the work to be done by the lawyer. This will be a drastic reset of consumer expectations. Consumers are not giving up the advantages of technology found in other industries, i.e. streaming entertainment, delivery services, or telehealth. AI will have a similarly disruptive effect on the law. AI will not replace lawyers, but it will fundamentally change how they find and work with their customers.

Focusing solely on the risk for lawyers is shortsighted. As the AI revolution plows forward, a human lawyer must manage the risks and benefits for themselves and consumers. While the risks may seem novel, this is not particularly different from the management of risk in any legal matter. The human lawyer must decide if cost effectiveness for clients, careful consideration, context, empathy, intuition, and human touch are found generally in their firm and now in the Generative AI used at their firm, in addition to producing correct large language answers. This will cause consumers to trust the AI robots *and* the lawyers who use those tools.

The real risk is, if lawyers do not find a path to show the public that lawyers plus AI are better, in a catastrophic result, for lawyers and clients, the public could turn predominantly to AI for their legal counseling.

Making a smarter, more profitable, law firm

Let us assume some lawyers will overcome vague ethical objections, the fear of change, and will reasonably analyze and address the risks and emerging power of AI. How might that turn out?

One recent survey concluded most law firm respondents (65 percent) either "strongly agree" or "somewhat agree" that the effective use of Generative AI will separate successful and unsuccessful firms within the next five years. Most in-house corporate legal counsel (61 percent) echoed those sentiments as well.[1]

Lawyers, no matter how hard they try, are still only one person. One person with only so many hours in a day. One person who is shaped by their own experiences. One person with a great deal of, but still limited, knowledge. AI will exponentially widen these horizons, streamlining process, improving efficiency, and supplying valuable insights.

The following question was posed to ChatGPT3.5. "How can AI make law firms more profitable?"

Automated Document Review: AI-powered tools can quickly analyze and review large volumes of documents, contracts, and legal briefs, saving time and reducing manual labor costs. This can be particularly useful in due diligence processes, contract management, and e-discovery.

Legal Research and Analysis: AI-powered research tools can help lawyers quickly find relevant case law, statutes, regulations, and legal articles. This not only saves time but also ensures that the firm's research is comprehensive and up to date.

Predictive Analytics: AI algorithms can analyze historical case data to predict outcomes, helping lawyers make more informed decisions and offering clients realistic expectations. This can lead to better settlement negotiations and potentially reduce the time spent on cases.

Chatbots for Client Interaction: AI-driven chatbots can handle initial client inquiries, schedule appointments, and provide basic legal information. This allows lawyers to focus on more complex tasks while providing clients with timely responses.

Billing and Time Tracking: AI-powered tools can automate time tracking and billing processes, ensuring accurate invoicing and reducing the risk of missed billable hours. This can lead to improved cash flow and increased revenue.

Compliance and Regulatory Assistance: AI can help monitor changes in laws and regulations, ensuring that the firm remains in compliance with legal requirements. This can reduce the risk of legal liabilities and penalties.

Personalized Legal Services: AI can help analyze client data to offer personalized legal advice and solutions. This can lead to stronger client relationships and potentially result in increased referrals and repeat business.

Workflow Optimization: AI can analyze workflows and suggest improvements to increase efficiency. This may involve optimizing processes such as case management, document filing, and client communication.

Language Translation and Interpretation: AI-powered translation tools can assist in handling cases involving clients or documents in different languages. This expands the firm's reach and potential client base.

Cybersecurity and Data Protection: AI can play a crucial role in identifying and mitigating cybersecurity risks, helping to protect sensitive client information and maintain trust.

Staff Training and Development: AI-powered platforms can offer ongoing training and development resources for legal professionals, ensuring that the team remains up to date with the latest legal trends and technologies.

To demonstrate that current AI needs a human eye and is significantly curtailed by the question it is asked, the above answer importantly overlooked that Generative AI will also be a powerful marketing tool for lawyers. It will be able to cost effectively create content, curate it, organize effective email and social media campaigns, and analyze client feedback and sentiment. What else did AI miss in answering the question?

Lawyers, particularly those in small firms or solo lawyers, may believe their work will not support an AI investment. Indeed, costs, the need for IT experience, training, customization, and a low-volume caseload may appear to be full roadblocks. This is deceiving. With careful planning, law firms can be more affordable to clients while not eroding profit. These law firms will attract more clients, including from an untapped market for legal services and from those lawyers who do not incorporate AI into their practice. Granted, the AI age will give a competitive advantage to those with resource superiority, i.e., large law firms and venture capitalists. The best strategy for smaller law firms will be carefully collaborating with trustworthy legal tech companies (and there are plenty) that can provide smaller firms with access to advanced technology and resources with less financial burden.

Conclusion

Is the AI boogeyman real for the legal profession and, for that matter, the entire world? No. However, the public has proven repeatedly it wants the convenience and lower costs delivered by technology. The legal profession, like other professions, does not have time to sit back and rely on old methods. AI could quickly and significantly marginalize lawyers and hurt the public, as AI may cause clients to turn away from the true value of lawyers' services. The profession must quickly but thoughtfully incorporate AI into its work to help more clients carry out what clients need. Meanwhile, the human touch will remain critical to the practice of law. The local attorney in any sized law firm must converge the convenience of technology with actual human-to-human connection. This combination of conditions is a workable path to serving the public, law firm success and increased profit.

References

1 www.wolterskluwer.com/en/news/survey-predicts-generative-ai-use-will-separate-successful-from-unsuccessful-law-firms, 26 July 2023.

Chapter 12:
Sustaining success along the profitability journey

By Madhav Srinivasan, CFO, Proskauer, and Mitch Spradlin, pricing director, Hunton Andrews Kurth

Overview

For most law firms, implementing client profitability initiatives can aptly be described as a journey, a perpetual work in progress, and more like a marathon than a sprint. Once a profitability program is in place, firms must be able to sustain and build upon their early achievements. This is a complex endeavor! Organizational change is gradual and must be reinforced regularly. It also requires thoughtful planning and a determined, persistent approach.

Drawing from our experience, we offer this guide to sustaining success in your profitability journey, organized around these five key areas:

1. Positioning – evaluate and refresh your messaging; provide an ongoing, comprehensive lawyer training program at various levels of experience and understanding; gradually roll out new reporting and tools to keep lawyers focused on profitability.
2. Goal-setting – to move lawyers to take the right action, set profitability targets at various levels within the firm.
3. Matter management – incorporate legal project management (LPM) into the profitability initiative to carry it further.
4. Matter lifecycle – infuse profitability thinking throughout the matter lifecycle.
5. Resourcing – build teams and tools to support and manage profitability.

The following narrative is a direct transfer of experience from the authors to the readers, the expected owners of the profitability process in their law firms, and thus relayed in a conversational tone.

Positioning

Most of us have probably used GPS apps at one time or another. If you take a wrong turn, the app will recalculate your path to get you back on course. Profitability initiatives can follow a similar pattern. Their initial implementation likely generated a lot of attention and focus, but over time, they perhaps fell somewhat out of focus for lawyers. Do not let this critical program get lost! You can help it get back on the right path through regular education, periodic refreshing of the message, and by introducing new reports and tools.

Lawyer education is an ongoing process, and you need to offer regular training and coaching opportunities at different levels of understanding. Newer lawyers may have missed the initial training, so they need to hear the basics – the purpose, the metrics, the reporting, and how this will impact them. Often, you can create on-demand modules that lawyers can view at their convenience. Some lawyers may need to see the metrics applied across various scenarios to fully illustrate actions for profit improvements. More advanced topics are better presented through in-person, live interactions that allow for Q&A. Other lawyers will only catch on when they can see profitability analysis applied to *their* clients and matters. Set up one-on-one sessions with these attorneys as "profitability check-ups". These meetings will go a long way to to anchor profitability in their minds.

In a busy firm, there are typically many initiatives that compete for lawyers' attention. You do not want profitability to be another "flavor of the month" that fades into the background after a short time. Keep your profitability initiative fresh and timely by sending periodic communications. You can use these messages to share firm-level progress reports, share insights and data from the industry, and offer advice on what lawyers can be doing *now* to positively impact profitability. Provide links to training materials or class registrations. Vary the senders – these communications should not always come from pricing or finance leaders. You can develop the message outline but have different leaders tailor the message and make it their own. Video messages are always highly impactful.

Continuous and high visibility of your firm's profitability efforts keeps them top of mind for lawyers. Profitability metrics should be disseminated in many ways – through the intranet, partner dashboards, and key financial reports. Partners don't always look at this data from their laptops, so you should ensure that reports and tools work on tablets and phones whenever possible. Client profitability should be high on the agenda at practice meetings and similar gatherings. The data must be updated frequently. To maximize effectiveness, profitability results need to be communicated quickly and easily. We recommend a gradual rollout of different reports and tools. This avoids overwhelming folks with too much new information, and it provides natural opportunities to bring profitability to the forefront.

Goal setting

The end result of a profitability initiative is to gain improvement over time. Information and well-designed dashboards will not move the needle until lawyers take the necessary actions to improve profits. Early in your journey, the top priority was gaining acceptance and adoption of profitability metrics. To propel your initiative forward, you must focus on profit *improvement*. One of the primary ways of motivating people to action is by setting goals. When lawyers become fluent in how profitability is measured and how to improve it, collaborate with them to develop aggressive yet achievable targets.

The first step in this process is to identify clients within a practice area with the greatest potential for profit improvement. From this analysis, create a target list of clients that merit the highest priority. Use this information to set profit margin goals for the practice area. With leadership support, the pricing team can begin working with individual partners to craft a strategy for each client on the list.

Our experience shows there is no one-size-fits-all plan for improvement. The challenges can be in different areas – low rates, high discounts, persistent write-offs, and/or suboptimal staffing. Sometimes you will have challenges relating more to clients who often push back or mandate onerous guidelines, while other times the attorney may need some coaching to correct prior habits or focus on value delivery. There can be client-specific issues at play that would impact the timing of some actions, such as asking for increased rates. Staffing issues can lead to higher write-offs and/or lower leverage. It can take a while to resolve some of these challenges, and other administrative leaders may need to be involved in finding a solution.

As you prepare to have these meetings, it is important to set the right tone. You are likely to propose that the lawyer make one or more changes. Recognizing that some level of anxiety and fear related to change is possible, the use of positive language is critical. This should revolve around support, help, opportunities, added insights, and enhanced performance. Try and build momentum with easier opportunities to notch some early wins. The result of these lawyer interactions should be action plans to improve profitability within a defined timeframe.

Matter management

At the heart of improving client profitability is effective matter management. Once a new engagement arrives, lawyers are tempted to start immediately to provide the best client service possible. However, a more thoughtful, disciplined, cost-conscious approach at the beginning can prove very useful. Efficient and effective management of matters comes naturally to some lawyers, while others will benefit from guidance and support. High quality matter management support from experienced and trained pricing and LPM professionals can be a strong resource for the firm. will enhance client profitability and satisfaction while improving service delivery. Experience shows that matter management should encompass some key factors:

- *Defining the matter scope*. This process frames the engagement in terms of what needs to be done and conversely what will not be done. The lawyer and client should agree on specific deliverables and timeframes. LPM resources include many good checklists to guide lawyers through the scoping process. It is also important to outline the process for managing any future scope changes. A solid matter scope sets the framework for creating an effective staffing plan and budget.
- *Staffing and budgeting*. Budgeting is an invaluable step, even on smaller matters, as it forces thinking through the required work scope and which timekeeper resource will specifically accomplish which task. Estimates of matter profitability can be modeled for different scenarios. Consider how alternative staffing, such as staff or project attorneys, can impact the budget and matter profitability. This process leads to informed, strategic decisions about how to move forward. There is a natural tendency to underestimate the amount of work for a desired level of legal service. Rigorous budgeting can be quite revealing and force critical actions to occur. Our experience indicates that crafting a budget, even when not required by clients, is a great learning opportunity. Over time, the firm will improve its budgeting skills. Sharing budgets with the matter team sets expectations and leads to fewer write-offs. Sharing budgets with the client fosters goodwill, reducing the likelihood of any future fee disputes.
- *Communication plans and reporting*. As the matter progresses, schedule regular times for the team to meet. Review actual performance against the budget. Spotting and correcting issues early is key to maintaining strong profitability. Keep the client in the loop on progress against the budget. If the budget and/or matter scope need adjustment, meet the

client as soon as possible to negotiate the change. It would not be fruitful to surprise the client with a large bill at the end of the matter.

- *End of matter debrief*. This is a critical step but is often skipped on the way to the next new matter. Avoid the temptation to bypass end-of-matter review, as this can lead to solid learnings, especially by comparing budgets to actuals and predicted profitability against actual profitability. Understand what went right and what, if anything, needs to be improved. Were there faulty staffing or hours assumptions? Did unexpected or unpredictable circumstances cause variances? Preparing a list of learnings and modified approaches can tremendously help towards efficient budgeting for future matters.

Matter lifecycle

A successful client profitability initiative should touch every part of the matter lifecycle, from the pitch to the close. Establish policies and best practices that will encourage a more disciplined approach to pricing and profitability. Such a broad mandate means the need to enlist and educate other business professionals in the firm – in business development, conflicts and intake, and client billing. Here are some recommendations to incorporate at the different lifecycle stages:

- *Engagement*. An ounce of prevention is worth a pound of cure. Getting the pricing and profitability team involved at the proposal stage is vital. Pricing can review all relevant documentation, including outside counsel guidelines. These guidelines often contain provisions that can have a material impact on profitability if not considered up front. Addressing and resolving issues early is much easier initially than in later phases. Committing to high discount levels or large AFAs without understanding the expected profitability can be detrimental. Requiring a profitability analysis of all proposals and RFP responses for engagements that cross a certain threshold can prove quite useful. In cases where anticipated profitability is below a defined threshold, leadership should be engaged to accept or reject decisions.
- *Planning*. You should require a matter budget for larger matters and when the client has relatively lower profitability. Over time, the "large" matter threshold can be reduced in order to capture more matters into a formalized budgeting process. Your pricing and profitability experts can review the budget and create a profitability estimate. Matter management resources can work the lawyer to make

budget adjustments – to hours, rates, and/or staffing – that will produce an acceptable result.

- *Executing.* Encourage regular reporting that tracks the budget to actuals. The reports should focus on the staffing mix as well as the overall hours and fees. Provide timely recommendations if mid-course corrections are needed. Set rules to enforce good timekeeping and billing practices. Financial hygiene in terms of time not recorded, late time and bills being written off, failure to adhere to client guidelines, etc. can lead to write-offs and lost profits.
- *Evaluating and closing.* Require matter debriefs for large matters and complex AFAs. If the matter resulted in a lower profit margin, determine why, and document the lessons learned. For clients with persistently low profitability, it would be worthwhile to mandate pricing and profitability team involvement.
- *Rate setting.* While LPM is episodic and focuses on a single client or matter, there is a larger picture to consider, which is the annual setting of standard rates and their realization in terms of collected rates. Billing rate management is a critical topic on its own. The essence of this process is to arrive at standard rates that are reflective of the value of legal services delivered, attorney experience, market conditions, external factors, and the law firm's cost base. Setting the right rate is based on being confident in the value provided to clients towards a win-win situation for the firm and the clients.

Resourcing

For profitability programs to remain successful, firms must invest in the necessary resources to sustain them. Since the journey to improved profitability is ongoing, continual investments can provide returns in the form of increased revenue and profits. Based on our experience, here are some thoughts and recommendations in several key areas:

- *Strategy.* Before you start buying or building tools, or hiring personnel, think about some of your end goals. How and when will the pricing team get involved? What level of "self-service" do you expect from lawyers? We recommend some form of triaged approach. The largest, most complex matters get personalized attention from pricing. Smaller, straightforward matters are ideal candidates for self-service. Matters in the middle would get varying levels of individual support, combined with input from technology tools.

- *Technology.* There are several products in the marketplace to assist pricing teams and attorneys. Many firms have IT departments that could potentially build in-house software that accomplishes the same or similar functions. There is a whole discussion to be had on the "build vs buy" question. In developing your technology resources, you should examine the following:
  - *Tool vs tools*. More than likely, you will need multiple tools to cover the full spectrum of tasks – modeling profitability, comparing profitability using different AFAs, building budgets (top-down or bottom-up), analyzing past data to develop cost estimates, developing alternative rate structures, etc. Our experience has shown that there is no one tool that does everything well and is suitable for both pricing team and attorney use. One may need to mix and match off-the-shelf products with in-house applications.
  - *The end user*. You need to have tools for both the pricing team and attorneys. While some attorneys will have the skills and desire to dive deep into more robust pricing and profitability solutions, most will want something where they can enter a few data points and "push a button" to get the results.
  - *Timing*. Do not wait until you have the "perfect setup" to begin deploying solutions. Gradually introducing new technology over time allows you to start making profit improvements sooner and is more easily digested by your team and the lawyers.
  - *The changing marketplace*. Legal technology is rapidly evolving. New providers pop up. Companies merge. The quest for the "silver bullet" is ongoing. One of the hottest topics today is Generative AI. While this technology has existed for a while and is already part of some software, we expect to see it fully integrated into most solutions. In terms of pricing and profitability, it will allow you to better analyze the historical data that informs so many decisions. Marrying that data with the facts of the matter at hand will help pricing teams better predict profitability and make more accurate recommendations on budgets and staffing. It should get you to better answers in less time.
- *Staffing*. No matter how good the technology is, you are going to need a solid team of professionals to really sustain the success of your initiative. When planning and building your team, consider these elements:

- *Structure*. Determine where the team will sit within the firm. Will it be part of finance, business development, or on its own? There are benefits and drawbacks to any setup, and you should consider what would work best within the firm's culture. You may also decide to have some staff positioned on the legal teams where there is enough need for dedicated support.
- *Leadership*. The leader of your team must have, of course, the respect of the firm and practice area leadership. To be effective, they must also have the authority to act on their behalf in most pricing and profitability matters. This can be a challenge in some firms where the partners are used to having a great deal of autonomy. Over time, the leader will prove their worth by building a track record of "wins" and similar successes.
- *Skillsets*. It almost goes without saying that you need people who excel in data analysis. These analysts are the solid foundation of the team. It is critical that the team also have individuals who have strong communication skills and high emotional intelligence. These are the folks who will initially interpret the data and develop recommendations on improving profitability. They will work directly with partners and need to evaluate all the circumstances, both financial and non-financial, to arrive at the best conclusion. They need to instill confidence in the partners and build successful relationships that carry forward from one matter to the next.
- *Recruiting*. The legal industry has matured to the point that there are now hundreds of professionals with some level of specific experience with pricing, profitability, and matter management. It is also wise to recruit from adjacent disciplines such as client billing or business development. They can bring valuable perspective to your team and improve the important relationship between the pricing team and related departments.

Summary

Our experience shows that, as firms progress, their outlook, challenges, and focuses mature. We provided the analogy of a long journey, and indeed as one goes over a hill, another appears; and calls for modifications and new actions. With widespread understanding, adoption, discipline, and accountability on the legal side, there are demands on pricing and LPM to continually modify their own objectives, toolkits, resourcing, communication, and goals. This journey is full of challenge and diligence, but it brings great satisfaction and accomplishments, making it evergreen and interesting.

Chapter 13:

The seven profit zones formula for higher profits – without working more hours

By Michelle Peters, former practicing solicitor and founder, The Business Instructor

Introduction

A dangerous myth pervades our legal industry. It keeps law firms – and the lawyers who work in them – stuck on the "time-for-money" treadmill, and it keeps them working too hard for too little reward.

The myth in question is that the benefit of higher profits is inextricably linked to the burden of working more hours. This keeps lawyers working longer than they need to.

When I was a practicing lawyer in London, I experienced first-hand the long hours culture of a large law firm – being constantly assessed on the basis of the number of chargeable hours I recorded each day, with no time to consider anything else.

In my last decade of working with smaller law firms to help them increase their profitability I have clearly seen how the myth of "more hours equals more profit" not only keeps lawyers working too hard but it actually prevents the firm from being more profitable.

This chapter will debunk that myth, and it will also demonstrate how small changes in each of the seven "profit zones" in a law firm can dramatically increase profits without the lawyers in that firm needing to work more hours. Not only are these small changes highly effective for increasing a firm's profitability, they are simple to implement and are therefore realistic for any law firm – regardless of its size or maturity.

The problem of the time-for-money model

Most law firms operate on a time-for-money model, whether or not they overtly acknowledge it. The "billable hour" is the ultimate time-for-money model, and most fixed fees are also based on an estimate of the amount of time required to complete the work. Even contingency fees (no win, no fee) are still a time-for-money trade-off, because the opportunity to receive a premium fee for a "win" is balanced with the risk of getting nothing if you "lose".

In a time-for-money model, the general assumption is that more time is required in order to generate more fee income and, in turn (assuming the work is actually profitable), more profits.

But this mindset assumes that the lawyers must work longer hours in order for their law firm to generate higher profits. It is also why so many lawyers and law firm owners feel stressed, burned out, and sometimes find themselves questioning whether they have chosen the right profession.

A better approach is to consider how to make each hour more profitable for the firm, and how to develop a law firm model where the systems and processes of the "business" work harder so that the lawyers do not have to.

The hidden cost of acquiring new clients

Acquiring new clients is expensive. Whilst marketeers love to encourage law firms to invest time and money in the latest marketing strategies or social media platforms to attract new clients, this incurs the expense (both in time costs and, usually, marketing costs too) of acquiring new clients.

This lowers the profitability of the work those clients bring. For example, if your firm spends £500 in marketing to acquire a new client, the profitability of a £2,000 instruction is immediately reduced by that £500 cost.

But even if your firm doesn't spend money directly on marketing, there will usually be a "time cost" for generating a new enquiry. For example, if one of your fee-earners spends an hour of their time (valued at their hourly rate of £300) networking or having coffee with a potential client in order to acquire them, this "cost" similarly reduces the profitability of the client's instruction. Even though you don't pay your fee-earner £300 to spend this time, it is an hour that cannot be billed to another client and so is a lost billing opportunity, costing your firm £300.

Because of the costs involved in acquiring new clients, existing or past clients offer the biggest opportunity to increase profitability. Doing more work for existing or past clients avoids any "acquisition cost", so the work is more profitable. In addition, it is generally easier and less time-consuming to provide an existing client with additional legal services than it is to service a new client – you do not need to spend as much time finding out about them and their circumstances. Also, because they already know your firm, they do not require as much "hand-holding".

As we shall see in this chapter, firms that prioritize acquiring new clients over maximizing the profitability of their existing or past clients will find it harder and slower to reach their profit goals.

A different approach – the seven profit zones formula for profitable growth

There are seven "profit zones" in every law firm. They are areas of your firm, represented by numbers or percentages that, if you improve them, will result in additional profit being generated. Five of the seven profit zones relate to making the most of existing or past clients, meaning the opportunity to increase profitability is greater than it is with new clients.

The seven profit zones are as follows:

1. *Number of enquiries.* Attracting more enquiries will (assuming you convert them into paying clients) result in additional client instructions, which should (assuming the work is profitable) generate additional profit. The amount of additional profit will depend on the underlying profitability of the additional work generated – for example, wills are often offered as a "loss leader" whereas the probate work that can follow may be the firm's most profitable work.
2. *Conversion rate.* Converting a greater percentage of the enquiries you receive will result in more new client instructions, which will in turn generate additional profit (assuming the work itself is profitable).
3. *Number of matters per year.* Increasing the number of times a client instructs the firm – either for the same service or a different service – will result in more client matters overall. This will generate additional profit without the time and expense of acquiring as many new clients, meaning higher profitability on the additional matters.
4. *Average value of a client matter.* Increasing the value (i.e. amount) of a client's instruction, by offering additional services or a greater scope of services, has a similar effect to increasing frequency – the additional services will generate additional profit. The extra work should also be more profitable because the cost of client acquisition will be a lower percentage of the overall value of the client's instructions.
5. *Profit margin.* Increasing the profit margin on the fee-earning work done by your firm – whether by raising fees, lowering costs, or increasing efficiency – will produce additional profit without the need for staff to work more hours. This is the ultimate "more profit without working more hours" strategy.
6. *Referrals from clients.* Getting more referrals from each client will (assuming they are converted into new clients) results in a greater number of new client instructions without the time and expense of marketing to generate those instructions.

7. *Average client lifetime.* Retaining clients for longer will increase the likelihood of additional or repeat instructions, as well as the opportunity to receive more referrals from those clients, further boosting profits.

The power of the compound effect

Increasing any one of the seven profit zones in your firm will usually create additional profit, but the real power of the seven profit zones formula lies in the compound effect of increasing each zone – even by just a small amount.

For example, a ten percent increase in each profit zone will usually result in a 75-80 percent increase in profitability overall (the exact result will depend upon the starting number in each profit zone).

The flexibility of the formula means you do not even have to increase every zone by ten percent to achieve this. You could instead increase some zones by more than ten percent and others by less (or even nothing) and still achieve 75 percent profit growth.

Moreover, the formula works with any size of law firm, whether your current fee income level is £100,000 per year, £500,000, or £1,000,000 or more.

Here's an example of how this compounding effect works. Let's assume that:

- A firm (or a department within a larger firm) attracts 1,200 enquiries per year (100 per month).
- 300 of those enquiries (25 percent) are converted into paying clients, each of which spends an average of £1,500, twice a year, at a 30 percent profit margin. Each client therefore generates £3,000 of fee income and £900 of profit for the firm.
- The firm receives 260 enquiries a year via referrals from these clients. These referred enquiries also have a conversion rate of 25 percent, producing an additional 65 clients who also each generate £3,000 in fee income and £900 in profits for the firm.
- Overall, these direct clients and referred clients generate £1,095,000 fee income per year, of which £328,500 is profit.
- These clients stay with the firm for an average of three years, and they continue to instruct and refer the firm at the same rate – meaning the client lifetime value of these clients (i.e. the profit from them over that time) is £985,500.

This is summarized in Figure 1.

Profit Zone	Description	Current
1	Annual Number of Enquiries	1,200
2	Conversion Ratio	25%
	Number of Clients	300
3	Number of Client Matters Per Year	2
4	Average Matter Value	£1,500
	Annual Fee Income	£900,000
5	Profit Margin	30%
	Annual Profits	£270,000
6	Annual Number of Referrals from Clients	260
	Conversion Ratio of Referrals	25%
	Number of Clients From Referrals	65
	Annual Fee Income From Client Referrals	£195,000
	Annual Profits From Client Referrals	£58,500
	Total Annual Fee Income (Turnover)	£1,095,000
	Total Annual Profits	£328,500
7	Average Client Lifetime (Years)	3
	Lifetime Value of Clients (without Referrals)	£810,000
	Total Lifetime Value of Clients (with Referrals)	£985,500

Figure 1: Example of the seven profit zones in a law firm.

Taking these starting figures and implementing some simple and inexpensive strategies that increase each profit zone by ten percent would result in increases to the annual fee income, annual profits, and lifetime value of clients indicated by the black arrows in Figure 2.

Profit Zone	Description	Current	Increase	Results	Cumulative Increase
1	Annual Number of Enquiries	1,200	10%	1,320	
2	Conversion Ratio	25%	2.5%	27.5%	
	Number of Clients	300		363	
3	Number of Client Matters Per Year	2	10%	2.2	
4	Average Matter Value	£1,500	10%	£1,650	
	Annual Fee Income	£900,000		£1,317,690	46%
5	Profit Margin	30%	3%	33%	
	Annual Profits	£270,000		£434,838	61%
6	Annual Number of Referrals from Clients	260	10%	286	
	Conversion Ratio of Referrals	25%	2.5%	27.5%	
	Number of Clients From Referrals	65		79	
	Annual Fee Income From Client Referrals	£195,000		£286,770	47%
	Annual Profits From Client Referrals	£58,500		£94,634	62%
	Total Annual Fee Income (Turnover)	£1,095,000	→	£1,604,460	47%
	Total Annual Profits	£328,500	→	£529,472	61%
7	Average Client Lifetime (Years)	3	10%	3.3	
	Lifetime Value of Clients (without Referrals)	£810,000		£1,434,964	77%
	Total Lifetime Value of Clients (with Referrals)	£985,500	→	£1,747,257	77%

Figure 2. Practice Growth Calculator, showing the effect of a ten percent increase in each of the seven profit zones. Note: each profit zone number has been increased by ten percent. However, where the numbers in the "current" column are percentages, the "increase" column next to it will not show "ten percent" but instead the percentage figure that is mathematically ten percent. For example, the current conversion figure of 25 percent is shown with a two-and-a-half percent increase, which equates to adding ten percent to 25 percent.

Figure 2 demonstrates the cumulative effect of the seven profit zones formula by demonstrating how just a ten percent increase in each zone results in:

- Annual fee income increasing by 46 percent to £1,604,460;
- Annual profits increasing by 61 percent to £529,472; and
- Total lifetime value of clients (with referrals) increasing by 77 percent to £1,747,257.

These are impressive results, but perhaps more interesting is that using this formula means profits can be increased substantially without the same level of increase in the number of new clients – avoiding the need to service more new clients. Figure 2 shows that these increases are generated with just 77 additional clients, made up as follows:

- Direct clients have increased by 63; and
- Referred clients have increased by 14.

This is a total increase in new clients of just 21 percent, which many law firms would be able to service without needing to recruit additional staff – making these additional clients even more profitable than the clients the firm already has.

Small (ten percent) increases in each of the seven profit zones are therefore enough to produce an overall profitability increase of 77 percent with only 21 percent more clients in total.

The seven profit zones growth formula contrasts with the approach taken by many law firms that focus primarily on getting more clients in order to increase their profits. In other words, they put all their efforts into just increasing the first profit zone – the number of enquiries.

This can, however, have an unintended – and negative – effect on profitability. Fee income will increase but profits may remain stagnant (with a lower profit margin overall), or even decrease.

For example, increasing the number of new enquiries by 50 percent without trying to increase any other profit zone would – assuming they were converted at the existing rate of 25 percent – bring a 50 percent increase in new clients and a 50 percent increase in fee income from those new clients. However, the profitability of the additional work generated from those new clients will be negatively affected by two factors:

- The increased marketing cost (money, time, or both) required to bring about such a dramatic increase in enquiries; and
- The time cost of servicing those clients, both in terms of dealing with the enquiries and onboarding those new clients and servicing them. This might well require additional staff, meaning recruitment costs and additional salary costs.

If these additional time and money costs result in the firm's profit margin reducing from 30 percent to 20 percent this would in turn reduce – or even wipe out – the additional profits the firm would expect to be generated by the new clients. To illustrate this, and using the same figures as in previous examples, a 50 percent increase in enquiries with a ten percent reduction in profit margin would result in fee income increasing by 41 percent to £1,545,000 but the annual profits would decrease to £309,000 (a six percent reduction) – see Figure 3.

There is now more work, and more risk, for less profit overall.

This example illustrates what I regularly see in firms who approach me for help – they have a high level of enquiries, which they are turning into new clients who produce a good level of turnover for the firm, but profits are dangerously low.

Getting practical – how to increase each profit zone

The opportunities to increase each profit zone in your firm will depend on many factors. They will include your practice areas, the types of clients you service (in particular, whether they are business clients or private individuals), and the size of your existing or past client base. Here are some tips to consider for each profit zone.

Profit zone one: Number of enquiries

Actively generating more enquiries (rather than passively waiting for them) means implementing more or better marketing strategies or other business development activities.

There are two main options for law firms to consider:

- Generating enquiries directly from your firm's target clients. Typical examples include increasing traffic to the firm's website, promoting the firm on social media platforms, email marketing to a database of prospective clients (for example, those who have enquired about services but not proceeded, or those who have downloaded resources

Profit Zone	Description	Current	Increase	Results	Cumulative Increase
1	Annual Number of Enquiries	1,200	50%	1,800	
2	Conversion Ratio	25%	0%	25%	
	Number of Clients	300		450	
3	Number of Client Matters Per Year	2	0%	2.0	
4	Average Matter Value	£1,500	0%	£1,500	
	Annual Fee Income	£900,000		£1,350,000	50%
5	Profit Margin	30%	-10%	20%	
	Annual Profits	£270,000		£270,000	0%
6	Annual Number of Referrals from Clients	260	0%	260	
	Conversion Ratio of Referrals	25%	0%	25%	
	Number of Clients From Referrals	65		65	
	Annual Fee Income From Client Referrals	£195,000		£195,000	0%
	Annual Profits From Client Referrals	£58,500		£39,000	-33%
	Total Annual Fee Income (Turnover)	£1,095,000	→	£1,545,000	41%
	Total Annual Profits	£328,500	→	£309,000	-6%
7	Average Client Lifetime (Years)	3	0%	3	
	Lifetime Value of Clients (without Referrals)	£810,000		£810,000	0%
	Total Lifetime Value of Clients (with Referrals)	£985,500		£927,000	-6%

Figure 3: Practice Growth Calculator, showing the impact of increasing enquiries by 50 percent without increasing other profit zones.

from the firm's website), sponsorship activities, speaking opportunities, and webinars.

- Generating enquiries via referrers. Typical examples include referrals from lawyers operating in non-competing areas (such as between a family lawyer and a private client lawyer), or other professionals who serve the same clients such as accountants, financial advisers, or business advisers. Referrals can also be generated from current or past clients, which is considered under profit zone seven below.

In both cases, firms should focus on attracting more of their "ideal" clients. These are the ones who need the most profitable services you provide and who are willing to pay the fees your law firm charges for those services. Increasing the number of these "ideal" clients will not only increase the fee income from those new clients but it will also increase the profitability of the work itself.

Effective marketing and business development to attract your "ideal" clients requires three key factors:

- *Market*. If you want more of your "ideal" clients you must identify who they are so you can then target them specifically.
- *Message*. To stand out from your competitors you need to create a marketing message that uses the words your ideal clients need to read or hear to understand why you are the "ideal" law firm for them (I call these "Magic Words").
- *Method*. You must get your message in front of your ideal clients by using the right marketing "method". Consider where your ideal clients spend their time – if they don't use a particular social media platform, don't waste your time promoting your law firm there, even if that platform is the current latest trend.

A good example of how to combine these three key factors into a successful marketing strategy is to use what I call a "client magnet". This is a written guide that helps one specific category of ideal client understand why they need your services. For example, if one of your ideal clients is a business owner wishing to sell their business, you can create a specific guide to explain the common mistakes business owners make that reduce the sale price of their business and how getting the right legal advice can help them avoid that.

The particular benefit of a "client magnet" guide is that you offer it as a download on your firm's website in return for a contact name and email – thereby enabling you to follow up with those who download it.

This technique was used to great effect by one of my law firm clients who specialized in setting up businesses in an offshore jurisdiction. This firm created a "client magnet" guide on the seven reasons why businesses should establish themselves in their specific offshore location, and they offered it for download from their website in return for a contact name and email address. Within two weeks of starting to promote it, the guide was downloaded more than 200 times – giving the firm a pipeline of potential enquiries to follow up, along with £50,000 in immediate instructions from new clients.

Profit zone two: Conversion ratio

Improving the percentage of enquiries your firm converts into paying clients has two key benefits:

- It increases the number of new instructions without the need to do any additional marketing, thereby saving the (time and money) cost of client acquisition and boosting profitability of the fee-earning work.
- It turns more of the time that fee-earners spend talking to prospective clients into new instructions, thereby reducing the amount of time "wasted" on free consultations that do not convert. Your fee-earners will not have to spend as much time giving free consultations because fewer consultations will be needed to achieve the target number of new clients. This frees up more time for fee-earning, which increases profitability per fee-earner.

Increasing the conversion rate can be the biggest growth opportunity in a law firm, particularly if the current conversion rate is below 50 percent. For example, if the conversion rate is 33 percent, it is realistic – with the right strategies – to double that to 66 percent. This would double the number of clients for the firm without requiring any additional marketing and – provided there is capacity amongst the staff to do the fee-earning work – double the firm's revenue and profits just from improving this profit zone alone.

Strategies for improving conversion rate include:

- Responding to new enquiries promptly – ideally within a few hours, and always on the same day;

- Helping prospective clients see the "value" of the legal service being offered, so they are more likely to invest in that service;
- Following up proposals or fee quotes in a structured and timely way (rather than assuming they will respond if and when they want to proceed);
- Training fee-earners and other team members who deal with enquiries on how to handle those enquiries in a more effective way (i.e., improving the quality of the response, not just its speed);
- Creating a conversion "process" to ensure consistency of results regardless of which staff members are involved; and
- Regularly analyzing where prospective clients get stuck in, or drop out of, the conversion process and fixing those "blocks" or "leaks" so that more of them convert into paying clients.

Helping prospective clients to see "value" in your law firm's services is perhaps the most challenging aspect of improving conversion. But the most significant improvements I have seen in conversion rates have been in those firms that really commit to excellence in this area. One of our law firm clients, who offered a wide range of legal services in a "high street" style firm, doubled its conversion rate from 40 percent to 80 percent, simply by addressing the "value" issue when responding to the initial enquiry by phone or email. When their fee-earners learned to ask what I call "value questions" – which help the prospective clients understand the value of the law firm's services to them as clients – their conversion rate doubled practically overnight.

Profit zone three: Number of matters per year

A firm's ability to increase the average number of matters per year from each client will depend on the practice areas offered.

Some practice areas lend themselves more readily to "repeat" instructions than others. Commercial, employment (when acting for employers), immigration, and wills are good examples of areas where clients may need to update or refresh legal documents or to seek updated advice on a regular basis.

The key to increasing the number of matters per year from each client is:

- Reminding existing (or past) clients about the need to update or refresh legal documents or to seek updated advice. Many firms wait for clients to return and to ask them to do this, but most clients don't know why or when they should do so. This means that the reactive approach misses opportunities to increase the average number of matters per client.

- Using the reminder as an opportunity to educate those clients about why they should update or refresh their legal documents or advice. Most clients won't understand the need to do this, but if it is explained to them why this is important and – more importantly – the dangers or risks associated with not doing so, they will be much more likely to take up the invitation.
- Repeating this process of reminding and educating regularly – clients who are reminded today may be too busy to respond or may have other priorities for now, but in a week, a month, or a year, they may be ready to take up the invitation to instruct your firm again.

The key to success in this area is to be proactive. A small immigration law firm I worked with was losing out on repeat instructions because their clients would ask them for help with renewing their immigration visas at the last minute. This meant they could not always help them in time due to lack of fee-earner capacity. So we created an outbound email campaign to clients whose visas were due for renewal within the next three months, explaining the importance of instructing the law firm now rather than waiting until nearer the renewal date. One email sent to 20 clients with upcoming renewals resulted in £12,000 of repeat instructions with plenty of time for the law firm to service the work. The law firm not only generated instructions that might otherwise have been lost, but they now had a strategy they could repeat every month with very little time or effort.

Profit zone four: Average value of each client matter

Where repeating the same service is not a likely occurrence due to the "one-off" nature of the legal service provided (such as litigation or company sales), there is still an opportunity to offer clients other legal services as a way of increasing their average number of matters per year. There are also obvious "pairings" of legal services that will help increase the overall spend of each client, such as wills with powers of attorney, or divorce with updated estate planning.

Tips for increasing the value of each client matter include:

- Using a "fact find" with all new clients to identify other legal services they require from the start.

- Spotting opportunities during the client relationship to offer additional services – for example, when new information becomes available about the client's circumstances or needs.
- Recommending complementary legal services to clients that are directly relevant to their existing matter – for example, recommending a new will to a client who is getting legal advice on their divorce, or recommending a future update to a business' terms and conditions at the same time as helping them resolve a dispute that has arisen based on their current terms.
- Taking opportunities throughout the client relationship to educate them about how other legal services would benefit them – for example, through seminars or newsletter articles or one-on-one discussions with fee-earners so they are more receptive to the recommendations given in the above scenarios.

If you can increase the average value of a client matter from £1,500 to £2,000, you not only have a 33 percent increase in fee income (and the resulting additional profit that comes from that) but the extra £500 of fee income comes without any additional cost of acquisition. This means the profit margin on that extra income is higher.

Profit zone five: profit margin

Your profit margin is the difference between the fee income you generate and your costs, usually expressed as a percentage. To increase your margin you have three main options:

- Generate more fee income without incurring more costs;
- Generate the same level of fee income with lower costs; or
- Use a mixture of the two.

Many law firms focus on cutting costs, but this can be a limiting strategy. If the costs you cut are actually *investments* that help you generate fees, cutting them will limit or reduce your ability to generate those fees – leaving you worse off.

For example, cutting the cost of support staff who free up fee-earners to spend more time on fee-earning could result in your fee-earners recording fewer chargeable hours and your fee income reducing.

Another popular cost-cutting measure is to reduce spend on marketing.

If marketing isn't producing a return on the investment you make it's a cost, and cutting it will be beneficial. But if that marketing brings you new client instructions that are profitable, cutting it will likely reduce your fee income and not improve your profit margin.

The other way to cut costs is to increase efficiency. If your staff can get the work done in fewer hours you will have fewer write-offs of chargeable time or overruns on fixed fees that the client may not be prepared to pay for. This reduces the time cost of providing the service to the client and it also frees up your fee-earners to do chargeable work for another client. This has a positive effect on your profit margin, but increasing efficiencies can be one of the hardest (and slowest) projects to implement successfully in a law firm.

Instead, I prefer a simpler strategy for increasing fee income in a way that does not involve any additional higher costs – increasing your hourly rates or fixed fees.

Even a small increase can make a big difference to your financial results.

For example, if you increase your hourly rate from £250 to £260, that's an extra £10 per hour.

If your fee-earners currently do 5,000 chargeable hours per year in your firm, then an extra £10 per hour would bring you an additional £50,000 in fee income per year. This would all be additional profit, because there wouldn't be any additional costs associated with that extra fee income.

If you raise your fees by £50 per hour, it would be £250,000 additional profit per year – without doing any extra work.

Many law firms would love to raise their fees like this, but they worry about losing clients as a result. Here are some tips for raising your fees without losing clients:

- Be clear about how many clients (or chargeable hours) you can afford to lose and still be better off from your fee raise – this will give you confidence to increase your fees. If your current profit margin is 30 percent and you raise your fees by ten percent, you can actually afford to lose 25 percent of your clients and still generate the same amount of profit. This would mean you would generate the same amount of profit for 25 percent less work. If you don't lose any clients as a result, you will make more profit from the same number of clients as you had before – meaning you will have increased your profits without working more hours.
- Raise your fees for new clients before existing clients – this will allow you to test reactions to the new fees without the risk of upsetting existing client relationships.

- Make sure your discussions with prospective or existing clients include demonstrating the "value" of your services before you tell them your fees – so they make a decision based on value rather than cost. The fee increase will then not impact your conversion rate.

One of my conveyancing law firm clients used the above strategies to increase its fixed fees by between 18 percent and 56 percent (depending on the value of the property being sold) without any reduction in conversion rate. In addition, by charging for additional services that the firm had previously included within its fixed fee (such as the cost of preparing a co-ownership deed) it was able to increase the average spend per client by £200. All these increases were additional profit, since there was no additional fee-earner time cost – it was the same amount of work as before, but now for a higher fee.

Profit zone six: Client referrals

If each client in your firm referred another client to you, you would double your number of clients without the time or money cost of any additional marketing. This would generate additional profits and the referred clients would be more profitable because they cost you less to acquire.

Referred clients can also be more profitable for firms. They are generally easier to convert (taking up less fee-earner time) and less sensitive to fees because they have already been told the value and quality of your services by the client who referred them.

The key to increasing the number of referrals from clients is:

- Be proactive – rather than waiting for referrals, ask for them, especially after a client has provided positive feedback or thanked you for your help; and
- Demonstrate capacity for more clients – make sure your existing clients know you would welcome additional clients.

Profit zone seven: Client lifetime

We have already seen that many of the profit increase opportunities in your law firm come from existing clients, so it is important to focus on keeping those clients as long as possible.

There are many factors that influence a client's decision to remain a client or go to a competitor, but happy clients are more likely to stay longer.

The key to keeping clients is:

- Use the *"Platinum Rule"*. This means *"treat clients as they wish to be treated"*. The well-known "Golden Rule" of *"treat others as you wish to be treated"* fails to take into account the reality that not all your clients are like you. Different clients value different things. To avoid having to deliver different bespoke services to every client (a logistical nightmare), create a Platinum level of service targeted at your "ideal" clients.
- *Keep in touch*. Many lawyers feel that clients will not welcome them staying in touch after a matter has concluded. They fear that following up will be viewed as a sales tactic. In reality, most clients will often consider you still to be "their lawyer" long after you have closed their file and archived it. So it is not only important to keep in touch with them, but in many cases, it is expected. If you do not stay in touch, your clients might assume you have either closed your firm or you are no longer interested in their business and go elsewhere.
- *Attract the right clients in the first place*. Not only will the right clients naturally stay longer but, if your law firm is set up to cater to the needs of your specific "ideal clients", they are even more likely to stay longer.

Increasing the average "lifetime" of a client at your firm will – for those who have repeat instructions or can refer you to others – create additional fee income and profit for your firm without the additional cost of acquisition of new clients.

Beyond ten percent increases – doubling your profits without doubling your clients

We have already established that trying to increase your profits just by significantly increasing your number of clients is unlikely to work. The time it takes to attract, convert, and onboard those new clients eats into fee-earning time and your profits.

A much easier option for doubling your profits is to use the seven profit zones formula, and to increase some of your profit zones by *more* than ten percent.

To illustrate how to achieve this, Figure 4 uses the same numbers we used in Figure 3 but – this time – profit zone one (number of enquiries) has only increased by ten percent, whereas the other six profit zones have increased by 20 percent each. As you will see, this more than doubles the annual profits of the firm.

Profit Zone	Description	Current	Increase	Results	Cumulative Increase
1	Annual Number of Enquiries	1,200	10%	1,320	
2	Conversion Ratio	25%	5%	30%	
	Number of Clients	300		396	
3	Number of Client Matters Per Year	2	20%	2.4	
4	Average Matter Value	£1,500	20%	£1,800	
	Annual Fee Income	£900,000		£1,710,720	90%
5	Profit Margin	30%	6%	36%	
	Annual Profits	£270,000		£615,859	128%
6	Annual Number of Referrals from Clients	260	20%	312	
	Conversion Ratio of Referrals	25%	5%	30%	
	Number of Clients From Referrals	65		94	
	Annual Fee Income From Client Referrals	£195,000		£406,080	108%
	Annual Profits From Client Referrals	£58,500		£146,189	150%
	Total Annual Fee Income (Turnover)	£1,095,000	→	£2,116,800	93%
	Total Annual Profits	£328,500	→	£762,048	132%
7	Average Client Lifetime (Years)	3	20%	3.6	
	Lifetime Value of Clients (without Referrals)	£810,000		£2,217,093	174%
	Total Lifetime Value of Clients (with Referrals)	£985,500	→	£2,743,373	178%

Figure 4: Practice Growth Calculator, showing the impact of doubling profits without doubling client numbers.

The increase in income and profits (highlighted by the top two arrows in Figure 4) shows that the fee income has increased by 93 percent and annual profits have increased by 132 percent. Further, the lifetime value of the clients (including their referrals) has increased by 178 percent (shown by the bottom arrow), which is more than three times higher than before.

What is particularly interesting in this example is that the number of clients has not doubled. The number of new clients in total has increased as follows:

- Direct clients from 300 to 396; and
- Clients referred by other clients from 65 to 94.

This means that, overall, client numbers have increased from 365 to 490. In other words, the firm has generated more than twice as much profit with only 34 percent more clients.

When you take into account the time and money saved by not needing to generate as many enquiries or spend as much time converting and onboarding new clients, but instead doing more for existing and past clients, it becomes feasible to double profits without working any more hours overall.

It is worth noting that this doubling of profits without doubling the number of clients does not require a 20 percent increase in profit zones two to six, as shown in Figure 4 – it can be achieved by many different combinations of percentage increases. Each firm will have the potential to increase different profit zones by different amounts. You might only be able to achieve five percent in some areas but you could achieve 25 or 30 percent in other areas. By using the Profit Growth Calculator[1] you can insert your existing numbers for each profit zone and see what is possible for your firm when you apply different percentage increases to each one.

How long does it take to double your profits?

The amount of time required to double your profits will depend on several factors:

- *Your starting numbers.* If you have a particularly low average client matter value or low conversion rate, there is more scope to increase them significantly.
- *Your firm's agility.* Some firms are better able to implement changes more quickly than others. This often depends on the management structure, priorities, and personalities.
- *How much time you devote to this.* If you could double your profits in the next 12 months, how much fee-earner and management time would you be prepared to devote to achieving this outcome?

- *Your support structure*. Firms that put in place the right support and accountability structure to track growth and troubleshoot "bottlenecks" get faster results.

Some of the law firms I have worked with have devoted focused time and energy to these strategies and have, as a result, achieved increases of 200 to 400 percent in just a couple of years. Others have, by following a structured process, doubled their profits within 12 months. Some firms that only "dipped in and out" have achieved slower (and lower) end results.

The speed at which you achieve these results is up to you and what you put into the process.

The implementation paradox – information vs action

If doubling your profits is as simple as adding between ten and 20 percent to a combination of the seven profit zones, why don't more law firms double their profits on a regular basis?

The answer lies in the quote attributed to Socrates: *"Knowing is not the same as doing"*.

Busy law firms, wrestling with the time-for-money model, rely on staff having the time (and inclination) to implement the strategies required to increase each profit zone.

Not only that, but with the notable exception of raising hourly rates or fixed fees, these strategies also need to be repeated regularly – and in a consistent way – to continue getting results. You may also need to modify or improve the strategies over time, depending on the results.

In my experience, the biggest challenge law firms face is not in understanding the principles of the formula but in *implementing* the strategies needed to improve the results in each profit zone on a regular and consistent basis.

Instead of relying on the manual labor and independent initiative of staff, law firms should explore ways to systemize and automate implementation of these strategies. For example:

- Instead of relying on fee-earners to remember to contact past clients to invite them to take up other services, systemize this by creating a monthly email to a database of past clients that covers different services each month, or by automating the sending of specific emails to a client at the start, middle, and end of their client matter to let them know about other relevant services your firm offers.

- Eliminate the inconsistent results that come from having initial consultations conducted in different ways by different staff through systemizing the process – for example, by using a framework for the consultation with suggested wording for the most critical parts.
- Remove the burden of staff remembering which prospective clients to follow up with and when by using software to remind them when to follow up or, if appropriate, automating the follow up process entirely.

Success in implementing the strategies to increase all seven profit zones is also dependent on the firm having the right culture. Increasing the profit zones should be the responsibility of all staff, not just the management team. This requires the right education, training, and support for staff to do this. In addition, the management team needs to recognize and reward efforts that are made by staff to increase the profit zones. Otherwise, if the only activities that are recognized and rewarded are getting time onto a timesheet, or getting invoices paid on time, those will be the only activities that staff will focus on.

Getting started

With seven profit zones to focus on, it can be difficult to know where to start. What I have found to be most effective with the law firms I have worked over the past decade is the following approach:

1. Begin with the end in mind. Define how much additional profit you want to generate, in which practice areas, and over what timescale.
2. Analyze which of the seven profit zones provides the biggest opportunities for profitable growth – using the Practice Growth Calculator[2] will enable you to see the results you could achieve from increasing each profit zone and which ones create the biggest impact on your profits with the least effort required to implement.
3. Choose your top three profit zones and put them in order of priority to implement.
4. Create an action plan to implement those profit zones over the next 90 days. This should include a mixture of implementing strategic systems and training and supporting staff to run those systems.
5. Implement the 90-day plan. For the clients I work with we also break down this 90-day plan into two-week "micro-plans", to ensure they take small steps on a regular and consistent basis.

6. Review progress at the end of 90 days and use that to decide on priorities for the next 90 days.
7. Create the next 90-day action plan, implement, review, and repeat the process.
8. Remember that this is not a "once and done" process. Sustained profit growth requires regular review and improvement in each profit zone. This is best supported through having both training and support for those who need to implement the systems and accountability for those responsible for the implementation.

Conclusion

The seven profit zones formula provides a realistic way for firms to double their profitability through a series of small, strategic improvements to each profit zone rather than by trying to achieve dramatic results in just one or two areas. It also provides a more profitable route to growth by minimizing the impact of the cost of acquisition of new clients or cost of hiring more staff to service more clients.

When implemented in a systemized way, the seven profit zones formula will ensure that your *law firm* works harder to generate profits, rather than *you and your staff* having to work more hours.

The key is to get started.

References

1 Practice Growth Calculator, available to download from www.thebusinessinstructor.com/profitability-book

2 As above.

Chapter 14: The human cost of boosting profitability

By Richard Martin, principal consultant, Byrne Dean and CEO of the Mindful Business Charter

Mental health in the legal profession

It is truism to say that there is a crisis of mental health in the legal profession, and that this is a global issue. It is also fair to assume that this has always been the case, albeit that in previous generations it tended to be disguised by alcohol and related substance abuse issues, but over recent years it has been getting worse. Readers who are unsure of, or unfamiliar with, the extent of the issue, should refer to the International Bar Association's (IBA) 2021 report – *Mental Wellbeing in the Legal Profession, a Global Study*,[1] and a white paper from the Mindful Business Charter published in October 2023, called *Raising the bar, Addressing the state of mental health in the legal sector.*[2]

To take one headline data point from the IBA report, using a World Health Organization wellbeing index that is calibrated from zero (very poor wellbeing) to 100 (excellent wellbeing) and where a respondent scoring 52 or below is recommended to seek a psychiatric assessment of their wellbeing, the average score for lawyers responding to the IBA survey was 51.

Although other professions also experience a higher-than-average prevalence of mental illness, lawyers are one of the most at risk professions. The reasons are complex, inevitably, but the IBA report analysis can be broken down into three main categories:

1. The sort of people who become lawyers;
2. The work lawyers do; and
3. The context or culture in which they work.

In terms of the sort of people who become lawyers, a useful starting point is the 2003 book by psychiatrist Tim Cantopher – *Depressive Illness, the curse of the strong.*[3] Cantopher talks about what we might nowadays call burnout. Early on he describes how, as a junior doctor, when first meeting with a patient experiencing this condition, he would sit and talk to them to get to know them and find out about their character, their personality. He then states that he does not tend to need to bother anymore because he knows what they are like, they are all the same, and then lists their common personality traits:

- Moral strength;
- Reliability;
- Diligence;
- Strong conscience;
- Strong sense of responsibility;
- A tendency to focus on the needs of others before their own;
- Sensitivity;
- Vulnerability to criticism; and
- Self-esteem often dependent on the evaluation of others.

As a description of the nature of the average lawyer it would be hard to beat this list. As Cantopher observes, these characteristics are noble and good; we love these people and recruit and promote them, they are the very people we turn to when the heat is on, because they do not say no, or give up when the going gets tough. All they know is to try a bit harder, until it can become too much, and something snaps. This of course is not to say that anyone with those traits is doomed to mental distress, but they create a higher level of risk.

In terms of the work lawyers do, they tend to move from one high pressure project to the next without pausing for breath. Further, lawyers are trained to catastrophize and to seek perfection, to see things in black and white terms, and to take a whole heap of personal and professional responsibility – all classic unhelpful thinking patterns from which therapists make a living trying to rescue their clients.

Those two create risk, which perhaps would be manageable in the right culture or context, the third element identified in the IBA report. If that culture, however, also creates risk then it can become unbearable. It is on that culture and context that this chapter is most focused.

This crisis of mental health comes at a cost. There is a very real human cost in terms of the lives lost or damaged. There are the good people we are losing from the profession, either broken by it or getting out before they become too damaged. There is the staff turnover and attendant costs – a

2022 Vitality report[4] in the UK suggests that average employees lose 20 percent of their hours per year due to mental health-related absence and lower levels of performance due to poor mental health. Pay is generally one of the biggest expenses of a law firm. If 20 percent is being lost each year, then one very obvious way to increase profitability would be to reduce that rate of loss by creating healthier and more sustainable and productive working cultures and practices. Sadly, as this chapter will explore, some of the traditional methods used to increase profitability do the very opposite.

A couple of caveats before we start

The legal profession is a vast spectrum. There is a world of difference between a sole practitioner on the high street in a provincial town, struggling to make ends meet, often dependent in part on public funded work for which the rates are pitifully inadequate, and big law. Most of what this chapter is focused upon is big law and the pursuit of profitability in that context. That is not to in any way ignore or dismiss the plight of that high street lawyer, but they have a very different challenge. The solution is almost certainly a very significant change in public policy and the value the state places on the importance of an independent legal profession and the respect governments and the wider public have for lawyers and the crucial role they play in free societies. That is beyond the scope of this chapter.

There are also huge differences between private practice and in-house lawyers. This chapter primarily focuses on private practice lawyers, but parallels can be drawn to the in-house profession.

Secondly, in discussing the workplace risks to our mental health, it would be wrong not to acknowledge the very positive benefits work can bring. The sense of purpose, achievement, and connection, as well as the financial security that work can provide, are hugely important protective factors for our wellbeing.

It ought to be a statement of the obvious that to *perform* well as individuals and organizations we need to *be* well. That logic would mean that wellness should be at the heart of any organization's strategy if it wants to succeed. That is very rarely the case in the legal profession.

Why lawyers become lawyers

Why anyone ends up joining, and staying, in a job or profession will of course be a complex and unique mix of many different motivations and influences. That said, however, there are a range of different influences, most of which are likely to have had some part to play in the choices of most lawyers:

- The intellectual challenge of analysing a situation and applying to it an expert understanding of the relevant law.
- Helping people, whether that is vulnerable people to enforce their rights or defend themselves, or corporate entities to conduct their commerce.
- The intellectual art of argument and negotiation.
- A desire to see justice and fairness.
- A calling to be part of a profession that upholds standards and ethics, and is respected in society.
- Holding power to account.
- Job security and the opportunity for advancement.
- For most, the prospect of a good level of remuneration.

The character traits described by Cantopher will also play their part in guiding people who share them to the profession.

These tend to be the common motivators at any stage in a person's legal career – from starting out at law school onwards. These are the values lawyers tend to hold, their personal sense of purpose. When asked by clients or their children or other loved ones why they do the job they do, and to an extent what it is they do, these are the things lawyers say.

While earning money is certainly a factor (and to an extent, its relative importance to an individual lawyer will help them decide the sort of law and firm in which they want to practice), it is rarely the only or the most important. The reality of most lawyers' daily life, however, is that revenue and profit are one of, if not the only, key metric against which they and their firm are managed and assessed. In years gone by, law firms would of course have had an eye on their profitability, in order to stay in business and in order to provide their lawyers with a level of income with which they felt comfortable, but it was largely a private matter, one that rarely got discussed outside of the partners' meeting.

The advent of legal directories – and the rankings central to them – changed that dramatically. Although there are many metrics the directories include, a key one, at least in so far as many firms are concerned, are the headline income rates – the salary paid to newly qualified lawyers and then the profits per equity partner or PEP. With a few notable exceptions, most firms feed the directories their numbers, and are then ranked on the basis of them. Most firms have a sense of where they are in those rankings and where they would like to be – some aspire to be at the top, others are comfortable lower down, but at the same time need to maintain their position in order to continue to attract and retain talent.

The pursuit of profit is of course a healthy thing, and a degree of competition is important to any functioning marketplace. Arguably, however, it has gone too far. There can be few other professions or business sectors where one of the key measures of an organization's success and standing is the amount of profit the owners are able to extract – indeed, in most other sectors, the perception of excessive profit is a source of concern and often outrage.

There is of course a valid debate to be had over what constitutes "excessive" for these purposes but that is perhaps not the point. The issue is the extent to which the financial metrics then permeate every level of a law firm and form one of the key bases on which individual lawyer performance is measured, and how lawyers are then rewarded, often to the virtual exclusion of other bases. Yes, there may be "balanced scorecards" that seek to take into account other factors but there is no arguing that revenue and profit form a core element.

For most associates, if they are eligible for an annual bonus, this is very likely to be almost entirely based upon the hours they record and/or recover. Depending upon the equity structure for partners and how the firm's profits are divided, it will be a key factor for them too and, even if their revenue in any one year may be based upon a lockstep or other arrangement, a failure to deliver the numbers expected in one year will almost always influence whether, and to what extent, they advance on that lockstep in future years. In some firms, data will regularly be shared, comparing the hours recorded and revenue generated by different partners and their teams. In a firm of any size where the financial management is delegated to a group of senior partners, the purpose of this is surely to enable comparison and to pressurize those perceived not to be pulling their weight. When managing partners stand up in partner meetings to report on the progress of the firm, much of the time will be taken up with the financials.

Again, sound financial management is important. Too many good law firms have failed in its absence. The question to be asked, however, is one of degree. If we go back to those factors that motivate someone to join and stay in the profession, generally speaking, only one plays an important role in how they are individually managed and rewarded, or how their firm is perceived. Those other values – the sense of individual and collective purpose – are nowhere to be seen. Sure, some of them may indirectly feed into the numbers, but how often does a lawyer get assessed by reference to any of them apart from revenue?

Law firms, and the legal profession as a result, have become less of a profession or calling and more a business. This matters because of the impact upon the individual lawyers. If your sense of purpose and values is reflected in the purpose and values of the work you do and the organization in which you work, this creates harmony and congruence, factors that create resilience and an enhanced ability to manage the stress that comes with a legal career. Where your individual purpose and values feel like they are not aligned with the work you do or the firm in which you do it, this creates incongruence or dissonance – tension and stress. It may not be immediately apparent and destructive, but it festers and gnaws away, reducing the resilience and capacity to manage that inevitable stress, and creating stress in its own right.

The concept of incongruence comes from humanistic psychology and was originally developed by Carl Rogers. It focuses upon the unpleasant feelings that can result from a discrepancy between our perceived and our ideal self. The perceived self is how an individual views the reality of themselves and the ideal self is how an individual wishes they were.

Of course, some will feel this more strongly than others. That may be because of the different weight attached to the different values and purpose factors by different individuals – for some, earning big money will be more important than for others – and it may be because some are more reflective than others, and perhaps more honest. For many, perhaps most, lawyers, however, it is a factor and, in a profession replete with inherent stress, any additional unnecessary stress is a risk factor.

Where's the balance?

As with many things, this is partly a question of balance. One cannot run any commercial enterprise without some level of focus on the financials. Too often, however, it will feel that the only, or at least the most important, way in which activity and performance is measured, on an individual or firm wide basis, is in financial terms, ignoring all those other values and sources of purpose that motivate lawyers. In a world of points-based lockstep and league tables of law firms' performance, where do those other factors get a look in? Where do we recognize, celebrate, and reward those other factors? Incentive-based rewards systems are designed to incentivize particular behaviors – they deliver a very clear message about what the organization wants and values, and behaviors will be directed towards those factors as a result, however much lip service may be paid to the importance of others.

There is a need within any firm to have an honest discussion among the partners about where they want the balance to lie. What is the level of profit they would like to achieve, for example, and how important is that relative to other factors of how they might recognize performance, such as quality of client service, important work done, integrity, client retention, contribution to a collegiate and supportive culture that nourishes and develops the next generation? These are not always going to be easy conversations, particularly where there are more than a handful of partners, and there will inevitably have to be compromises, because no two partners are going to agree all of the time about where the balance lies. But that complexity is not an excuse for ignoring the question and simply adopting the lowest common denominator of cash. For all but the very few lawyers who are in it solely for the money, that is a sure-fire recipe for incongruence.

Some of this does of course take place. Most informed partners will have a sense of where they feel their firm sits and where other firms may sit. A firm may well have a set of values and a statement of purpose. But those statements mean nothing, and can add to the problem, if the day-to-day reality is, or is perceived to be, based on something else. What this means, therefore, is that the firm's values and purpose need to be constantly kept front and center and as much as possible of what a firm does, and how it does it, needs to be judged against them. This needs to feed down into discussions about performance and reward. That way, the lawyers in the firm, at every level, can properly decide for themselves whether the firm feels right for them. The firm needs to be ready and brave enough to have honest conversations with its partners and other lawyers about whether there is sufficient fit in terms of values and purpose – even if they are rainmakers!

How profit is increased and the impact of that

It is also important to focus on how a firm goes about increasing or maintaining a particular level of profit, a broad subject that is of course more fully explored in other chapters of this book. For the purposes of this chapter, it is sufficient to think about the four levers most firms tend to think they have available to them to increase profitability:

- Do more work;
- Charge more for work done;
- Reduce costs; and/or
- Improve financial management of work that is done.

Each will have a potential impact on mental health. The intention in focusing on them is not to say that they are therefore off limits, but rather that, in thinking about which, if any, of the levers to use, there should be due consideration of the potential impact upon the wellbeing of your people, which consideration might also take into account how people are already, and what, if anything, might be done at the same time to ameliorate that impact.

Doing more work

Assuming the work is there to be done, in the standard law firm model of the billable hour, doing more chargeable work should mean more profit. You could employ more junior lawyers to build out the classic pyramid model but that does add more payroll and other cost. The easier way is to get your existing lawyers to bill more hours. There may need to be bonuses paid to incentivize this but otherwise, at face value, you get more income for the same base cost, which ought to deliver pure profit.

There are of course potential downsides:

- If your people are already working at or close to their limits then asking them to do more will increase the risk of mental illness, perhaps most obviously burnout, which in layman's terms is a sense of emotional, physical, and mental exhaustion. The World Health Organization describes burnout as a syndrome resulting from chronic workplace stress that is not successfully managed. There is no inevitable correlation between hard work and mental illness, but working excessively hard for prolonged periods without respite increases the risk for most people. Increases in the targets for billable hours may often appear quite small but if they are repeated on a regular basis, it may be much like boiling a frog.
- It is also important to keep in mind that by asking people to spend more time at work, they risk, inevitably, spending less time on the things that enhance their wellbeing – other interests, relationships, hobbies, rest, and sleep being obvious examples.
- You can try to ameliorate that risk, part of which might be to take steps to increase the efficiency of your lawyers, getting rid of processes and activities that distract them from billable work. If your people are already working flat out, then asking them for more of one thing ought to be accompanied by a reduction of something else. In simple terms, if you want to drive higher performance then you need to take

greater care. We see this in most other aspects of human performance. A Formula One driver has a great deal of safety built into the system to protect them from the risks of their ultra-high performance. They train hard to enable them to perform at that level, they prioritize rest, and they have a lot of other stuff done for them to allow them to focus solely on the job in hand.

- There may be an increased risk of the incongruence discussed earlier if your lawyers feel that the gap between their perceived real selves and their ideal selves is being increased by the demand that they record more billable time. This increases the risk of mental distress, as well as the risk of increased staff turnover if people recognize that gap and take steps to address it by finding an alternative home for their skills. You may also lose client relationships as a result.
- Aside from that incongruence, there may be increased turnover if people feel that the firm culture is changing from that which they felt they joined and/or that the increased demands upon them are no longer being adequately compensated for by the reward in return.

This is probably the right point to mention something about time recording. Inevitably, in a billable hour-based revenue construct, time sheets slavishly completed by lawyers have become an accepted part of the job, even if they are not actually what lawyers are trained and employed to do. While most lawyers accept them, however reluctantly, there have always been some who seemed to struggle, but with little sympathy or empathy from those around them. Wider society and workplaces have thankfully become more attuned to neurodiversity over recent years. People who are high on the spectrum for dyscalculia, ADHD, and dyslexia are more likely to find timesheets (because of the particular executive functioning involved) a real challenge. That does not mean that a particular individual with those neurodiversities will experience that challenge or that others without those conditions will not, but it is more likely. That will create stress for them. Is it still good enough, in an age of greater awareness and inclusion, simply to ignore that and insist they conform along with everyone else? Or is it time we found ways to help them, given they may be excellent at lawyering, which is, after all, what we have employed them to do?

Reducing costs

Again, simple math would suggest that if you keep income the same but reduce overheads, then you increase profit. There may obviously be some overheads you can reduce without a potential impact upon your people – negotiating lower rent, bills, and insurance premiums might be examples.

What we have seen in many firms over the last few decades, however, is a reduction in the roles that traditionally sat alongside lawyers that enabled them to do their job more efficiently. If lawyers doing billable legal work is where you get your income, then logic dictates you want to reduce as far as possible asking them to do other things. Instead, we have seen ratios of lawyers to EAs, for example, increase significantly. Obviously, part of that is a reduced need for typing – many lawyers would rather type themselves. Communication by email is much faster and more efficient than typing and signing letters. But how much time do lawyers spend organizing their diaries and filing, for example – is this an efficient use of their time, or could that be done by someone else, freeing lawyer time for billable work? Gone are the days when access to a lawyer on the telephone was closely guarded by their EA – most lawyers have, perhaps without questioning, given clients and everyone else they work with direct access through their cell phones. The risk of regular interruption and distraction can get in the way of billable focused time.

Keep in mind that lawyers generally like doing law, delivering good legal advice, and other legal services to clients. Stuff that gets in their way of doing so will be an irritation and potentially generate stress. Additionally, it makes sense that if you have a highly prized professional who has spent many years training to do something and for which you are paying a high cost, get them doing the thing they are good at rather than something they do not like and may not be so good at.

Of course, there are some other things lawyers need to do alongside the law, particularly as they become more senior, whether that is managing, mentoring, and supervising their teams, developing and sustaining client relationships, firm management, and more. Some will actively thrive on that while others will find it a nuisance. Find out and direct people to what they enjoy and are best at and where you will derive the most value, and do what you can to take away the other stuff. Crucially, when you are thinking about a scheme to reduce overheads, factor into the decision the potential impact on your people. Yes, your lawyers may be able to take on some more administrative work, but it potentially comes at a price. The more you add, the greater that risk.

Charging more or differently for work done and improved financial management

The nuances of how lawyers charge and the impact on profitability, as well as how to improve profitability by reducing the time between work being done and the firm being paid for the work, are for other chapters of this book. From a mental health perspective, there are probably only a few factors to keep in mind.

Keep it as simple as possible for most lawyers. There is a reason they did law and not accountancy. Let them focus on what they trained for and enjoy, and do not distract them more than is necessary with financial management. As ever, it is a balance, but exercise thought in that balance and think about what you can get out of the way of good lawyering rather than what you can put in the way.

Keep in mind that if you send a lawyer something, they will generally feel obliged to read it and try to understand it. How many firms routinely send substantial financial reports around to all the partners on a regular basis? How much of that do they really need to see and understand? What is the intended purpose of sending it to them? Openness is a good thing but that does not mean everyone needs to see everything all of the time.

A different approach

In 2017, in-house lawyers at Barclays Bank, in discussion with counterparts at two of their London panel law firms, Pinsent Masons and Addleshaw Goddard, began a conversation that has turned into a global movement. They recognized that stress was the primary cause of mental and physical illness for professionals, and that it also causes people to work less effectively. They also noted that most workplace efforts to address poor mental health were focused on raising awareness and supporting people in distress. Instead of applying a band aid to an infected wound, how about trying to address the cause of the distress? What about trying to remove some of the unnecessary stress in the ways we work so that we can work more effectively as well as more healthily?

The result was the Mindful Business Charter, a community of law firms, their clients, and other business organizations, which was launched in October 2018 with three signatory banks and nine law firms and has now grown to over 130 organizations around the world.

The Charter recognizes that some stress is inevitable in the work we do, but some is not, and often comes from the ways we work and interact with each other, within our teams and organizations but also, critically, between our organizations and most obviously in the client–law firm dynamic. Most of us do not mean to cause each other stress, but we do, and then we do not talk about it. What if we could all try to be more aware of the impact of our behaviors on ourselves and each other, and what if we gave each other the permission to talk about it? That way, we ought to be able to identify the unnecessary sources of stress in the ways we work so that we can work more healthily and more effectively.

The Charter is deliberately not a prescriptive rulebook full of dos and don'ts, but rather a permissive framework, a common language and, crucially, a permission and invitation to talk about what we each need to deliver of our best, and to call out things that inhibit that.

It is based around four pillars of which the first – openness and respect – is the key. This calls for us to seek to be more respectful of ourselves and our fellow professionals and to commit to a relationship of brave (but respectful) openness in talking about how we work. What are our working hours, our preferred methods of communication, and expectations of turnaround time, for example? Why not tell each other about holidays we have booked and key family and personal events we need to attend? That way, we can usually find a way to work around them, rather than facing the stress of trying to negotiate a compromise in the moment, or missing them altogether. By being open about this we can work more effectively and build stronger relationships that rehumanize the workplace, and perhaps dispel unconscious assumptions about what the client expects and demands, for example.

The other three pillars then apply that starting point to different aspects of how we work:

- *Meetings and communications*. Let's try to only have meetings that need to happen, let's make them as short as possible, and only invite people who need to be there. If we provide a clear agenda, people can take a view as to whether to attend, or which part of the meeting to attend. Let's try to avoid meetings at lunch time and let's be mindful of time zones when working internationally. With email and other communications, let's only send messages that need to be sent. Let's only copy people who need to see them. Let's make sure they make sense and that the subject line accurately reflects the content. Let's be mindful of the time of day we are sending them. If we are using multiple communication platforms, let's agree what they are for and let's avoid spamming each other with multiple messages across different platforms. Of course, there will be times when we need to work, and collaborate and get answers, outside of normal working hours but do we really want all of us sitting with our family and friends, or in the gym or wherever we choose to relax, with our devices immediately at hand just in case a colleague sends an important message? Might we agree that if we need each other outside of agreed core hours we will call and ask?

- *Respecting rest periods*. We know rest and downtime is important, so what can we do to enable people to have that while still delivering great client service? Just because I can be always on, it does not mean I should be or need to be. Might we, for example, think about how to maximize the chance of someone taking their vacation undisturbed? The Charter does not seek to lay down rules but rather encourages signatories to think and talk about what would work and make a difference in the context of their work and their culture. When clever people dare to think differently, amazing things can happen that no one thought were possible.
- *Mindful delegation*. When we are asking someone to do something, make sure that they know what is being requested, where it fits into the wider context, who the key people are and so on, and, rather than impose deadlines, where we can, let's try to discuss them.

None of this is about not working hard. Rather, it is about working more effectively. The flexibility the Charter embraces means it can apply to a white shoe firm with the highest expectations of billable hours just as much to a firm with lower output expectations. The 130+ members are a community, sharing their successes, challenges, ideas, and resources, and providing each other with a sense of energy and common purpose to address the mental health challenges in the legal profession and business more widely.

On a basic level, it is about having the permission, language, and courage to talk about the things that cause us stress, that get in the way of our doing our work effectively, on the basis that, if we can talk about them, we might be able to do something about them.

The Charter is a challenge to dare to think differently, to change. For too long we have known our working practices are unhealthy and are hurting us all, some more dramatically and visibly than others, but we have collectively shrugged our shoulders and said it is just the way it is. It only is the way it is if we all carry on doing it. If, together, we try to do things differently then we can make a difference. As Barack Obama put it, "*Change doesn't happen, change won't happen, while we sit around waiting for the right person or the right time. We are the people we have been waiting for.*" The Charter does not claim to solve all ills, but it is a start and is a commitment from an increasing part of our global profession to try to rebuild a profession that is profitable while at the same time sustainable and healthy, for this generation of lawyers and those that are coming.

As Richard Foley, then the senior partner of Pinsent Masons, observed at the launch of the Charter in 2018, if we are not more profitable as a result of doing this then we are doing it wrong.

References

1 www.ibanet.org/document?id=IBA-report-Mental-Wellbeing-in-the-Legal-Profession-A-Global-Study
2 https://lnkd.in/eWVN4xJ2
3 *Depressive Illness: The Curse Of The Strong*, Tim Cantopher, Sheldon Press, 2020.
4 www.vitality.co.uk/media/britain-sees-128bn-productivity-loss/

About Globe Law and Business

Globe Law and Business was established in 2005. From the very beginning, we set out to create legal books that are sufficiently high level to be of real use to the experienced professional, yet still accessible and easy to navigate. Most of our authors are drawn from Magic Circle and other top commercial firms, both in the United Kingdom and internationally.

Our titles are carefully produced, with the utmost attention paid to editorial, design and production processes. We hope this results in high-quality publications that are easy to read and a pleasure to own.

In 2021, we were very pleased to announce the start of a new chapter for Globe Law and Business following the acquisition of law books under the imprint Ark Publishing. Our law firm management list is now significantly expanded with many well-known and loved Ark Publishing titles.

We are also pleased to announce the launch of our online content platform, Globe Law Online. This allows for easy search and networked access across firms. Key collections include the Law Firm Management Collection and the Banking and Finance Collection. Details of all titles included can be found at www.globelawonline.com. Email glo@globelawandbusiness.com for further details and to arrange a free trial for you or your firm.

We'd very much like to hear from you with your thoughts and ideas for improving what we offer. Please do feel free to email me at sian@globelawandbusiness.com. Happy reading and thank you for your time.

Sian O'Neill
Managing director
Globe Law and Business
www.globelawandbusiness.com